Scientific and Tech Translation

Routledge Translation Guides cover the key translation text types and genres and equip translators and students of translation with the skills needed to translate them. Concise, accessible and written by leading authorities, they include examples from existing translations, activities, further reading suggestions and a glossary of key terms.

Scientific and Technical Translation focuses on texts that are typically translated in scientific and technical domains, such as technical instructions, data sheets and brochures, patents, scientific research articles and abstracts, popular science press releases and news reports. In seven chapters, this practical textbook:

- introduces readers to the typical contexts in which scientific and technical translators work;
- shows how corpus resources can be used for terminological and phraseological research;
- considers how translation technologies are employed in technical and scientific translation;
- explains a range of technical and scientific genres and their translation.

Including a wide range of relevant tasks and activities, examples from the most commonly taught language pairs and a glossary of key terms, this is the essential textbook for modules on scientific and technical translation and specialized translation.

Maeve Olohan is Senior Lecturer in Translation Studies at the University of Manchester, UK. She is author of *Introducing Corpora in Translation Studies* (2004, Routledge).

Scientific and Technical Translation

Maeve Olohan

Routledge
Taylor & Francis Group

LONDON AND NEW YORK

First published 2016
by Routledge
2 Park Square, Milton Park, Abingdon, Oxon OX14 4RN

and by Routledge
711 Third Avenue, New York, NY 10017

Routledge is an imprint of the Taylor & Francis Group, an informa business

Every effort has been made to contact copyright-holders. Please advise the publisher of any errors or omissions, and these will be corrected in subsequent editions.

British Library Cataloguing-in-Publication Data
A catalogue record for this book is available from the British Library

Library of Congress Cataloging-in-Publication Data
Olohan, Maeve.
Scientific and technical translation: a coursebook/by Maeve Olohan.
    pages cm. – (Routledge Translation and Interpreting Guides)
Includes bibliographical references and index.
1. Translating and interpreting–Research–Methodology. I. Title.
P306.5.O565 2015
418'.02072–dc23   2015011443

ISBN: 978-0-415-83784-2 (hbk)
ISBN: 978-0-415-83786-6 (pbk)
ISBN: 978-1-3156-7960-0 (ebk)

Typeset in Sabon
by Sunrise Setting Ltd, Paignton, UK.

Contents

List of tables   *vi*
List of abbreviations   *vii*

Introduction   1

1   Scientific and technical translation as a
    professional activity   6

2   Resources for scientific and technical translation   26

3   Technical instructions   51

4   Technical data sheets and technical brochures   80

5   Patents   106

6   Scientific research articles and abstracts   137

7   Popular science   173

    Appendix 1   206
    Appendix 2   212
    Appendix 3   214
    Appendix 4   236
    Appendix 5   240

    Glossary   242
    Index   246

List of tables

1.1 Translation parameters for a translation project specification 20

2.1 Top 20 items in a simple word count of a 2014 Joint Research Centre report, as generated by Sketch Engine 30

2.2 Top 20 items in a lemmatized word count of a 2014 Joint Research Centre report, as generated by Sketch Engine 31

2.3 Top 20 candidate terms in a 2014 Joint Research Centre report, as generated by Sketch Engine 32

2.4 All multiword candidate terms generated by comparing the Joint Research Centre corpus to a reference corpus 33

2.5 Word sketch for *reactor* 36

2.6 Word sketch for *nuclear* 37

2.7 Word sketch for *nucleare* 38

2.8 Word sketch for *reattore* 40

6.1 Top 30 nouns, top 15 verbs and adjectives and top 5 adverbs from the Academic Vocabulary List organized by lemma 147

6.2 CARS model of rhetorical moves and steps 151

Abbreviations

ARIPO	African Regional Intellectual Property Organization
ASTM	American Society for Testing and Materials
BootCaT	bootstrapping corpus and terms
BNC	British National Corpus
BT	back translation
CARS	Create a Research Space
CAT	computer-assisted translation
CIoL	Chartered Institute of Linguists
CLIR	Cross Lingual Information Retrieval
CNRS	Centre National de la Recherche Scientifique
COCA	Corpus of Contemporary American English
CQL	Contextual Query Language
DGT	Directorate-General for Translation (of the European Commission)
DTP	desktop publishing
EAP	English for academic purposes
EAPO	Eurasian Patent Office
ELF	English as lingua franca
EMT	European Masters in Translation (Network)
EPO	European Patent Office
ESA	European Space Agency
ESP	English for specific purposes or English for specialized purposes
EU	European Union
GHS	Globally Harmonized System (of Classification and Labelling of Chemicals)
IMRAD	introduction, methods, results and discussion
INID	Internationally agreed Numbers for the Identification of (bibliographic) Data
IP	intellectual property
IPC	International Patent Classification
IPRP	International Preliminary Reports on Patentability
ISR	international search report
ITI	Institute of Translation and Interpreting
JRC	Joint Research Centre (of the European Union)

LSP	language service provider
MSDS	material data safety sheet
MT	machine translation
OAPI	African Intellectual Property Organization
PCT	Patent Cooperation Treaty
PDF	Portable Document Format
REACH	Registration, Evaluation, Authorization and Restriction of Chemicals
SaaS	software as a service
SDS	safety data sheet
SI	Système Internationale (d'Unités)
SL	source language
SMT	statistical machine translation
ST	source text
STS	science and technology studies
TBX	TermBase eXchange
TDS	technical data sheet
TEP	translation, editing, proofreading
TESOL	teaching English to speakers of other languages
TL	target language
TM	translation memory
TMX	Translation Memory eXchange
TT	target text
UN	United Nations
URL	uniform resource locator
USPTO	United States Patent and Trademark Office
WIPO	World Intellectual Property Organization

Introduction

The intellectual challenge

It's springtime in Life Before Internet. I pick up the large brown package from my mailbox and open it excitedly to discover that it contains a hefty volume of technical papers published by a German research centre. I'd written a letter to the centre, in the best formal German and the neatest handwriting I could muster (it's also Life Before PCs and Desktop Printers), and they'd replied by sending me this most impressive tome!

I'm working on my undergraduate translation dissertation on the topic of superconductivity. Superconductivity is the property of some materials to conduct electricity with no resistance when they're cooled to extremely low temperatures. In 1986 ceramics were discovered that superconducted at temperatures somewhat higher than before, that is, above 90 K, which is equivalent to $-183°C$. That was a significant breakthrough, because liquid nitrogen boils at 77K. So liquid nitrogen could now be used to cool superconductors for experiments and applications, making both suddenly much more practical and affordable than before. Since superconductors also repel magnetic fields, they have many possible applications. Superconductors are what makes the maglev trains levitate and they're a crucial component in the magnetic resonance imaging (MRI) machines now widely used in hospitals around the world.

Two scientists, Bednorz and Müller, were awarded the Nobel Prize for Physics in 1987 for their discovery of these high-temperature superconductors. The excitement around superconductivity was infectious, even touching a young undergraduate translation student working on her translation project. The enormous potential of the new materials led to extensive coverage in the popular press, usually accompanied by a photograph of a small magnet hovering, as if by magic, above a piece of superconducting ceramic immersed in liquid nitrogen. Scientists and engineers were also working hard on applications to exploit some of that promised potential.

I had chosen to translate a report on high-temperature superconductors for my project and was busy gathering material for my research. So letters had been posted and lots of bulging packages received. No websites, no online journals, no Google, no Wikipedia!

The point of this account is not to fill you with sheer incomprehension as to how anyone could have existed in such a state of technological deprivation. Rather, it is to say that researching and learning about a scientific or technical topic in preparation for translation is exciting and intellectually challenging, whatever the tools and ways of working. It involves identifying and accessing relevant texts in both languages, and reading them to gain an understanding of the topic and its terminology. It involves gaining familiarity with the ways specialists communicate, whether they're producing technical data sheets, patent specifications or scientific research articles. It involves developing familiarity with genres that lots of people never have occasion to experience but that are essential in doing science and developing and exploiting technologies. Translation is also an essential part of scientific and technological activities.

I had a lot more time to work on my student project than anyone does for a professional translation job, where the specialized information has to be processed and assimilated very quickly. But encountering technical and scientific concepts, as a linguist, and learning something about them can be immensely interesting and satisfying. That intellectual challenge may be one of the main reasons why the activity of technical or scientific translation interests you. You may have heard of the two-cultures debate initiated in 1959 by C.P. Snow (1959, 1963), criticizing the gulf between the arts and the sciences. Many say the gulf has narrowed or been bridged somewhat since then, though it's often still socially acceptable for someone to proclaim that they're no good at mathematics or that they don't understand something technical (while they may be more reluctant to admit ignorance of Shakespeare or the literary canon). As technical and scientific translators, we aspire to be inquisitive and knowledgeable in a broad range of disciplines, spanning languages, sciences and technologies. That is the challenge to be relished.

Purpose of the book

Many of the world's translators work on scientific or technical texts, and many translator-training programmes deliver some tuition in scientific or technical translation. In spite of this, there are relatively few pedagogical resources in English for students and teachers of scientific and technical translation. This book is designed to fill that gap by providing a coursebook for a postgraduate (Masters level) course unit or module on scientific and technical translation. It is structured so that you can work through it, chapter by chapter, accumulating knowledge and skills and practising relevant tasks, thus becoming increasingly adept in analysing and translating scientific and technical texts. It assumes no prior specialized translation experience. Used as a learning resource, the book will help you to achieve a set of learning aims, enabling you to develop the knowledge and skills you need for the activities of scientific and technical translation. Specifically, you will be able to

- understand some of the specific situations in which scientific and technical specialists communicate;
- recognize discursive and rhetorical purposes of scientific and technical texts;
- understand how professional translators operate in scientific and technical domains;
- analyse texts in your source and target languages using concepts and metalanguage of the field, in preparation for translation;
- apply a range of resources in your scientific and technical translation practice;
- generate your own translations of scientific and technical texts;
- justify your own translation decisions, using the metalanguage of the field;
- evaluate your own translations and the translations of others.

The book should be a useful resource for any higher-education programme in which technical or scientific translation is taught, as core or optional course units, between English and any other language, but it can also function well as a self-study resource for translators who have not had training or experience in scientific or technical translation.

Rationale and approach

In many countries entry barriers to the translation profession are low, that is to say, anyone can say they are a translator and can offer their services as a translator. In the past translators often entered the profession with degree-level language competence but little formal education in translation. Their effectiveness as translators was developed on the job; over time they developed their own approaches to translation and their own personal theories of translation, perhaps without knowledge of existing formal theories. Now in the UK and in many other countries there is a proliferation of translator-training programmes that formalize the acquisition of knowledge and skills for translation, and it is increasingly expected by employers that their translators will have undergone some postgraduate training in translation. Without replacing the on-the-job experiences and learning, academic training programmes can offer you theoretical and conceptual tools to help you to develop your knowledge and skills more efficiently than if you had to discover everything through trial and error on the job, as your predecessors often had to do. Academic programmes also develop your analytical and reflective abilities. These form an important part of professionalism and allow you to have a rational and analytical understanding of your translation activities, so that you will be able to respond to previously unencountered situations and will be able adapt to new practices as they emerge. This is particularly pertinent in the case of the increasing technologization of translation activities. Therefore, these higher-level thinking skills will be a tremendous asset to you in the professional workplace. Those are the benefits of targeted training in scientific and technical translation that underlie this book and inform its approach.

The book does not reduce translation to a set of prescriptions or formulae. Rather, it focuses on familiarizing you with texts that are typically translated in scientific and technical domains. On many occasions you may be aiming to produce a text that is accepted as belonging to the scientific or technical domain in the target culture, so knowing what is typical or characteristic of the target language and culture will provide a useful guide as to what translation options to choose. However, you will also be guided in your decision making by what you know or assume about the expectations and needs of your translation commissioner and the end users of the text; and of course having such in-depth knowledge, understanding and awareness also enables you to decide whether to conform to or challenge conventions or expectations.

Throughout the book you are encouraged to research the texts and practices that you are learning about, so that you can relate the book's perspectives to the local, regional, national or international practices that are of particular relevance to you. You are also encouraged to familiarize yourself with published research on relevant topics to help you to inform and justify your own judgements and decisions. Emphasis is placed on developing higher-order thinking skills of analysing, evaluating and creating (see Krathwohl 2002 for a discussion of Bloom's revised taxonomy of educational objectives). These skills help you to become reflective professionals who can behave responsibly towards clients, apply specialist knowledge and exercise autonomous thought and judgement in your work.

Material, languages and structure

The coursebook focuses on scientific and technical genres for which translations are likely to be commissioned. There are two main areas of focus, mapping onto technical and scientific translation domains respectively. The first area pertains to the design, delivery and use of technical products. Here, you learn about technical material aimed at end users, that is, instruction manuals (Chapter 3), product data sheets and technical brochures (Chapter 4), as well as technical documentation written by specialists for specialists, in the genre of patent specifications (Chapter 5). The second area of focus is the communication of scientific knowledge. Here, you learn about specialized scientific research (Chapter 6) and popular science reporting (Chapter 7).

The book also provides guidance on some of the resources that can help you in yourwork, with a particular focus on corpora (Chapter 2). Throughout the book examples give you insights into professional translation practices, to help prepare you for aspects of professional life.

In many cases English-language examples are used as a basis for discussion in the book, but you are encouraged to use similar analytical approaches to deal with texts in other languages, making the coursebook language-independent and of use for translator training and education in any language pair. Examples from other languages are integrated where practicable. Exercises at the end of each chapter aim to extend your experience further by encouraging you to find and work with additional examples for analysis and translation. They also prompt you to engage in discussions about your own linguistic and cultural contexts and your own translation work. Depending on organizational factors and the time and resources available, the exercises can be used for self-study or classroom activities. Many of them lend themselves well to group work, thus encouraging you to develop your team-working, collaborative and interpersonal skills too.

References

Krathwohl, David R. (2002) 'A Revision of Bloom's Taxonomy: An Overview', *Theory into Practice* 41(4): 212–18.

Snow, Charles P. (1959) *The Two Cultures and the Scientific Revolution*, Cambridge: Cambridge University Press.

—— (1963) *The Two Cultures: And a Second Look*, Cambridge: Cambridge University Press.

1 Scientific and technical translation as a professional activity

This chapter provides an introduction to scientific and technical translation as a situated activity, by outlining some of the typical workplace configurations for translators and other professionals in the sector. It also notes the kinds of competences that may be expected of scientific or technical translators. It explains the notion of genre, as a way of understanding how the texts you translate are part of communicative events and fulfil communicative purposes. The translation brief and the translation project specification are introduced as tools that can be used to help you in your translation preparation and production.

Introducing science and technology

Science and technology are often paired together in general language usage, as well as when we talk about translation. However, science and technology designate different, though related knowledge domains. A simple indication of this is found in dictionary definitions, for example in the online *Oxford Dictionaries*, where science is defined as 'the intellectual and practical activity encompassing the systematic study of the structure and behaviour of the physical and natural world through observation and experiment' and technology as 'the application of scientific knowledge for practical purposes, especially in industry' (www.oxforddictionaries.com). As if to emphasize the close relationship between the two domains, the first contextual example of usage of the word 'science' offered by the *Oxford Dictionaries* is 'the world of science and technology'. As well as reflecting the close relationship between them, these definitions seem to imply that technology emerges from science and gives priority to the ends rather than the means ('application . . . for practical purposes'). Science, on the other hand, seems to value the means by which knowledge is obtained, that is, through the scientific method of 'observation and experiment'. Although perhaps simplistically formulated here, this perspective on both activities is common throughout pre-modern and modern eras, particularly in anglophone contexts. However, like the well-known conundrum of the chicken and the egg, the primacy of science and the subordination of technology is now disputed by some scholars. Forman (2010), for example, argues that this relationship has been reversed in the postmodern era, claiming that, from around the late 1970s or early 1980s, we have become more interested in ends than means, and technology has become the 'principal model for all our social and cultural activities' (ibid.: 162). This means, he continues, that resourcefulness, risk-taking and utilitarian entrepreneurship are now more highly valued in society than scientific means and methods.

The question of the standings of science and technology in society is a fascinating but complex one, explored in sociological disciplines, including science and technology studies (STS). It is beyond the scope of this book to pursue it much further, but Sismondo (2010) offers an accessible overview for those who are interested. A key point to be made here, and borne in mind throughout this book, is that traditional views of science as a neutral, objective, value-free activity carried out by disinterested scientists is heavily challenged by much of that scholarship. On the contrary, it is argued that science is a culturally and socially contingent activity, which can be ideologically and politically driven. Likewise, technology, often portrayed as the means by which many of the world's problems and our human imperfections can be fixed, must also be examined closely for its motivations, influences and effects. On that topic, Morozov (2013) offers a thought-provoking and polemical challenge to what he calls solutionist and Internet-centrist mindsets.

In the chapters that follow, we can adopt the convenience of grouping science and technology together, while recognizing that the nature of the domains and the dynamic relationships between them can be understood in different ways. Bringing them together in this book implies that they share some features, challenges or approaches. Rather than reflecting on how some things might be labelled as scientific and others as technical, we will focus on the ways in which texts and language are used to perform specific communicative functions in technical and scientific contexts. The analytical concept of genre, discussed in more detail below, will be helpful to us in highlighting those aspects. Before that, the next section introduces the translation landscape, to give you an insight into the settings in which scientific and technical translators work and the key competences they acquire and exercise.

The translation landscape

Apart from the enticing intellectual challenge that scientific and technical translation presents, there are other factors that may motivate you to pursue a career in this area. Firstly, the language services sector is a growing one (MarketWatch 2014). Secondly, a large proportion of professional translation work is technical or scientific; the sectors of industry that spend most on translation globally include manufacturing, software and healthcare, alongside defence in the USA (Kelly 2012). Thirdly, some surveys of professional translators (Aparacio et al. 2001) show that translators who offer a specialization can command higher rates of pay for their work. In addition, commissions from direct clients, rather than translation agencies, are also more lucrative (CIoL and ITI 2011) and are perhaps easier to secure in a specialized domain. The next sections outline some of the typical configurations in which scientific and technical translators work professionally.

Freelance translation

Many or most translators work freelance, in many parts of the world (Kelly 2012). This means they are self-employed – they are not employees of the companies who give them commissions. This is an important distinction when it comes to financial matters like paying income tax (you should consult relevant information for your national or regional situation regarding self-employed status), but it also has implications for finding work and keeping a steady supply of work. Freelance translators generally only get paid for the translation work they do, but they also have to set aside time for marketing themselves, networking, doing test translations for prospective clients, kitting out their office with the necessary equipment and resources and maintaining it, learning about new developments, keeping their own financial records, and lots of tasks that employees of a company might take for granted. For example, unless they work in a very small company, employees can often call on someone in the IT support department or elsewhere when they have technical problems with their computer or their internet access; freelancers have to sort this out themselves or commission and pay someone to work on the problem.

Working freelance has both advantages and disadvantages. One of the key advantages is that it can give you the flexibility to organize your work around your own circumstances, location and preferences. One of the key disadvantages is the lack of a guaranteed regular income. Other pros and cons to consider may revolve around aspects such as contact with people during the working day, variety in translation work and range of other activities.

Most freelance translators (e.g. 82 per cent of the respondents in the last CIoL/ITI survey in 2011) receive their translation commissions from a translation company or agency, often referred to as a language service provider or LSP.

Translator cooperatives and partnerships

A variation on individual freelance work may be seen in partnerships or cooperatives of translators; this is where translators group together, sometimes just to share translation work but sometimes to set up a joint approach to organizational matters too, for example they may hire a shared work premises or market themselves collectively.

An example can be seen on the website of the Swedish group called Lund Translation Team. They present themselves as a group of translators who market themselves under one name, share office space and meet once a week to share experiences and offer mutual advice. They present the advantages for them of working in this way as: 'greater resources, broader reach, greater expertise, more inspiration, more ideas, and of course more fun' (www.lundtranslationteam.se/what-is-lund-translation-team). They see the group as offering advantages to clients too, namely access to a variety of skills and entrepreneurial expertise.

In-house translation

While the vast majority of today's translation work is done by freelance translators worldwide, some in-house/salaried positions for translators continue to exist. Some of the more common configurations are as follows.

A translation company employs in-house translators

'In-house' refers to something which happens within an organization, so in this case we are talking about translators who are employed or salaried. An LSP is more likely to employ in-house translators if it specializes in a specific set of languages or subject domains. For example, the UK-based Sandberg Translation Partners (stptrans.com) specializes in translation of Nordic languages, and around half of its employees are in-house translators for those languages. Fry & Bonthrone (www.fb-partners.com) is a German company specializing in translation for the financial services sector and they employ in-house translators for their most specialized work. For this set-up to make sense for an LSP, they usually have to be sure they have enough regular work for specific language pairs or specialisms to keep in-house staff occupied.

It is seldom the case that an LSP covers all its translation needs with in-house staff; they will usually commission freelancers too, as is also the case with the two companies just mentioned. It is also worth noting that 'in-house' does not necessarily mean that the translators work on the company premises; in some situations they may have the flexibility to work from home.

A company or organization whose core business is not translation has a translation department employing in-house translators

This set-up makes sense for specialized companies which require very regular translation work, perhaps for a limited set of languages. A major advantage of having an in-house translation department is that there can be communication between the translators and technical writers, engineers or other specialists engaged in the company's core activities. Indeed this liaison may be a crucial part of the translator's role, and it is vital that translators have an appropriate set of interpersonal skills, as well as linguistic and technical ones. Another advantage of in-house translation is that the company can manage its own quality assurance and quality control more closely than when translation is outsourced. A potential disadvantage for translators is that the translation department can sometimes be seen within the company as less important than the core business and thus perhaps less valued as an ancillary support service.

A useful insight into running an in-house translation department is given by the then head of the translation department at SMA Solar Technology AG, Germany (Salisbury 2010) in an article in the online magazine *tcworld*. The company produces equipment for solar energy installations and distributes its products to numerous locations around the world. Salisbury describes in-house translation as 'the hard way', but also 'the better way'. He writes about some of the aspects of the work of the internal language services team that make it a successful configuration for that company. These aspects revolve around optimization of communication channels, terminology and project management. Some scientific research centres employ in-house translators, so can be included in this category.

An international organization employs in-house translators

Among others, the European Union (EU) and the United Nations (UN) fall into this category. The ranges of languages and translation activities vary in accordance with the institutional remits. The translation services of the EU institutions are the largest in the world in terms of the number of languages and specialist fields covered. To illustrate the scale of activities, based on 2013 data (European Union 2013), the European Commission's Directorate-General for Translation (DGT) employs around 1,700 translators. The European Council and the Council of the European Union share a translation service employing over 600 translators. Another translation service is shared by the Court of Justice, the General Court and the Civil Service Tribunal, and this also employs around 600 translators, known as lawyer–linguists because they have to be qualified lawyers as well as well as translators. The European Court of Auditors employs around 150 staff in its Translation Directorate. The Committee of the Regions and the European Economic and Social Committee have a joint Directorate for Translation, employing around 350 translators. Translators are employed by the European Central Bank and the European Investment Bank. Finally, the Translation Centre for the Bodies of the European Union is a service providing translation for 50 other EU agencies, institutions and bodies; it employs around 200 staff.

The work done by these translators is often described as institutional translation, and legislation is a core part of that. However, it is useful to note that the EU makes policy in domains of science and technology, among others, and this process requires the translation of scientific and technical reports and papers as well as legislative instruments.

It is common for international organizations to commission translation agencies or freelancers to provide translation services to supplement the translation work of their in-house staff; for example, of the 2 million pages of text handled annually by the DGT of the European Commission, around one-quarter is translated by external contractors (European Union 2013).

The remit of other international organizations may be more overtly scientific. The European Space Agency (ESA), for example, employs translators in-house to translate between English, French and German, and most of the work is of a scientific or technical nature. As noted in a recent recruitment advertisement, ESA translators are required to have an ability to understand scientific and technical concepts and to be able to translate source texts (STs) of considerable complexity, accurately and quickly under pressure.

A national governmental organization employs in-house translators

Governmental organizations, bodies or agencies in countries or regions may employ translators in-house. Like companies with in-house translation departments, these organizations benefit from maximum control over their translation services, which can be important for achieving high levels of quality, but may also be crucial for ensuring confidentiality. Countries with more than one official language or where specific language policies apply may do a lot of translation at various levels of government, but perhaps mostly between the two (or more) official languages. This is the case in Canada, where the Translation Bureau provides translation and terminology services to the federal government and the parliament. Government bodies in non-bilingual countries may also translate for the purposes of international exchange and employ translators in-house. Examples in Germany, with a strong focus on technical or scientific translation, include the language services of ministries such as the Ministry for the Environment, Nature Conservation, Building and Nuclear Safety (Bundesministerium für Umwelt, Naturschutz, Bau und Reaktorsicherheit).

Other roles for trained translators

Your main interest may be to work as a translator, but it is useful to consider the range of other roles for which skilled linguists with translation competences are potentially suited.

Translation project manager or account manager

LSPs usually employ translation project managers in-house, but many prefer to appoint linguists with a translator profile to the role, since a detailed understanding of what translation involves is essential. Project managers liaise with clients and translators and often assume responsibility for the smooth running of the translation project from start to finish. The role usually does not involve translation, but may involve checking and proofreading translations, as well as many other tasks. In the UK context, the project management role is often considered as a graduate entry-level position. For an overview of translation project management, consult Dunne and Dunne (2011) or Rodríguez-Castro (2013).

Terminologist

Larger institutions or organizations may employ terminologists to research terminology and compile and maintain documentation and termbases (see Chapter 2) for use by translators and others. An example of an organization, discussed in Chapter 5, that employs terminologists in that capacity is the Language Division of the World Intellectual Property Organization (WIPO). The ESA, mentioned above, also employs in-house terminologists, recruiting people who have very good terminology research skills, as well as good organizational and communication skills. As for translation, the ability to grasp concepts in scientific and technical fields is also essential. Finally, an overview of the work of terminologists at the Canadian Translation Bureau can be read in Pavel and Nolet (2001).

Reviser or proofreader

Labels to designate processes of checking translations are used in the sector in diverse and potentially confusing ways. To be consistent, we will use the labels set out by the European standard for translation services, EN15038:2006 Translation services – Service requirements (British Standards Institution 2006). In that standard, revision is a bilingual operation, defined as 'examin[ing] a translation for its suitability for the agreed purpose, compar[ing] the source and target texts, and recommend[ing] corrective measures' (ibid.: 6). Review is monolingual, defined as 'examin[ing] a target text for its suitability for the agreed purpose and respect for the conventions of the domain to which it belongs and recommend[ing] corrective measures' (ibid.: 5). Proofreading is then the final checking of proofs before publishing. All, any or none of these processes may be applied to a translation, depending on the circumstances of production, what the client requires and what the LSP has agreed to provide. Some translators choose to take on revising or reviewing tasks at times, or indeed to move into those roles more permanently. Although mostly outsourced, like translation, some LSPs employ people in-house for these activities.

To this category we could add post-editing, that is, editing the raw output of machine translation systems (see Chapter 2). This usually requires a combination of revising and reviewing, as defined above.

Related roles requiring additional expertise

For those interested in the technicalities of document layout and production, there are roles in the translation sector for DTP (desktop publishing) specialists, freelance and in-house. Additionally, expertise in website design, web editing, search-engine optimization and other technical aspects of developing multilingual websites is often required as part of the translation project. The localization sector requires linguists for translation roles, but also those who have additional expertise, for example in testing software products. Translator training programmes may cover aspects of these activities, but you may also benefit from additional training as you move further into roles that focus less on language.

The focus on language is key to the role of the technical writer (also referred to as technical author), but it may be a monolingual rather than a multilingual focus. Technical writers deal with the production of technical documentation, which may then form the ST for the translation process. There is substantial convergence and similarity between technical writing and technical translating, so your expertise as technical communicator, gained through translation, may help you to change direction if you are interested in pursuing a career in technical writing.

Technical writers are usually responsible for creating, maintaining and managing documentation of various kinds, for example technical specifications, product descriptions, service descriptions, instruction manuals, user guides, wikis and tutorials. Technical writers usually need to liaise closely with designers, manufacturers or developers in creating the documentation. Like translators, their focus is on assessing audience needs and producing documentation that addresses specific readerships; this can include adapting technical information for non-technical users. Employers of technical writers tend to look for people with excellent communication skills, preferably including some technical writing expertise, who can work independently or in teams, perhaps with experience of the product, service or sector. Technical writers, like translators, are also required to have an eye for detail and precision in writing, problem-solving skills, an ability to acquire knowledge quickly from various sources and familiarity with software used for document production and management.

Following earlier observations by Risku (2004), Gnecchi et al. (2011) draw on survey data from North America and Europe to explore the growing convergences between the two activities in the professional sphere and to make recommendations about cross-training. The interface between these activities is also discussed by Suojanen (2010).

Knowledge and skills

Many contributions have been made to the translation-studies literature on topics of competences, skills, knowledge expertise and related notions. However, that is an area of scholarship where definitional clarity and empirical research are still lacking. It is well beyond the scope of this book to set out what has been done so far, but if you would like to read more, contributions by Kiraly (2000), Kelly (2005) and the PACTE group (Beeby et al. 2009) are useful places to start. Competence, broadly defined, is also a topic broached by initiatives such as the European Masters in Translation (EMT) Network that try to relate the professional profile to the curriculum by setting out a set of competences and subcompetences for translator training and education programmes to address. There are disadvantages to thinking about what translators do as a static, componential model that attempts to list and define competences and discrete subcompetences, but the EMT approach has become a convenient mapping used both within and beyond the EMT Network.

The main competence areas, as defined by the EMT (European Commission Directorate-General for Translation 2009), are:

- translation service provision competence
- language competence
- intercultural competence

- information mining competence
- thematic competence
- technological competence.

The subcompetences are too numerous to list, but can be consulted via the EMT section of the DGT website (European Commission Directorate-General for Translation 2009). They are not formulated specifically with scientific and technical translation in mind, but are broadly relevant for translation in any specialized domain.

For our purposes, it is useful to note that you certainly need to acquire knowledge and understanding beyond your command of your source language (SL) and target language (TL), that you need to be able to perform lots of different tasks as part of your translation process, with a good understanding of what you are doing and why. Domain-specific (thematic) knowledge is important; here this means understanding the technical or scientific ideas communicated through the texts you are translating. Knowledge and understanding of how professional translation activities are organized is also important. The practice of technical and scientific translation involves the ability to process information, often using technology (addressed in more detail in Chapter 2), so you need to develop your computational expertise alongside your linguistic and domain-specific knowledge. Translation, as communication, is inherently social and intercultural, thus also requiring you to acquire knowledge, understanding and skills to communicate and act as an intercultural specialist.

Training programmes certainly help you to develop some of these competences. As noted in the Introduction, they also offer you theoretical, conceptual, analytical or reflective tools to help you to develop your knowledge and skills more efficiently than if you had to discover everything on your own, through trial and error. Practice and professional experience will then deepen your knowledge and enhance your skills further, throughout your entire working life. However, your earlier academic training, particularly at postgraduate level, should have helped you to develop an analytical understanding of what you are doing. That can help you to know how to respond to situations you are confronted with for the first time or how to grasp new practices that have recently emerged. We can be certain that the translators of the future will encounter many new situations and new practices, presenting interesting challenges for those of you who embark on that path, and requiring you to exercise your flexibility and adaptability.

Communicative purpose

Chapters 3–7 introduce you to various ways and settings in which technical or scientific communities communicate. Our focus is on the purposes of their communications. For communication within the community to be successful, its communicative purpose must be recognized and understood by others. For example, a patent application would not fulfil the purpose of making claims for a novel invention if it was not accepted as such by patent offices, patent lawyers, etc. On the basis that the inventor is making those claims for novelty, others can then agree or challenge the claims. The parties involved have a shared understanding of the communicative purpose of the application. This is the basis on which the concept of genre is defined: 'a recognizable communicative event characterized by a set of communicative purpose(s) identified and mutually understood by the members of the professional or academic community in which it regularly occurs' (Bhatia 1993: 13, drawing on Swales' (1990) work).

For the members of the community to recognize and understand the communicative purpose, they have to be familiar with the structure that the communication normally or typically takes. They learn this through their training and their own recurrent experience of the genre in their professional lives. A genre is therefore described as 'a highly structured and conventionalized communicative event' (Bhatia 1993: 14). As we will see in Chapter 5, patent specifications are constructed in a certain way. The inventors writing them have some linguistic constraints to follow, as well as some freedom in how they formulate their ideas. But if they step far outside of the accepted rules and conventions of the genre, other members of the community are likely to not recognize the contribution as an example of the genre (Swales 2014: 313). It will not be accepted as belonging to the genre and it will fail to fulfil its communicative purpose. As we will see in Chapter 6, an author submitting an article to a prestigious scientific journal may have their article rejected if it does not conform to the journal's explicit rules, but also to a set of conventions that may not be explicitly stated but that are recognized by the established members of the community. Perhaps the author has used very colloquial language in the article. Established members will review the article; they themselves may be regular readers of the journal or they may have had their own articles accepted for publication. The journal editor also acts as gatekeeper and decides whether the genre conventions have been met. The colloquial language may result in rejection of the article or a request for revision before it can be published. However, similar instances of colloquial language may be acceptable to the audience listening to a conference presentation at a scientific conference or in a science lecture to students; the topics under discussion may be the same in each case, but they are different genres, with different communicative purposes and different conventions.

Translators often aim to translate a text in such a way that it will be accepted by the target discourse community as recognizably belonging to a genre, conforming to the rules and conventions of the genre, fulfilling identifiable communicative purposes. To do that is far from straightforward. It means translators have to be as knowledgeable about the genre as the expert members of the discourse community, although they have not trained or worked as engineers or scientists. It requires an understanding of the socio-cultural context of the discourse community and its activities, the communicative purposes of the genre, and the conventionalized structure and the linguistic resources typically employed in the genre. While engineers and scientists pick up the genre conventions through their training or their own engineering and science work, translators can familiarize themselves with genre conventions through their ability to analyze texts, and to be expert and sensitive readers and authors themselves. Expert members of a discourse community may have the skill to push the genre boundaries and exploit the genre in ways that may be deemed creative but acceptable by the community, but novice members are less likely to be able to do that. As noted in Chapter 6, translators may also reach that level of genre expertise and may indeed be in a position to subvert genre conventions, in pursuit of other goals.

However, we should remind ourselves that the key defining characteristic of genres is not their linguistic similarities, it is their shared character as 'communicative vehicles for the achievement of goals' (Swales 2014: 305). In thinking about genre in this way, we are paying attention not only to the participants in the discourse and the discourse itself, but also the environment in which the discourse is produced and received. As we explore genres in Chapters 3–7, certainly discussing linguistic choices, we will also bear in mind the discourse community, the socio-cultural contexts of the communicative event and the communicative purpose. It is also worth emphasizing that genres may have sets of communicative purposes (ibid.: 307). The main purpose of the conference presentation may be to communicate new research findings to the discourse community, but it may have other purposes too – to increase the visibility and profile of the speaker, to challenge or endorse research done by others and to entice collaborators to come forward for the next stage in the research, among others. The audience members, who are also members of the scientific community, will probably recognize these functions as they listen to the presentation. Students – as apprentices rather than fully fledged members of the community – may recognize some but not all of them, and people who are not part of the scientific community at all, for example the audio-visual technician who sets up the equipment for the lecture, may or may not recognize any of those purposes.

'Text type' is a concept that is closely related to 'genre'. Indeed, some researchers use these terms interchangeably. Although our main focus is genre, to avoid terminological confusion we will make a distinction here between the communicative event and its purpose, external to the text (i.e. genre), and the rhetorical purpose fulfilled by texts in their context (i.e. text type). Text types therefore cut across genres. A longstanding classification of text types is Werlich's (1976), according to which texts can be descriptive, narrative, expository, argumentative or instructive. Numerous variations on this text typology can be found in the literature (Biber (1995) proposes eight text types for English). Most classifications are based on rhetorical purposes realized by internal linguistic features. Hatim and Mason's (1990) typology of argumentative, expository and instructional text types is among the best known in translation studies; Trosborg (1997) also provides further discussion and exemplification of text typology in translation.

This book deals with recognized communicative events in professional settings and therefore the notion of genre is most useful to us. We will also refer to rhetorical purposes served by texts in their contexts, where this serves our explanatory and analytical needs. A final point to be made about classifying purposes is that texts are often multifunctional and can therefore be described as hybrid. Hatim and Mason (ibid.: 146) point out that texts tend to have a dominant rhetorical purpose, with other purposes then assuming secondary importance. In analyzing STs and producing our translations, we will need to be aware of both dominant and secondary purposes, and to recognize this potential for hybridity and multifunctionality.

The translation brief

Our translation practice can be informed by our ever-increasing familiarity with genre, and we can foreground the communicative purposes of the genre, as communicative event, and the knowledge and expectations of the discourse community for which our translation is destined, if we know it. Typically we are commissioned to translate by a client, either directly or via the intermediary of the LSP. There will be an explicit statement of what the client is commissioning. In its most basic form, this may simply be a purchase order specifying what texts are to be translated and by when, how many words they contain and the agreed payment. If we need to know more, we will have to ask. Depending on circumstances, we may learn something about the intended purpose, use and readership of the translation. We might receive some information about the context of production, for example explanation of a company brand or image. If we cannot glean more than the most basic information, we may have to make some assumptions or educated guesses about purpose and readership; our genre expertise will help us a lot in that situation. All of this information can be considered as forming the translation assignment, the translation commission or the translation brief. In the 1970s translation scholars began to think about these aspects of translating, through Holz-Mänttäri's theory of translatorial action (1984) and Vermeer's skopos theory (1989). Nord (1997a: 47–8, see also 1997b) further developed the idea of the translation brief, particularly as a pedagogical tool. In her view, it should contain explicit or implicit information about:

- the target-text addressee(s)
- the prospective time and place of text reception
- the medium over which the text will be transmitted
- the motive for the production or reception of the text.

Mason's (2000) work on audience design for translation is also useful in that he encourages us to think about the target text in relation to the socio-textual practices of the target culture. This approach accommodates the notion that translators may design their texts for more than one possible receiver group as addressees, depending on the context of situation in which they are producing the translation.

Translation project specification

As noted above, it varies very much from case to case how much information is specified to the translator as part of a translation brief. The UK's Institute for Translation and Interpreting, in advice to commissioners of translation, suggests that they provide information on the following 10 points, as part of a barebones commission (Durban and Melby 2007):

- audience
- purpose of the translation
- deadline
- price
- subject area and type of text
- source language and regional variation
- format
- volume (how many words, characters, etc.)
- target language and regional variation
- steps to be followed during the production phase (e.g. translation, bilingual checking, monolingual checking, and translation, editing, proofreading (TEP)).

In the international technical specification for translation projects, ISO/TS11669:2012 Translation Projects – General Guidance (British

Standards Institution 2012), an attempt is made to set out, in greater detail, what a professional translation project specification should look like, in an ideal case. Twenty-one parameters are used to define various aspects of the translation project. An explanatory version of these is reproduced in Table 1.1. If clients were to specify each of these parameters, translators would have a detailed translation brief to guide them.

Table 1.1 Translation parameters for a translation project specification

1. Source characteristics	1A. Source language
	1B. Genre
	1C. Audience(s)
	1D. Communicative purpose(s)
2. Specialized language	2A. Subject field (e.g. chemical engineering)
	2B. Terminology (here the client specifies if they want ST terms translated in a certain way, e.g. by providing a glossary of source terms)
3. Volume	(The amount of translation, usually measured in words)
4. Complexity	(Any factors that make the project difficult, e.g. special file formats, special use of graphics, particular linguistic difficulties of the ST)
5. Origin	(Any details about the ST authoring or provenance)
6. Target language information	6A. Target language
	6B. Target terminology (as 2B above, but also encompassing any particular TL terms that the client wants to use, e.g. as specified in a bilingual glossary or termbase)
7. Target audience	
8. Target purpose	
9. Content correspondence	(How the target content is expected to match the source content, e.g. a complete or abridged translation, a full or summary translation, an overt or covert translation)
10. Register	(Level of formality of language)
11. File format	
12. Style	12A. Style guide (from client, if available)
	12B. Style relevance (i.e. an indication of how relevant style is to the project)

(*Continued*)

Table 1.1 (Continued)

13. Layout	
14. Typical production tasks	(Preparation, initial translation, self-checking, revision, review, final formatting, proofreading)
15. Additional tasks	(E.g. additional sample/spot checks for quality)
16. Technology	(What technologies will be used in the translation process?)
17. Reference materials	(E.g. documents, glossaries, translation memories – see Chapter 2)
18. Workplace requirements	(E.g. any restrictions on where the work is to be performed)
19. Permissions	19A. Identification of the copyright holder of the translation (this is usually the client once the translation has been delivered and paid for)
	19B. Recognition (i.e. will the translator or LSP's name appear on the document?)
	19C. Restrictions (i.e. are there any restrictions on use of translation memories developed for the project?)
20. Submissions	20A. Qualifications (e.g. does the LSP have to meet any requirements, such as accreditations or standards certifications?)
	20B. Deliverables (i.e. what is to be delivered, including the translation but perhaps also an updated translation memory, glossaries or style guide created by the translator or LSP)
	20C. Delivery (i.e. means by which the translation is to be delivered)
	20D. Deadline
21. Expectations	21A. Compensation (i.e. payment, how calculated, what rate, any discounts, how long after invoicing?)
	21B. Communication (e.g. procedures for asking and answering questions of client, contact person in LSP and client company)

Source: adapted from British Standards Institution 2012: 16–28

For any translation tasks you complete, it would be useful to develop a hypothetical translation brief. At the very least, this could involve specifying the hypothetical addressees of the target text and its purpose. However, you may find it useful to build on the more detailed specifications to help you to design the brief (from the hypothetical client's perspective), and then to think about the implications of that brief for you, as the translator, before you translate.

Exercise 1.1: Familiarizing yourself with professional associations

(i) The ITI (Institute of Translation and Interpreting, www.iti.org.uk) is the UK's association for translators and interpreters. Focusing on the ITI or a professional association in another country or region, find out what resources, services, training and networking opportunities the association offers (i) freelance translators and (ii) student members.

(ii) The UK's professional association for technical writers is the Institute of Scientific and Technical Communicators (www.istc.org. uk). The European Association for Technical Communication, also known as tekom (www.technical-communication.org), is Europe's largest professional association for technical communicators. Find out if there is a similar association in your country. From the associations' websites, find out more about the technical-writing profession and draw up a list of similarities and differences between technical writing and technical translation.

Exercise 1.2: Considering translation as part of the technical communication process

The e-magazine published by tekom is called *tcworld* (www.tcworld. info). It has a section dealing with translation and localization. Read a selection of recent articles to observe how translation is perceived as fitting into the wider technical communication context. Discuss your findings.

Exercise 1.3: Understanding the scope of international standards

In this chapter we mentioned two international standards defining translation services and translation projects:

* EN15038: Translation Services: Service Requirements
* ISO/TS 11669:2012: Translation Projects: General Guidance.

An American equivalent of the first one is:

* ASTM F 2575-06: Standard Guide for Quality Assurance in Translation (ASTM 2006).

The texts of international standards (e.g. ISO or those published by your national standards organization, like the British Standards

Institution in the UK) are normally expensive to purchase, but university or municipal libraries may have a subscription to your national standards organization. If you have subscription access, consult these standards and consider the extent to which they could be relevant to you as a freelance translator.

Exercise 1.4: Developing a hypothetical translation brief and translation project specification

For a text and translation task of your choice, design (i) a basic translation brief and (ii) a detailed translation project specification.

Further reading: Learning more about the study of scientific and technical translation

Read Olohan (2013) for an overview of approaches to the study of scientific and technical translation.

Key points from this chapter

- Scientific and technical translators work in a variety of professional configurations – mostly freelance and for LSPs, but also in-house and in institutional contexts.
- Scientific and technical translators need to be knowledgeable and skilled in a range of domains; it is also essential to be intellectually curious, to have the capacity to learn and to be adaptable.
- Scientific and technical translation form part of the larger technical communication environment, and there are some parallels between technical writing and technical translation.
- Genre is a useful concept for understanding how texts are used in conventionalized ways in discourse communities to fulfil communicative purposes.
- Translation is facilitated by being defined by a translation brief or a translation project specification.

References

Aparacio, Antonio, Michael Benis and Graham Cross (2001) *Rates and Salaries 2001*, London: Institute of Translation and Interpreting.

ASTM (2006) *ASTM F 2575-06: Standard Guide for Quality Assurance in Translation*, Philadelphia, PA: ASTM International.

Beeby, Allison, Mònica Fernández, Olivia Fox, Amparo Hurtado Albir, Inna Kozlova, Anna Kuznik, Wilhelm Neunzig, Patricia Rodríguez, Lupe Romero, Stefanie Wimmer (2009) 'Results of the Validation of the PACTE

Translation Competence Model: Acceptability and Decision Making', *Across Languages and Cultures* 10(2): 207–30.

Bhatia, Vijay K. (1993) *Analysing Genre: Language Use in Professional Settings*, London: Pearson Education.

Biber, Douglas (1995) *Dimensions of Register Variation*, Cambridge: Cambridge University Press.

British Standards Institution (2006) *EN 15038:2006 Translation Services – Service Requirements*, London: British Standards Institution.

—— (2012) *ISO/TS 11669:2012 Translation Projects – General Guidance*, London: British Standards Institution.

CIoL and ITI (2011) *2011 Rates and Salaries Survey for Translators and Interpreters*, London: Chartered Institute of Linguists and Institute of Translation and Interpreting.

Dunne, Keiran J. and Elena S. Dunne (2011) *Translation and Localization Project Management: The Art of the Possible*, Amsterdam and Philadelphia: John Benjamins Publishing.

Durban, Chris and Alan Melby (2007) *Translation: Buying a Non-commodity*, London: Institute of Translation and Interpreting.

European Commission Directorate-General for Translation (2009) 'European Master's in Translation (EMT) Project', online at: http://ec.europa.eu/dgs/translation/programmes/emt/index_en.htm (accessed 5 March 2010).

European Union (2013) *Interpreting and Translating for Europe*, Brussels: European Union, online at: http://ec.europa.eu/dgs/translation/publications/brochures/interpreting_translating_europe_en.pdf (accessed 15 January 2015).

Forman, Paul (2010) '(Re)cognizing Postmodernity: Helps for Historians – of Science Especially', *Berichte zur Wissenschaftsgeschichte* 33(2): 157–75.

Gnecchi, Marusca, Bruce Maylath, Birthe Mousten, Federica Scarpa and Sonia Vandepitte (2011) 'Field Convergence between Technical Writers and Technical Translators: Consequences for Training Institutions', *IEEE Transactions on Professional Communication* 54(2): 168–84.

Hatim, Basil and Ian Mason (1990) *Discourse and the Translator*, London and New York: Longman.

Holz-Mänttäri, Justa (1984) *Translatorisches Handeln: Theorie und Methode*, Helsinki: Suomalainen Tiedeakatemia.

Kelly, Dorothy (2005) *A Handbook for Translator Trainers*, Manchester: St Jerome Publishing.

Kelly, Nataly (2012) 'Clearing up the Top 10 Myths About Translation', *The Blog, The Huffington Post*, online at: www.huffingtonpost.com/nataly-kelly/clearing-up-the-top-10-my_b_1590360.html (accessed 15 January 2015).

Kiraly, Donald (2000) *A Social Constructivist Approach to Translator Education: Empowerment from Theory to Practice*, Manchester: St Jerome Publishing.

MarketWatch (2014) 'Market for Outsourced Translation and Interpreting Services and Technology to Surpass US$37 Billion in 2014', *MarketWatch*, online at: www.marketwatch.com/story/market-for-outsourced-translation-and-interpreting-services-and-technology-to-surpass-us37-billion-in-2014-2014-07-01 (accessed 15 January 2015).

Mason, Ian (2000) 'Audience Design in Translating', *The Translator* 6(1): 1–22.

Morozov, Evgeny (2013) *To Save Everything, Click Here: The Folly of Technological Solutionism*, New York: PublicAffairs.

Nord, Christiane (1997a) 'Defining Translation Functions: The Translation Brief as a Guideline for the Trainee Translator', *Ilha Do Desterro* (33): 41–55, online at: https://periodicos.ufsc.br/index.php/desterro/article/download/9208/9484 (accessed 15 January 2015).

—— (1997b) *Translating as a Purposeful Activity: Functionalist Approaches Explained*, Manchester: St Jerome Publishing.

Olohan, Maeve (2013) 'Scientific and Technical Translation', in Carmen Millán Valera and Francesca Bartrina (eds) *The Routledge Handbook of Translation Studies*, London and New York: Routledge, pp. 425–37.

Pavel, Silvia and Diane Nolet (2001) *Handbook of Terminology*, Ottawa: Canadian Government Publishing, online at: www.bt-tb.tpsgc-pwgsc.gc.ca/btb.php?cont=692 (accessed 15 January 2015).

Risku, Hanna (2004) 'Migrating from Translation to Technical Communication and Usability', in Gyde Hansen, Kirsten Malmkjaer and Daniel Gile (eds) *Claims, Changes and Challenges in Translation Studies: Selected Contributions from the EST Congress, Copenhagen 2001*, John Benjamins Publishing, pp. 181–95.

Rodríguez-Castro, Mónica (2013) 'The Project Manager and Virtual Translation Teams: Critical Factors', *Translation Spaces* 2: 37–62.

Salisbury, Gerald A. (2010) 'Running a Successful In-House Translation Department', *tcworld*, April 2010, online at: www.tcworld.info/e-magazine/translation-and-localization/article/running-a-successful-in-house-translation-department/ (accessed 15 January 2015).

Sismondo, Sergio (2010) *An Introduction to Science and Technology Studies*, 2nd ed., Chichester: John Wiley & Sons.

Suojanen, Tytti (2010) 'Comparing Translation and Technical Communication: A Holistic Approach', in Tuija Kinnunen and Kaisa Koskinen (eds) *Translators' Agency*, Tampere: Tampere University Press, pp. 47–60, online at: http://tampub.uta.fi/handle/10024/65639 (accessed 15 January 2015).

Swales, John M. (1990) *Genre Analysis: English in Academic and Research Settings*, Cambridge: Cambridge University Press.

—— (2014) 'Genre and Discourse Community', reprinted from Swales (1990), in Johannes Angermuller, Dominique Maingueneau and Ruth Wodak (eds) *The Discourse Studies Reader*, Amsterdam and Philadelphia: John Benjamins, pp. 305–16.

Trosborg, Anna (ed) (1997) *Text Typology and Translation*, Amsterdam and Philadelphia: John Benjamins Publishing.

Vermeer, Hans J. (1989) *Skopos und Translationsauftrag*, Heidelberg: Universität Heidelberg.

Werlich, Egon (1976) *A Text Grammar of English*, Heidelberg: Quelle & Meyer.

2 Resources for scientific and technical translation

This chapter focuses on the exploitation of a range of resources for scientific and technical translation. You learn about concepts and terms and procedures for using corpus resources to research terms and other aspects of specialized language use. We also discuss ways of managing and storing your terminological data for future reference and outline how other computer-assisted translation (CAT) tools, like translation memory and machine translation, may be used as part of your translation process. In the case of the various technologies, we focus on general principles and functions rather than specific software applications, thus ensuring that the information is useful, irrespective of your access to specific tools.

Introducing terminology

One of the striking features of many technical and scientific genres is that they contain specialized vocabulary that is often not readily understandable to people who are not part of that discourse community. Terminology is not the only distinguishing feature of those genres, and future chapters will introduce other features, some of which offer interesting challenges to translators. However, technical and scientific translators also need strategies for dealing with terminology. This chapter first explains briefly what terms and concepts are and then guides you through some uses of corpus analysis tools to help you to research the terminology of a specialized subject domain or text.

Terms and concepts

A specialized subject domain is made up of objects with specific properties. The objects might be parts of machinery, electronic components, engineering equipment, chemical compounds, atomic particles or manufacturing processes, to give just a few examples. We could describe an object in terms of its properties, for example what it is made of, how it looks and how it is used. We can regard those individual objects as belonging to a set or class of objects, and we can form a conceptualization or mental image of that class. From the range of properties displayed by the individual objects, we could also abstract a set of common characteristics, for example related to composition, form, function and usage. This abstraction or mental representation of the object is known as the **concept**, and the concept can then be defined using the set of **characteristics**. Thus, the concept is our mental representation of an object from a specialized domain, not the (physical) object itself but an abstracted unit of knowledge. To organize, refer to and communicate something about a concept, we give it a label or a designation in our language; that designation is the **term**. The collection of terms for a subject domain is the **terminology** (specialized vocabulary) of that domain. So, when authors of texts want to refer to concepts of a subject domain, they will use terms. When we translate those texts into another language we generally need to know and use the corresponding term in the target language (TL), so that the target text also refers to that same concept in that specialized domain.

Terms therefore play an important role in communicating about concepts, particularly in those settings where there is a need to avoid ambiguity or vagueness. Many terms are well known and widely accepted within a discourse community, but sometimes a concept may be designated by two different, competing terms, making communication about a specific concept and mutual understanding less clear-cut. Sometimes terms fall out of use, to be replaced by alternative terms which gain acceptance. Sometimes a concept is new or unknown and a new term has to be created to designate it in a particular language. Terms typically represent just one concept in a subject domain, but the same term could designate different concepts in different domains. Finally, it is also common for word forms that do not have specialized meanings in general language use to be used as terms, to designate a specific concept in a specialized subject domain. These scenarios can pose challenges for translators and highlight the need for careful terminological research and thorough conceptual understanding.

Most terms are nouns or noun phrases, but verbs and adjectives can also be terms. A term can be a single word (**simple term**) or a multi-word expression (**complex term**), but symbols, formulae and abbreviations can also be terms. Terms may commonly co-occur with other expressions; recurrent patterns of phrases in discourse are called **phraseology**.

The next section focuses on how we can identify and research the terminology and phraseology of technical and scientific discourse, in preparation for translation tasks.

Corpus-based terminology research

An electronic collection of texts, compiled according to some organizing principles, is called a **corpus**. In this section we focus on how we can use **corpora** (plural form of corpus) to carry out terminological and phraseological research, both monolingually and bilingually, in preparation for translation.

Corpus software or corpus tools help us to extract data of various kinds from a corpus. Typically, corpus users are interested in gathering data about patterns of language usage, frequencies of use and information about likely co-occurrence of words, terms or phrases. Likely co-occurrences may be categorized into **collocations**, the co-occurrence of two or more words, and **colligation**, the occurrence of grammatical structures with other structural patterns or words. Frequency and co-occurrence data about both SL and TL can be very useful to us in our translation preparation and translation production. If our corpus texts belong to a specialized genre, then we are likely to be able to extract usage data which will tell us something about the terminology and phraseology of that genre, as well as terminology related to the particular concepts belonging to that subject domain.

To illustrate this kind of corpus-based terminological research in very concrete terms, we will work through a specific example below. The following tasks have been completed using Sketch Engine, www. sketchengine.co.uk (Kilgarriff et al. 2014) which is available via monthly individual or annual institutional subscriptions, and offers a 30-day free trial. Sketch Engine provides an online corpus query interface and access to many pre-existing large corpora, monolingual and multilingual, as well as functions to enable you to create your own corpora. However, other corpus software could be used to perform some or all of these tasks; the principles of the terminological research are more important here than the choice of specific tools. Alternative corpus tools in widespread use include Wordsmith Tools (Scott 2015) and the freeware AntConc (Anthony 2014).

Before we start on our terminological research, it would be useful for you to explore and familiarize yourself with the main tools that corpus software can offer you. Concordancing is a key function of all corpus software, enabling users to find patterns of usage through a visual display. A concordance tool extracts all instances of a node or search word or phrase from the corpus, together with a short excerpt of the co-text to its left and right. It then displays the lines of text, with the node or search word or phrase highlighted, aligned and centred on the screen, with its co-text either side of it. This is also called a **concordance** or a **KWIC** (Key Word in Context) display. If you have access to Sketch Engine, select any pre-existing corpus and use the 'Concordance tool' to generate data from that corpus, by searching for word forms of your choice. If you do not have access to Sketch Engine, search the British National Corpus (BNC) or the Corpus of Contemporary American English (COCA) using the online concordancing tool at corpus.byu.edu. If you would like to learn more about how concordances can be used in linguistics research, consult Sinclair (2003). The other key tools of most corpus software are word lists and keyword lists, both of which we will use in the task below.

Let us assume that the text we have been commissioned to translate is a report issued by the European Union's Joint Research Centre (JRC) in 2014, entitled 'Science for Nuclear Safety and Security', available at ec.europa.eu/jrc/en/publication/science-nuclear-safety-and-security. As noted in the accompanying blurb, the report

> aims to give a comprehensive overview of the JRC's work in rela-
> tion to nuclear safety and security. It highlights the JRC's rele-
> vant scientific output in nuclear safety; nuclear security; reference
> measurements; materials and standards; nuclear knowledge
> management; training and education and, in the last chapter,
> innovation.

At the time of writing, the report is available in English only. The document comprises 35 pages, of which the last 5 are lists of references and links. Depending on your chosen TL, you could hypothe-size that (i) the JRC is commissioning translations of the report into other EU languages or (ii) that a national or regional nuclear research centre in a non-English speaking country is commissioning a transla-tion into their language to familiarize themselves with the JRC research activities.

Creating a corpus from the ST and identifying terms

Having been tasked with the translation, a first stage in our termino-logical research could be to explore the most prevalent terms and their behaviour in the ST. We can do this by creating our own small corpus, consisting of the ST. We can then use some of the software's functionality to compile a list of single- and multi-word expressions that are likely to be terms. We can also examine the collocational and colligational patterns of their usage.

We can use the 'Create corpus' facility in Sketch Engine to upload the ST (a range of file formats are accepted, including PDF). The soft-ware then compiles the corpus, which involves some automatic pro-cessing (parsing, tagging) to produce it in a format on which the corpus analysis tools can be used. The word count tells us there are 21,589 words in the corpus.

The most basic word-list option in any corpus software is to generate a simple **word list**, that is, a list of all the words in the corpus, in order of most frequent to least frequent. Table 2.1 shows the top 20 words from our text (i.e. an extract from the full list that includes all words in the corpus). As is typical for English-language

Table 2.1 Top 20 items in a simple word count of a 2014 Joint Research Centre report, as generated by Sketch Engine

Word	Frequency
the	1,187
and	977
of	874
in	436
to	388
nuclear	382
for	351
JRC	254
a	206
The	203
on	184
is	169
Nuclear	162
safety	131
European	130
materials	122
as	117
with	114
are	107
by	99

corpora, function words like *the, and, of, in* and *to* are by far the most frequent in our ST. However, the content words that also appear here look like they may form parts of terms designating concepts from our specialized subject domain: *nuclear, JRC, safety, European* and *materials*.

However, for the purposes of identifying terms, this simple word list contains a lot of distracting data, in the form of function words and words repeated in different orthographic or morphological variants (e.g. singular and plural noun forms or different forms of the same verb). We can improve the results of this operation by generating a listing by **lemma** (word stem) rather than by word. Doing so results in word forms such as *is* and *are* being combined into the lemma *be*. Two more content words now appear in the extract of the top 20 items, namely *fuel* and *reactor* – see Table 2.2.

For English and some other languages (Kilgarriff 2013), Sketch Engine has the additional functionality of producing a frequency

Table 2.2 Top 20 items in a lemmatized word count of a 2014 Joint Research Centre report, as generated by Sketch Engine

Lemma	Frequency
the	1,386
and	977
of	876
in	481
nuclear	417
be	397
to	388
for	364
JRC	254
a	223
on	187
material	164
safety	135
European	130
Nuclear	128
as	126
fuel	122
with	118
by	100
reactor	97

word list by term, rather than by word or lemma. These are Sketch Engine's proposals for terms, that is, they are **candidate terms**. As we can see just from looking at the top 20 items from that list, shown in Table 2.3, the function words have disappeared and we have a list made up of items that we would certainly recognize as terms for this domain (e.g. *fuel, reactor, Euroatom, radioactivity*), as well as more general lexis typical of scientific discourse (e.g. *field, work, support, knowledge*). However, we might also note that a frequent candidate term, *JRC*, occurring 254 times in the corpus, is not listed here, so this word list generated by term is a good starting point, but further work is needed.

A refinement on the lemma-based word list, and an option for all languages, is to ask Sketch Engine to extract keywords and possible multiword terms by comparing our nuclear safety corpus with a large reference corpus of English (for this example the reference corpus was the enTenTen corpus (2012), which contains over 10 billion

Table 2.3 Top 20 candidate terms in a 2014 Joint Research Centre report, as
generated by Sketch Engine

Terms	Frequency
safety	135
fuel	89
research	72
security	70
reactor	62
nuclear safety	45
training	45
energy	44
management	41
material	41
field	36
reference	36
Euratom	34
work	34
information	33
uranium	33
support	31
knowledge	29
laboratory	28
radioactivity	28

words of English obtained as a result of web crawling). This list is
present in order of **keyness**. Keyness is a quantitative calculation
reflecting the increased frequency of words and phrases in the specialized corpus compared with their frequency in the reference corpus (Kilgarriff 2012). All multiword terms in our text, according to
Sketch Engine's analysis of keyness, are listed in Table 2.4. We can
identify among them numerous terms that designate specialist
nuclear safety concepts. However, we might also spot some phrases
which are also prevalent in general language, for example *severe
accident*, and some which might be more frequent in scientific
discourse but are not specific to nuclear safety, for example *scientific
support, knowledge management, innovation flow*. To illustrate
how not all multiword units identified are, in fact, terms, we can see
further down the list that *following policy* is proposed as a term.
The ST contains five text boxes introduced by the following identical
sentence each time: *JRC activities in this area provide scientific*

support to the following policy initiatives. These occurrences are responsible for *scientific support* and *following policy* entering the list of candidate multiword terms. We might also note that, although many of the candidate terms are two-word units (also called bi-grams), the list also contains some longer units, such as *sodium-cooled fast reactor* (a 3-gram or tri-gram) and *routine uranium isotope ratio* (a 4-gram).

Sketch Engine provides a shortcut for the procedure just outlined by offering an 'Extract keywords and terms' function (for some languages) to facilitate the comparison between a specialized corpus and a reference corpus, but this kind of keyword or keyness analysis can be done, more or less as described above, with other corpus tools and applications. The searches above can also be carried out to find multiword sequences only, by changing settings for **n-grams** (i.e. word sequences) so that the results contain only bi-grams, or tri-grams or 4-grams, etc.

Table 2.4 All multiword candidate terms generated by comparing the JRC corpus to a reference corpus (enTenTen 2012)

Terms	Frequency
nuclear safety	45
nuclear security	27
illicit trafficking	14
nuclear fuel	21
nuclear material	14
knowledge management	18
nuclear energy	26
nuclear field	11
severe accident	11
fuel cycle	12
nuclear knowledge management	10
fuel safety	10
nuclear knowledge	10
nuclear research	9
nuclear reference	8
fast reactor	8
scientific support	8
innovation flow	7
mass spectrometry	8
innovative reactor	6

(Continued)

Table 2.4 (continued)

Terms	Frequency
proliferation resistance	6
nuclear energy sector	6
reactor safety	6
physical protection	6
nuclear fuel cycle	6
nuclear reactor	8
nuclear fuel safety	5
in-house science	5
process monitoring	5
following policy	5
nuclear non-proliferation	5
source information	5
waste management	11
in-house science service	4
nuclear data	4
science service	4
novel test	4
uranium isotope	4
certified reference	4
open source information	4
environmental sampling	4
safe management	4
training programme	7
safety assessment	4
emergency preparedness	5
radioactive waste	5
environmental monitoring	4
nuclear waste	5
nuclear technology	4
modified total evaporation	3
routine uranium isotope	3
routine uranium isotope ratio	3
uranium isotope ratio	3
sodium-cooled fast reactor	3
routine uranium	3
high burn-up	3
total evaporation	3

Table 2.4 (continued)

Terms	Frequency
advanced inspection	3
environmental radioactivity	3
energy sector	6
small punch	3
isotope ratio	3
nuclear waste management	3
direct research	3
stress corrosion	3
final disposal	3
conformity assessment	3
nuclear reaction	3
light water	3

From the above operations, we would have an extensive list of the terms used in our ST. Exploration of the concordance lines for any dubious candidates also helps to clarify matters. As noted above, concordance lines give us a visual display of all instances of a node or search word or phrase from the corpus, together with a short excerpt of the co-text to its left and right. The concordance lines for *small punch*, for example, show us that all three instances of *small punch* are in the compound term *small punch test*, so we can add that to our list of terms.

Identifying recurrent phrases

A particular feature offered by Sketch Engine is the 'Word sketch', a one-page summary of a word's collocational and grammatical behaviour. It should be noted that some of the same collocational and grammatical patterning may be retrieved from corpora using other corpus-processing tools, with varying degrees of convenience and user-friendliness. In those cases it will not be called a 'word sketch' and it will be displayed differently. Depending on the software, you may also have to make your own judgements on parts of speech and grammatical structures. We can use the word-sketch function to generate a display of grammatical and collocational patterns for any word in our corpus. For example, if we look at the word sketch for *reactor* (Table 2.5), we can see that there are few patterns which recur more than three times but they are (in bold typeface) *fast reactor, nuclear reactor, reactor design* and *reactor safety*. Of the others, several are also terms, particularly if we focus on modifiers of *reactor*,

Table 2.5 Word sketch for *reactor*

reactor *(noun)* Nuclear safety freq = 97 (3,608.89 per million)

object_of	7	0.90
cool	3	12.58
gas-cool	1	12.00
test	1	10.61
investigate	1	10.14
relate	1	9.91

subject_of	6	1.20
contain	1	11.54
provide	1	8.43
be	4	8.21

adj_subject_of	2	3.70
hollow	1	12.42
important	1	10.61

modifier	66	1.50
fast	8	11.62
future	4	10.54
Generation	4	10.51
sodium-cooled	3	10.38
IV	3	10.11
light	2	9.87
dedicated	2	9.83
high	3	9.80
water	2	9.56
nuclear	11	9.37
power	2	9.37
temperature	2	9.21
salt	1	8.93
Phenix	1	8.93
water-water	1	8.93
exemplary	1	8.91
lead-cooled	1	8.91
water-cooled	1	8.91
modular	1	8.91
supercritical	1	8.89
molten	1	8.89
sodium	1	8.83
small	1	8.83
flux	1	8.81
fission	1	8.77

modifies	44	1.00
design	8	11.33
core	3	10.73
concept	2	10.09
environment	2	9.71
type	2	9.70
BR	1	9.48
condition	2	9.42
park	1	9.42
size	1	9.42
kinetics	1	9.42
fleet	1	9.39
conversion	1	9.33
embrittlement	1	9.27
safety	5	9.14
structure	1	9.02
system	3	8.99
technology	2	8.79
fuel	3	8.64
application	1	8.48
behaviour	1	8.42
authority	1	8.27
activity	1	7.49

and/or	9	0.40
Petten	1	11.54
III	1	11.19
conversion	1	11.00
generation	1	10.83
production	1	10.25
technology	1	8.18
fuel	1	7.27

pp_obj_in	10	4.40
experience	1	11.30
foresee	1	11.30
specie	1	11.09
rod	1	9.96
operation	1	9.71
component	1	9.45
test	1	9.30
use	1	8.40
fuel	1	7.27
material	1	6.42

pp_obj_of	9	1.80
lifetime	1	11.30
variety	1	10.91
embrittlement	1	10.83
generation	1	10.83
core	1	10.48
evaluation	1	9.91
assessment	1	8.33
safety	2	8.01

pp_obj_for	6	3.20
prototype	1	12.00
rule	1	11.83
criterion	1	10.42
technology	1	8.22
system	1	7.71
fuel	1	7.29

pp_in	3	1.30
world	1	11.68
operation	1	10.00
France	1	9.68

predicate_of	1	4.40
tube	1	12.00

for example *sodium-cooled reactor, water-cooled reactor, light reactor*, and *reactor* as modifier, for example *reactor core, reactor kinetics*.

A second example is the word sketch for *nuclear* (Table 2.6). As an adjective, it occurs mostly with nouns which it modifies. As we can see from the bold typeface, there are numerous significant patterns. As we look down the 'modifies' list we can ascertain that all are good candidate terms, including the less frequent patterns. Obviously we can take a similar systematic approach to data for other terms or components of compound terms from our ST.

As outlined above, we can also use the concordance function to examine the immediate co-text of a word or term. In our ST, we can use concordances and sorting functions (or n-gram word lists) to spot recurrent phrases such as: *establish a framework for, maintain high levels of nuclear safety, knowledge, skills and competences* and proper nouns such as *Sustainable Nuclear Energy Technology Platform (SNETP)*.

The next stages of our research could then focus on finding equivalents for our terms in the TL.

Researching TL terms

Assuming we want to translate our text into Italian, it would be useful to compile an Italian corpus for this subject domain and to extract

Table 2.6 Word sketch for *nuclear*

nuclear (adjective)
Nuclear safety freq = <u>417</u> (15,514.5 per million)

modifies	<u>398</u>	3.3	and/or	<u>79</u>	1.1
safety	<u>39</u>	10.95	radiological	<u>14</u>	11.97
material	<u>46</u>	10.93	future	<u>6</u>	10.93
field	<u>17</u>	10.15	forensic	<u>4</u>	10.51
safeguard	<u>17</u>	10.07	undeclared	<u>4</u>	10.48
security	<u>14</u>	9.83	certified	<u>2</u>	9.52
fuel	<u>15</u>	9.68	current	<u>2</u>	9.52
installation	<u>10</u>	9.55	various	<u>2</u>	9.49
plant	<u>10</u>	9.47	special	<u>2</u>	9.45
management	<u>11</u>	9.47	major	<u>2</u>	9.42
reactor	<u>11</u>	9.31	structural	<u>2</u>	9.42
forensics	<u>8</u>	9.26	radioactive	<u>2</u>	9.31
facility	<u>9</u>	9.14	innovative	<u>2</u>	9.26
datum	<u>9</u>	9.11	national	<u>2</u>	9.21
energy	<u>7</u>	8.97	other	<u>2</u>	9.14
sector	<u>6</u>	8.89	international	<u>2</u>	8.84
technology	<u>6</u>	8.61	European	<u>2</u>	8.83
cycle	<u>5</u>	8.55			
activity	<u>6</u>	8.52			
system	<u>6</u>	8.49			
measurement	<u>6</u>	8.36			
non-proliferation	<u>4</u>	8.29			
science	<u>4</u>	8.28			
research	<u>5</u>	8.28			
power	<u>4</u>	8.25			
application	<u>4</u>	8.2			

term candidates from that corpus, to help us to identify possible corresponding terms for those we encountered in the ST. A small corpus of texts from the same genre or on the same topic, compiled relatively quickly, for the purposes of researching the language and terminological patterns of a subject domain, is known as an **ad-hoc corpus,** but may alternatively be referred to as a DIY (do-it-yourself) corpus or a disposable corpus. A specialized *ad-hoc* corpus can be much smaller than corpora that are used to gain a more general view of linguistic behaviour (Sinclair 2005).

Sketch Engine has a built-in tool called WebBootCaT that enables us to compile an *ad-hoc* corpus from the web using some key terms which are known as seeds (perhaps based on the principle of cloud seeding). If you do not have access to Sketch Engine you can download and install the BootCaT software as a stand-alone tool, free of charge, at bootcat.sslmit.unibo.it and use it to compile your corpus (see Kilgarriff 2013). 'BootCaT' stands for 'bootstrapping corpus and terms'.

As seeds, we could start with Italian terms we already know to be relevant, like *sicurezza nucleare, materiale nucleare, combustibile nucleare, reattore nucleare*. With these terms as seeds and using WebBootCaT, Sketch Engine compiles a corpus of 53 files and 169,674 words at the time of writing. Using the same tools as above, that is, word lists and word sketches, we can extract candidate terms and examine their behaviour.

In the English text, *nuclear installation, nuclear plant* and *nuclear facility* were used with equal frequency and seem interchangeable. By contrast, according to the patterns in the word sketch for *nucleare* (Table 2.7), we have a clear frontrunner as a potential translation equivalent in Italian, *impianto nucleare*, which is much more frequent than the also acceptable *installazione nucleare*. The Italian corpus is much larger and clearly also covers issues such as nuclear weapons, not the subject of the JRC report. But it is also important to observe

Table 2.7 Word sketch for *nucleare*

nucleare (adjective)
IT nuclear safety freq = 1,652 (7,886.5 per million)

NofA	1,278	4.7	e_o	137	1.3	pp_in	29	0.8	pp_al	6	0.4
centrale	251	11.94	centrale	12	11.05	giardino	3	11.16	fine	3	9.56
reattore	197	11.3	modulare	5	10.09	funzione	4	10.3			
energia	143	11.12	operativo	9	10.08	costruzione	5	9.82	pp_da	5	0.7
impianto	87	10.53	commerciale	5	9.96	modo	4	9.38	parte	3	8.4
fusione	60	10.32	civile	5	9.85						
fissione	61	10.2	italiano	5	9.85	pp_di	14	0.1			
sicurezza	64	10.15	attivo	4	9.78	ricerca	3	10.13			
arma	41	9.93	radioprotezione	3	9.46	potenza	5	10.12			
reazione	45	9.89	presente	4	9.45						
scoria	45	9.89	recente	3	9.41	pp_per	11	0.6			
materiale	30	9.08	europeo	4	9.37	uso	4	8.89			
rifiuto	21	8.65	industriale	4	9.31						
installazione	15	8.53	tedesco	3	9.3	pp_del	12	0.3			
incidente	15	8.35	francese	3	9.29	impianto	5	7.95			
proliferazione	11	8.1	naturale	5	9.29						
esausto	11	8.0	giapponese	3	9.23	pp_con	11	1.0			
programma	8	7.62	primo	3	7.94	unità	3	11.38			
propulsione	7	7.47				plutonio	4	9.65			
Il	7	7.47	pp_a	72	3.3						
bomba	6	7.17	catena	15	11.43	pp_nel	9	0.8			
fonte	6	7.11	fissione	35	11.17	paese	3	9.91			
tecnologia	6	7.07	fusione	9	9.82						
"	6	7.07				pp_ad	7	1.3			
industria	5	6.96				livello	4	9.05			
settore	5	6.96									

that the Italian corpus offers us only one plausible term for *nuclear safety* and *nuclear security*, namely *sicurezza nucleare*, signalling that this term most likely designates both of the concepts referred to in the English text. This hypothesis can be confirmed by searching for both *nuclear safety* and *nuclear security* in other corpora, for example in the Europarl English–Italian parallel corpus (available via Sketch Engine, or from www.statmt.org/europarl/ or via the OPUS collection of corpora at opus.lingfil.uu.se; OPUS, n.d.), where the only Italian translation offered is *sicurezza nucleare*.

Some of the word-sketch patterns for *reattore* (Table 2.8) also reveal terminological correspondences, like *fast reactor* and *reattore veloce*. However, we need to investigate further, looking at the six instances of *raffreddato* (cooling) using the concordancing function to find other compound terms needed. There we see *reattore raffreddato a gas* (gas-cooled reactor), *reattore raffreddate ad acqua* (water-cooled reactor) and *reattore raffreddate ad elio* (helium-cooled reactor). Although not in our data, we might propose *reattore rafreddate a sodio* for *sodium-cooled reactor*, and this term can be verified through other sources.

Finally, as we did for the English ST, we can use Sketch Engine to extract keywords by comparing our *ad-hoc* Italian corpus with a reference corpus for Italian (e.g. the itTenTen corpus, a 3-billion word corpus created by Web crawling and made available in Sketch Engine). As well as generating single-word (simple) term candidates, we can generate lists of keywords based on n-grams to help us to identify compound terms. As noted above, bi-grams are sequences of two words, 3-grams are sequences of three words, etc. Since Italian terms are sometimes formed by nouns or noun phrases linked by prepositions, it is worth looking at longer n-grams too, that is, 4-grams or 5-grams. Examples from this corpus data include *ciclo del combustibile* (fuel cycle) and *ciclo del combustibile nucleare* (nuclear fuel cycle).

Other corpora for terminological research

This kind of terminological, domain-specific research can be carried out with various corpus resources and tools. Another resource worth mentioning here is the Wikipedia corpus, accessible to all at corpus.byu.edu/wiki (registration required) (Wikipedia Corpus, n.d.). This is a 1.9 billion-word corpus made up of 4.4 million Wikipedia articles in English. Searching the entire corpus may be useful for some purposes; however, much more useful for our purposes is the facility to create what the developers call a 'virtual corpus' on a particular topic. This is a sub-corpus of Wikipedia, of up to 1 million words from up to 1,000 articles. It can be created based on titles of pages (e.g. select all pages with *nuclear* in the title), or on the basis of words occurring in the article (e.g. select pages with *nuclear security* in the article) or

Table 2.8 Word sketch for reattore

reattore (noun) IT nuclear safety freq = 1,044 (4,984.0 per million)

n_modifier	16	2.3
pebble	4	12.42
numero	4	8.5

preN_V	142	1.7
uranio	10	11.07
alimentare	7	10.27
costruire	6	10.08
esistere	7	10.07
Un	5	9.98
raffreddare	5	9.84
I	4	9.53
sviluppare	4	9.46
impiegare	3	9.24
essere	32	9.19
rappresentare	3	8.94
affiancare	2	8.81
giudicare	2	8.81
spegnere	2	8.71
utilizzare	6	8.66
chiamare	2	8.59
contenere	3	8.5
In	2	8.38
l	2	8.29

AofN	410	2.5
nucleare	197	11.75
primo	39	10.89
veloce	22	10.61
nuovo	13	9.68
commerciale	8	9.23
raffreddato	6	8.87
tradizionale	6	8.82
stesso	5	8.35
autofertilizzanti	4	8.31
autofertilizzante	4	8.31
odierno	4	8.29
moderato	4	8.28
sperimentale	4	8.23
piccolo	4	8.09
-ale	5	8.0
pronto	3	7.89
avanzato	3	7.89
problematico	3	7.89
grosso	3	7.86
cosiddetto	3	7.85
francese	3	7.84
occidentale	3	7.83
ultimo	3	7.79
civile	3	7.77
naturale	3	7.52

postN_V	164	2.9
autofertilizzanti	16	11.48
raffreddare	9	10.52
RBMK	4	9.58
autofertilizzante	4	9.56
funzionare	4	9.44
incoraggiare	3	9.15
divenire	3	9.11
entrare	3	9.11
progettare	3	9.06
essere	27	8.92
costruire	3	8.91
succedere	2	8.62
distinguere	2	8.61
utilizzare	6	8.6
basare	3	8.59
refrigerare	2	8.55
intendere	2	8.53
nascere	2	8.52
possedere	2	8.49
produrre	5	8.46
fare	3	8.43
trovare	2	8.32
ridurre	2	8.12
raggiungere	2	8.11
avvenire	2	8.02

pp_di	46	0.6
generazione	17	11.67
potenza	11	10.98
ricerca	7	10.9
tipo	8	10.04

pp_a	46	3.5
sala|sale	5	11.32
seconda	2	10.19
sale	2	10.14
nebbia	2	9.87
metallo	3	9.86
onda	2	9.79
fusione	8	9.77
neutrone	8	9.63
fissione	5	8.44
gas	2	8.42

pp_ad	46	14.5
acqua	42	10.23
uranio	2	6.66

e_o	30	0.5
bomba	2	9.13
isotopo	2	8.46
numero	2	7.45
impianto	2	6.59

pp_per	13	1.0
ciclo	3	9.28
produzione	2	8.42
periodo	2	8.12

pp_in	11	0.5
funzione	4	10.57
costruzione	2	8.65
modo	2	8.52

pp_della	8	0.5
centrale	7	8.12

n_modifies	8	1.1
grado	2	9.52

pp_del	5	0.2
tipo	3	8.88

using a combination of both criteria. As illustration, the latter approach produces a corpus of 39 texts totalling 110,276 words. Once you have compiled a corpus, you can search it and generate word lists of various kinds, including what are called 'keywords' in this tool, namely lists based on parts of speech, for example a list of all nouns, all noun+noun patterns and all adjective+noun patterns. Tools are also available to generate KWIC displays and collocates. It is also possible to compare data from your specialist sub-corpus with data from a set of available reference corpora, including COCA (the Corpus of Contemporary American English) and the BNC (British National Corpus).

Finally, if you have access to a parallel corpus for your language combination, that is, a set of texts in one language and their translations in the other, then you can also use corpus tools to analyse how words and terms have been translated by others. Some of the most widely and freely available parallel corpora (e.g. the EuroParl corpus of speeches from the European Parliament, available via the OPUS corpus collection at opus.lingfil.uu.se) are not specialized in science and technology, but you may find parallel corpora that could be useful for your work, for example the EMEA (European Medicines Agency) biomedical corpus in 23 EU languages, also available via the OPUS collection. In addition, if you can collect a set of relevant texts and their translations, you may build your own *ad-hoc* parallel corpus to enable you to conduct your preparatory research.

In later chapters we will see some other uses of corpora, namely to identify vocabulary that tends to occur frequently in texts written by academics, including scientists; not necessarily because they are terms related to a specialist field, but because they are lexical items related to the activity of researching and reporting on research (e.g. *study, group, system, research, level, experiment, process, development, policy, table*). That work shows how corpora can provide us with other useful information about language use, beyond terminology, which has been our main focus here.

This exercise illustrated the kind of information, particularly terminological, that can be extracted from monolingual corpora in the source language and in the TL using frequency lists, keyword lists, concordances and collocational data. If you have relevant parallel corpora, then corresponding TL terms may be identified more easily, using the same tools, including parallel concordancing. While such data can be generated by the software automatically, it is important to note that final judgements about what is and is not a term must be made by you, as translator. Likewise, judgements about likely correspondences between SL terms and TL terms are also made by you, through your interaction with your corpus texts, reference material and other relevant documentation.

Managing and storing terminology

Once you have identified terms in your ST and you have established correspondences with terms in the TL (using corpora or other resources) it is useful to store this data for any future work on texts in this domain. It is not realistic to expect yourself to remember the vast quantity of terminology you encounter, in two or more languages, as a translator. Preparing and keeping terminological records should prove much more reliable than your memory, and it is a much more efficient use of your time to store the fruits of your research than to have to repeat the same research time and again.

The simplest form of terminology storage used by translators is a bilingual glossary, often simply a list of terms in one language and equivalent terms in another language, with no or little other information recorded. This can be produced in a document using a table or a spreadsheet. You can order your lists alphabetically and you can use the 'Find' function to search for specific items. It is quite common to receive glossaries like this from clients or from translation project managers in LSPs as they attempt to standardize some of their terminology for their translators. However, this is not an ideal way of storing your own terminology, for several reasons:

- By storing no additional information about the terms and the concepts they designate, you limit the future usefulness of the data. Additional information that could be extremely useful when you consult your data later include indications of the subject domain, definitions of the concept, examples of term usage, details of the sources you used in your research, notes on term usage, including information on client-specific usage, etc.
- A table or spreadsheet is likely to become unwieldy as it grows. Searching or scrolling through thousands of items is not the most efficient way of accessing the information. As your term list grows, you will not necessarily know whether a given term is in your records, potentially leading to fruitless searches in your lists.
- You are likely to do a lot of your translation work within the editors of translation memory software, designed to assist you in the translation process (see below). It would therefore be preferable to be able to access your terminology records from within the editor of the CAT (computer-assisted translation) tool, rather than having to work with a word-processing or a spreadsheet application at the same time.

The solution to most of these issues is offered by software which has been developed specifically for the storage and management of terminology, in the form of a **termbase** (a terminology database).

A termbase is organized by concept; each concept is given its own entry. A termbase entry therefore typically consists of fields containing information about the particular concept (e.g. subject domain, definition, illustration) and information about the terms in one or more languages used to designate that concept (terms, contextual examples of the terms in use, perhaps grammatical or usage notes). Other fields may be used for administrative purposes to record client and project details, or information about creation, modification or validation processes, particularly for large, shared or institutional termbases. Examples of the latter are the EU's termbase IATE (n.d.; iate.europa.eu), the UN's termbase UNTERM (United Nations Multilingual Terminology Database, n.d.; unterm.un.org) and the Canadian Government's termbase Termium Plus (n.d.; www.btb. termiumplus.gc.ca).

Terminology-management software designed for translators to use for that function is very likely to be integrated with translation memory software. This means you can then benefit from an automatic search for your recorded terms as you encounter them in your ST during the translation process; the software will automatically display the search results, so that you do not have to decide whether to search. If you have recorded a TL term in your termbase already, this automatic retrieval makes it easy for you to copy or insert it into your translation, if you wish. If nothing is found, the software also allows you to add a new term entry quickly as you translate. This will then provide a TL term suggestion for you the next time you encounter the SL term.

Working with dedicated termbases has other advantages, including the possibility of importing and exporting termbase data in a range of formats, which allows data to be shared between translators, LSPs and clients. For example, if you have never worked with a termbase but have term data stored in a Microsoft Excel spreadsheet, this can be converted and imported into a termbase relatively easily. Similarly there are numerous possibilities for exporting data from termbase entries, for example to import into other termbases. The **TBX** (TermBase eXchange) file format is an international standard for terminology data, and all terminology-management software should allow you to import and export data in that format, thus making it easier to switch between terminology-management tools or to import existing termbase data. For example, the Sketch Engine term candidate lists we generated earlier can be saved in TBX format and imported. So too can Microsoft terminology collections, made available in many different languages, in TBX format, from www.microsoft.com/Language/en-US/Terminology.aspx (Microsoft Terminology Collection, n.d.). It is also possible to export data from termbases in other formats, including formats which might be readily accessible to those who do not have access to the termbase software (e.g. for use with office software suites).

The choice of terminology management software may depend on its compatibility with other tools you are intending to use. Many translation memory tools have an integrated terminology management tool which can be used either in conjunction with the TM software or as a stand-alone application. To give just one example, SDL Studio translation memory uses SDL Multiterm for term management, and Multiterm termbases can be accessed from within the translation memory interface. Multiterm can also be run in a stand-alone mode, without the TM, or as a desktop widget.

It is becoming more common generally for us to use 'software as a service' (SaaS), for example the software is not installed locally on our own computers, but instead we use applications installed on servers elsewhere (cloud-based), which we simply access via a website interface. Translation memory and terminology tools are also increasingly used as cloud-based software. One example is MemSource Cloud.

Much of the data that you work with as a translator cannot be shared with others (you may sign non-disclosure agreements with clients or LSPs to guarantee that you will not divulge the content of their confidential texts). However, if you have no impediments and a desire to share your terminology data with others, it is possible to do so using terminology networking sites which are not unlike social media sites. TermWiki (n.d.; www.termwiki.com) is an example of this.

Translation memory

In the previous sections we mentioned **translation memory** (TM) on several occasions. This is software that stores your translations in such a way that segments of text can be retrieved and reused in later translation work, if required. The database of ST and TT segments, mostly organized by sentence, is called a translation memory. The software includes not only this repository, but also usually a comprehensive interface and editor so that you complete all your translation work within the TM application. As you already know, it can interface with your terminology-management software to retrieve terminology matches from your termbase. In a similar manner, as you translate, it also retrieves matches (in accordance with your predefined settings) from your translation memory, showing you how the same or a similar segment of text in the SL was translated on a previous occasion. A principal advantage of using TM is that it is possible to achieve consistency of terminology and phraseology in and between texts, and in one and several translators' work, and at different places and times. Other features of TM use that remain open to debate, and for which more research is required, are to do with expectations of gains in productivity and efficiency.

It is beyond the scope of this book to go into much more detail on how TM works and on how translators use it. However, it is important to recognize that use of TM is taken for granted in many commercial scientific and technical translation settings; you will be expected to be able to use TM software and sometimes you will be required to use a specific TM package, for example one of the market leaders. However, as with termbases, data can be imported and exported in formats that allow exchange between TM systems (the **TMX** format is the international standard for Translation Memory eXchange), so it does not always matter so much which particular software you use, as long as you are proficient at importing, exporting and managing the data. It is also generally the case that, once you are familiar with one TM system, you will find it relatively straightforward to learn how to use others. Widely used, commercially marketed TM systems (with integrated termbase management) include SDL Studio, MemoQ, DéjàVu, Transit, Wordfast and Across, though numerous others are also available, including the open-source Omega-T and MateCat.

When you start working with TM software, you may start with an empty translation memory. It is often possible to use the TM's alignment tools to build up a translation memory from texts and their existing translations, if you have access to some. It is also possible to download ready-made TMs and import them in the TMX format. For example, the DGT of the European Commission makes its TM freely available for this purpose, at www.ec.europa.eu/jrc/en/language-technologies/dgt-translation-memory.

Finally, TMs can be downloaded and uploaded in TMX format via initiatives like TAUS (www.tausdata.org; TAUS Data 2013), where an online search tool also enables you to search for terminological correspondences in existing TM data.

Machine translation

While TM and terminology-management tools are usually described as computer-assisted translation (CAT) tools, machine translation (MT) usually refers to software that produces a translation automatically, without the translator's intervention. Recent advances in **statistical machine translation** (SMT) technology (using corpora as datasets from which statistical models of language and translation are developed) mean that the quality of MT output has improved considerably, compared with what was possible with previous MT approaches. For an accessible overview of SMT technologies, consult Kenny and Doherty (2014).

For some language pairs, and with an SMT system specially developed for specific subject domains or genres, the output can be useful enough for translators or translation agencies to work with. This often means they take the MT output and edit it (a process called **post-editing**) to make it fit for purpose, particularly if the intended purpose is for publication or dissemination outside of an organization, but there are also purposes for which the unedited MT output may suffice. As we will see in Chapter 5 on translating patents, the European Patent Office uses a customized SMT system, called PatentTranslate, developed in collaboration with Google Translate.

Unfortunately it is also common to find organizations relying on the freely available Google Translate, without customization, to provide translations of their externally facing documentation. One example, among many we could cite, is UK-based Soil Machine Dynamics Ltd, or SMD. It describes itself as one of the world's leading manufacturers of remote intervention equipment, including remotely operated vehicles for use in oil and gas industries, and for oceanographic research and other applications. A Google Translate link is offered on their website at smd.co.uk for anyone who wants to access its extensive range of promotional and technical material in a language other than English. It could be argued that their international market is not particularly well served by doing so. A very brief glance at translations into other languages throws up some very obvious issues, like the fact that the company name is translated or partly translated, where it would make more sense to reproduce it in English, with or without a gloss; for example the company name becomes *Bodenmaschinendynamik Ltd* in German, *Terreno macchina Dynamics Ltd* in Italian and *Maaperän Machine Dynamics* in Finnish. Other problems abound throughout the MT-produced website.

A novel, apologetic approach to Google Translate is taken by German renewable-energy institute IWR on their website at www.iwr.de/welcomee.html. They warn the English-language reader that the translation is done by Google Translate, so 'quality of translation is not always well, but you can read our news always "just in time"'. A second point explains to the reader that, whenever a news item begins with the word *cathedral*, 'it means the town Muenster in Germany and is one of the machine-translation problem by google'. Münster, also written Muenster, is a city in Germany (referred to in some of the IWR news items), but the same word also designates a cathedral. The readers of Google's translations are therefore forewarned!

Further reading: Learning more about terminology

The Pavel Tutorial is an online tutorial made available by Public Works and Government Services Canada (www.bt-tb.tpsgc-pwgsc.gc.ca/btb.php?lang=eng&cont=308) and produced with substantial input by the Canadian Translation Bureau. Although it is archived material and therefore no longer updated (a point to bear in mind if reading the sections on tools and technologies), it nonetheless provides very accessible training in the fundamentals of terminology research, and is available in English, Arabic, Dutch, French, Italian, Portuguese and Spanish. Read Chapters 1–3 to learn about the principles of terminology work.

Exercise 2.1: Evaluating the usefulness of institutional termbases

There are numerous institutional termbases that you can consult online, for example:

- IATE, the EU's termbase: http://iate.europa.eu
- UNTERM, the UN's termbase: http://unterm.un.org
- Termium Plus, the Canadian Government's termbase: www.btb.termiumplus.gc.ca.

For these or other online termbases for your language(s), explore them to find out what subject domains and languages they cover. Examine the types of data they store alongside the terms; for example, do they include definitions and contextual examples, information about validation or reliability? Which termbases do you find most useful, as a translator, and why?

Exercise 2.2: Designing your own termbase

If you have access to dedicated terminology-management software, create a termbase in which you will store your scientific and technical terms. If you do not have access to that kind of software, start by recording your terminology in a spreadsheet (e.g. using any office software application). In both cases, consider how you can strike a balance between the kinds of institutional practices you observed in the previous exercise and the practical needs and limited time and resources of a freelance translator. What is the most important information to record, to ensure that you, or your fellow translators with whom you might share your data, will have confidence in the data when you or they consult it in the future?

Exercise 2.3: Accessing reference corpora online

Many reference corpora are freely available online and can be useful in your linguistic analysis and production. They also provide a reference against which you can compare or identify specialized aspects of your specialized texts. For English, two well-known reference corpora, available to consult online, are:

- British National Corpus, BNC: www.natcorp.ox.ac.uk
- Corpus of Contemporary American English, COCA: http://corpus. byu.edu/coca.

Other online corpus resources for English include:

- WebCorp, a synchronic English web corpus: http://wse1.webcorp. org.uk/cgi-bin/SYN/index.cgi
- Collins Wordbanks Online, www.collins.co.uk/page/Wordbanks+ Online (1-month free trial).

Find out whether you can access a reference corpus for your other language(s). Sometimes such corpora are made available as 'national' corpora (e.g. following the BNC model) or they are produced by dictionary publishers (as Collins Wordbanks, above), but there may be other sources of useful reference corpus resources, for example corpus linguistics research groups in universities.

Exercise 2.4: Using corpus tools for your own research

If you cannot gain access to licence-based corpus tools such as Sketch Engine, Wordsmith or ParaConc, identify freeware (e.g. AntConc) that you can download and use. Familiarize yourself with the main functions, for example compiling a corpus, generating concordances and sorting them to examine patterns, generating word lists and keyword lists.

To compile your own *ad-hoc* corpora from the web, download and use BootCat: www.bootcat.sslmit.unibo.it. You can then import these corpora into your corpus software. To work with *ad-hoc* corpora without downloading software, try out the functionalities for compiling and querying corpora on specific topics from Wikipedia at http://corpus. byu.edu.

Further reading: Learning more about corpus-based linguistic and translational analysis

Read Wynne (2005) for guidance on using corpora for linguistic analysis generally and Olohan (2004) or Zanettin (2012) for corpora in translation studies.

Further reading: Learning more about TM and SMT

Read Kenny and Doherty (2014) for an accessible overview of SMT technologies. Read Schjoldager and Christensen (2010) for a review of research on translation memory in the 2000s and Moorkens (2012) for an example of a study focusing on TM and consistency.

Key points from this chapter

- An understanding of the nature of concepts and terms helps translators to deal with specialized texts, enabling them to ascertain what research is required to gain an understanding of the concepts and to become familiar with the relevant SL and TL terms.
- Scientific and technical translators need to be proficient in the use of a variety of technologies used during the translation process, including research or preparatory phases.
- *Ad-hoc* and reference corpora can be very useful resources for terminological and phraseological research in preparation for translation.
- It is important to develop good practices for storing and managing your terminology.
- TM is widely used for scientific and technical translation and can help with consistency and productivity.
- Machine translation is increasingly used in scientific and technical translation contexts, but works better when extensive resources are put into developing customized, domain-specific and/or genre-specific systems. In most cases, raw MT output is unlikely to meet professional standards for essential, external-facing documentation.

References

Anthony, Laurence (2014) *AntConc*, Tokyo: Waseda University, online at: www.laurenceanthony.net/ (accessed 15 January 2015).

IATE: Interactive Terminology for Europe (n.d.) online at http://iate.europa.eu (accessed 30 January 2015).

Kenny, Dorothy and Stephen Doherty (2014) 'Statistical Machine Translation in the Translation Curriculum: Overcoming Obstacles and Empowering Translators', *The Interpreter and Translator Trainer* 8(2): 276–94.

Kilgarriff, Adam (2012) 'Getting to Know Your Corpus', in Petr Sojka, Aleš Horák, Ivan Kopeček and Karel Pala (eds) *Text, Speech and Dialogue: 15th International Conference, TSD 2012, Brno, Czech Republic, 3–7 September 2012. Proceedings*, Berlin: Springer, pp. 3–15.

—— (2013) 'Terminology Finding, Parallel Corpora and Bilingual Word Sketches in the Sketch Engine', in *Proceedings of ASLIB 35th Translating and the Computer Conference, London*, online at: www.mt-archive.info/10/Aslib-2013-Kilgarriff.pdf (accessed 30 January 2015).

Kilgarriff, Adam, Vít Baisa, Jan Bušta, Miloš Jakubíček, Vojtěch Kovář, Jan Michelfeit, Pavel Rychlý and Vít Suchomel (2014) 'The Sketch Engine: Ten Years on', *Lexicography* 1(1): 7–36.

Microsoft Terminology Collection (n.d.) online at: www.microsoft.com/Language/en-US/Terminology.aspx (accessed 30 January 2015).

Moorkens, Joss (2012) 'A Mixed-Methods Study of Consistency in Translation Memories', *Localisation Focus*: 11(1): 14–26.

Olohan, Maeve (2004) *Introducing Corpora in Translation Studies*, London and New York: Routledge.

OPUS: The open parallel corpus (n.d.) online at: http://opus.lingfil.uu.se/ (accessed 30 January 2015).

Schjoldager, Anne Gram and Tina Paulsen Christensen (2010) 'Translation-Memory (TM) Research: What Do We Know and How Do We Know It?', *Hermes* 44: 89–101.

Scott, Mike (2015) *Wordsmith Tools*, Liverpool: Lexical Analysis Software, online at: www.lexically.net (accessed 15 January 2015).

Sinclair, John (2003) *Reading Concordances*, Edinburgh and London: Pearson Education.

—— (2005) 'Corpus and Text – Basic Principles', in Martin Wynne (ed) *Developing Linguistic Corpora: A Guide to Good Practice*, Oxford: Oxbow Books, pp. 1–16, online at: www.ahds.ac.uk/linguistic-corpora/ (accessed 12 January 2015).

TAUS Data (2013), online at: www.tausdata.org/ (accessed 30 January 2015).

Termium Plus (n.d.) online at: www.btb.termiumplus.gc.ca (accessed 30 January 2015).

TermWiki (n.d.) online at: www.termwiki.com (accessed 30 January 2015).

UNTERM: United Nations Multilingual Terminology Database (n.d.) online at: https://unterm.un.org/ (accessed 30 January 2015).

Wikipedia Corpus (n.d.) online at: corpus.byu.edu/wiki (accessed 30 January 2015).

Wynne, Martin (ed) (2005) *Developing Linguistic Corpora: A Guide to Good Practice*, Oxford: Oxbow Books, online at: www.ahds.ac.uk/linguistic-corpora/ (accessed 12 January 2015).

Zanettin, Federico (2012) *Translation-Driven Corpora*, Manchester: St Jerome Publishing.

3 Technical instructions

This chapter focuses on a genre that plays an important role in the supply and use of technical products, that is, instructional texts aimed at helping users to install or operate those products. These come in the form of instruction manuals, user guides, operating or installation instructions. In the context of international trade and distribution of goods, documents of this kind are frequently translated, often from one source language into multiple target languages. We consider the communicative purposes of this genre, we think about what it means for a set of instructions to be usable, and we examine typical rhetorical features of instructions and their composition. Drawing on examples, we discuss some common translation issues.

Introducing instructions

Many of us may have become frustrated at some point with deficiencies in the set of instructions we were working with when trying to use or install something, especially for the first time. Perhaps we lost our way because the instructions were pictorial only? Perhaps there were verbal instructions but none available in our preferred language? Perhaps the instructions were in our language but we could not make sense of them for some reason? We may even have suspected that flaws in a translation were to blame for our problems.

In this chapter we examine the genre of technical instructions. We start by thinking about what it means for instructions to be usable. We then focus on the genre in more detail by considering the different types of information contained in instruction manuals and the ways in which they can fulfil a range of communicative purposes. We conclude by discussing some common difficulties faced by translators of technical instructions.

Usability

A key criterion for designers of any technical documentation is usability. This is particularly salient in the case of technical instructions. Instructions must enable users to perform a given task. This operative function is a key aspect of the genre. However, as noted by Alexander (2013) and others (and as captured in the exasperation of the crude instruction in English slang to RTFM!), users often have negative perceptions of instructions and try to proceed with their task without reading them or may merely skim them. Ganier (2004) points out that instructions are often written to be followed in a linear fashion (to be read before performing the task), but that users frequently use the instructions in a more interactive fashion, turning to them (only) when they need help with a particular feature, function or problem. Eiriksdottir and Catrambone (2011: 750) also make the point that users often opt for a technical product to improve performance in some way and, if the product is used incorrectly or inefficiently, this potential productivity gain is lost and users may be rather dissatisfied. For these reasons it is important for instructions' authors and designers to focus on producing instructions which are usable, so that the operative function can be fulfilled.

There is an extensive literature on usability and usability testing, often related to products, for example consumer goods. The usability of instructions can form part of the usability testing of the products. For many purposes usability is understood, as in the ISO definition, as 'the extent to which a system, product or service can be used by specified users to achieve specified goals with effectiveness, efficiency and satisfaction in a specified context of use' (British Standards Institution 2010). 'Effectiveness' relates to the accuracy and completeness with which users achieve intended goal(s). 'Efficiency' refers to the resources (time, effort) expended by users in achieving the goal(s). 'Satisfaction' is about users' attitude towards the experience (ibid.).

Another aspect of the user's experience that is sometimes also discussed in relation to instructions is meaningfulness. Steehouder et al. (2000), for example, argue that a set of instructions might enable people to complete a task, but that it is not enough to measure success in terms of accuracy or time taken. They suggest that instructions have to be meaningful too, that is, they have to 'enable the users to build a mental representation or model of the technological device and its use' (ibid.: 464).

Some research on instructions (Eiriksdottir 2011) also distinguishes between usability and learnability, that is, a distinction between instructions that enable users to carry out a one-off task and instructions from which users learn and can transfer their knowledge. For example, Eiriksdottir and Catrambone (2011) show how users perform well when given quite specific instructions, requiring relatively low cognitive effort to process. However, users appear to learn and transfer their knowledge better when they work from more general or more abstract instructions, which require more cognitive effort for processing in the first instance.

Quesenbery (2003) developed an approach to usability (of products and systems, including websites, for example) which incorporates these criteria in the easy-to-recall '5 Es'. For a system to be regarded as usable it must be effective, efficient, engaging, error tolerant and easy to learn. This taxonomy can be extended to technical documentation and translation (see also Byrne 2006).

While efficiency is often measured in terms of time, it is also interesting to think about it in terms of cognitive resources. Research findings of relevance for document designers includes Ganier's (2004) analysis of the cognitive effort required in performing a task at the same time as trying to follow instructions. He notes that effort has to go into first finding the appropriate instruction in the text, then understanding it, then applying it, and he also draws attention to the difficulties of switching between task and text (which he calls macro-switching) and between text and graphics in the document (micro-switching).

Readability

Another criterion by which technical documents, including instructions, may sometimes be judged is readability. While usability focuses on how well the product or document works for its context of use, readability is a measure based on formal aspects of the text such as sentence length, word length, average number of words per sentence, average number of syllables per word, proportion of complex words (e.g. words of three or more syllables) in English. These are considered as being approximate measures of syntactic or lexical complexity. The readability score is calculated based on a formula drawing on some of those aspects. The score may also be equated to a reading age or a school grade level. Commonly used readability indices for English are the Flesch-Kincaid Reading Ease, the Gunning Fog Score and the SMOG Index, though there are also others. To give an example of the kind of calculation involved, the Flesch-Kincaid score is based on a 0–100 scale. The higher the score the more readable the text. The formula to calculate it is:

$$206.835 - 1.015 \times (\text{words} \div \text{sentences}) - 84.6 \times (\text{syllables} \div \text{words})$$

Similar indices or modifications of the English-language ones tend to be applied to other languages, for example the Amstad score or Wiener Sachtextformel for German, or the Flesch-Vacca score for Italian.

It is important to note that these kinds of readability scores do not tell us much about usability. They do not take any account of text organization, meaning, domain specificity, etc. Ongoing research on readability tries to approach the issue of readability in a more nuanced way, by seeking to take account of morphological information, but also other lexical and syntactic measures which may be more indicative of simplicity or difficulty of texts than, for example, number of syllables in words. Similarly, languages like Chinese may require analysis at sub-character as well as character level. Other lexical measures being considered in current research on readability include comparison against basic vocabulary lists for the language in question, or calculation of the **lexical density** (ratio of content words to the total number of words) or the ratio of nouns to verbs. Syntactic features of clauses and clause constituents may also be analysed (e.g. numbers and length of noun phrases, verb phases, prepositional phases). Morphological analysis is a crucial aspect for languages with rich derivational and inflectional morphologies. Readability measures could therefore try to take account of verb inflections for person, tense, mood and case, and derivational suffixes for nouns. See Hancke et al. (2012) and Dell' Orletta et al. (2011) for examples of how this kind of research is being developed for German and Italian respectively.

Words and images

In this chapter we will focus on instructions that have a substantial verbal component, produced as print-based texts and disseminated with products and made available on support or documentation sections of websites. These remain the norm, but it is worth noting that there are alternative ways of designing instructions. Many of us may be familiar with Ikea's wordless assembly instructions (see www.ikea.com). Their widespread use seems to imply that cross-cultural understanding of such diagrams is unproblematic, but it is important to note that images are used to represent concepts and require us, as readers, to draw on particular understandings and experiences of the structures and relations of our conceptual world. The representation offered by images reflects and embodies cultural, social, iconic and symbolic conventions.

Many instructions rely on a combination of words and images. The kind of diagrams that are included in instruction manuals are often used iconically, to resemble particularly salient or abstracted aspects of the concept in an informative way; they do not aim to offer a close physical resemblance. Indeed, it is often the case that adding more detail to a diagram detracts from its informativeness or usability. Some diagrams used in instruction manuals are symbolic, in that they are part of a conventionalized set of symbols that do not rely on resemblance, but rather on readers learning the symbols and their fixed meaning. Examples include the symbols to inform us how to care for clothes (indicating whether washing, dry-cleaning, tumble-drying, etc. is advised or not) or the symbols to warn us about handling toxic or hazardous substances. See Amare and Manning (2008) for further explanation of the iconic and symbolic nature of visuals in technical documentation, drawing on Piercian semiotics.

The use of diagrams and other forms of images may be carefully considered by technical writers and document designers at the time of authoring, but on many occasions it is assumed by clients and others that translated texts can simply reuse the same images. Sometimes this is unproblematic, but translators and clients should also be aware of the potential for cultural specificity and of the necessity to make judgements about cultural appropriateness, extending also to use of specific colours, for instance (see Cyr et al. 2010 for one of very few studies that considers the cultural specificity of colour, in this case focused on how trust in websites may be built among culturally diverse users).

Many of us have also made use of video instructions, often as online tutorials, for example as used by Microsoft. We will not focus on video instructions here, but the genre is an interesting one for future consideration. It is a prime example of multimodal communication, where a combination of images (moving, still, animated, etc) and text (on-screen writing, voice-over narration, etc) is employed to instruct users. If you wish to explore visual elements and multimodality further, Kress and van Leeuven's (2006) grammar of visual design offers a useful set of analytical tools. Alexander (2013) gives an informative overview of previous research into the usability of video instructions before reporting on her own experiment to see whether video or print instructions are more usable for relatively simple computer-based tasks. The video instructions were considered more usable in terms of effectiveness and level of comprehension. Users of the video instructions made fewer errors and they retained more information, because they had to watch or re-watch the entire video. But that was also a source of frustration and made them slower in their performance. Using the print instructions, participants could locate information faster and complete tasks faster. The print instructions therefore elicited higher user-satisfaction ratings and a higher preference overall for that task. Although more research is called for, that study is also a useful one because it highlights the potential tensions between different usability components; efficiency and user satisfaction were higher for the print instructions despite lower effectiveness and learnability.

Features of instructions

Instructions may be presented as a short text in leaflet or booklet form or as a lengthy manual or handbook. Depending on length and medium of production, the booklet or manual may consist of a range of different sections or components, apart from the main body of instructions. This could include front and back covers, a title page, a table of contents, an edition notice, trademarks, disclaimers, warranties, licence agreements, precautionary/safety notices, appendices, glossary, index, user registration form, user comment form, among others.

Below we will focus our attention on what is generally the main body of the text, the instructions. Instructions for use of consumer goods are very frequently translated and some of these are used as examples below. Longer excerpts come from the English-language instruction booklet for the Lakeland Bread Maker Plus (Model 17892), reproduced here courtesy of Lakeland (www.lakeland.co.uk). Lakeland is a UK-based company which distributes household appliances from a range of international brands and their own Lakeland brand. For their own small kitchen appliances (e.g. kettles, toasters, coffee machines, blenders), Lakeland provides operating instructions in English, German and Arabic, to cater for the German-speaking consumers who access their products via an online German-language store and the Arabic-speaking consumers who shop at their 10 physical stores in the United Arab Emirates, Saudi Arabia, Kuwait, Oman and Qatar. Short excerpts are quoted from a range of other sources where additional exemplification is needed.

Transitions from one state to another

The most essential type of information in instructions is procedural information. This comprises the steps that users need to perform. Procedural discourse guides users in their performance of the task, detailing conditions for actions, actions, and results from actions. Farkas (1999) and van der Meij and Gellevij (2004) describe usefully how procedural discourse help users to move from one set of circumstances, or state, to another state. The goal, as presented to the user, is the **desired state**. The **prerequisite state** is a condition for moving towards the desired state. As users move towards the desired state, they pass through **interim states**, and they avoid **unwanted states** (Farkas 1999: 42–3).

Excerpt 3.1, from the start of the Bread Maker booklet, outlines the prerequisite state (you want to bake your own bread) and the desired state (producing a range of delicious breads and cakes, in sizes to suit you, for many years to come):

EXCERPT 3.1

We are sure you will be delighted with the performance and will enjoy many years of baking your own delicious bread. This Bread Maker makes two sizes of loaf – 700g and 1000g. This allows you to choose a medium or large loaf depending on your needs. This versatile

machine has 12 settings allowing you to make basic, wholemeal,
French and sweet breads as well as excellent cakes, dough and
quickbreads.

The next section of the booklet, entitled Safety Cautions, outlines
some of the unwanted states (of electrocution or burns), in cautioning
against certain human actions or undesirable system responses; for
example: *To protect against fire, electric shock or personal injury, do
not immerse cord, plug or unit in water or other liquids*; or *Do not
place hands in the oven chamber after the bread pan has been removed
as it will be very hot.* Other unwanted states may arise from external
factors, for example if your electricity supply does not match the voltage shown on the appliance.

The instructions then guide users through set-up of the appliance
and operation of the pre-defined baking programmes (Basic, Whole
Wheat, French, Quick, Sweet, Cake, etc.). Successful operation of
those programmes may be a desired state in itself or may be seen as an
interim state towards a more ambitious desired state, as indicated by
the description of the Custom function in Excerpt 3.2:

EXCERPT 3.2

When you have become very proficient and have mastered the art of
bread making you may wish to change the way the bread maker pre-
pares and cooks your loaf. The CUSTOM function allows you to set
your own timings to produce a loaf to your own specification.

User background knowledge and expectations

To fulfil its key communicative purpose of guiding users through a set
of procedures, the Bread Maker instruction booklet has been written
with a specific set of prospective users in mind. Instructions for use of
a consumer product such as this are generally written so that a layper-
son or non-specialist can understand, and this is also the case here.
However, a little understanding of bread or cake baking is assumed,
so, for example, concepts such as *muffin batter, French style bread,
gluten-free flour* are not further elaborated in the text. Assumptions
are also made that the user is already equipped with items such as a
non-stick spatula, an oven glove, a cooling rack, etc. The use of British
English (e.g. through orthographic choices of *-ise* over *-ize* and *-our*
over *–or*, and use of lexis such as *jams* and *marmalades*) is also indicative of an non-US anglophone target readership. The product and the
instructions aim to make the baking process straightforward, so there

is no technical detail on the internal functioning of the machine; users learn nothing about how the heating elements of the machine work, apart from being reassured that a slight burning smell is normal when it is used for the first time.

Promotional function

As we will see in greater detail below, the instructions guide the user through certain procedures. However the rhetorical function of promotion is also important here. The user needs to be convinced not only of the usefulness of the product, but also of the usefulness of reading the instructions. The instructions therefore not only guide the user through the operation, but must also be authoritative enough to convince the user of their reliability and usefulness. As noted by Farkas (1999: 44), credibility can be established, at least initially, through professional appearance of the documentation. In this case, complemented by its professional presentation, our text also seeks to establish the company's credibility through the introductory passage reproduced in Excerpt 3.3, which appears immediately before the booklet's table of contents. Here several positive attributes of the company's operation and ethos are mentioned, and the company's longevity and quality control procedures are emphasized.

EXCERPT 3.3

An award winning family-owned business, here at Lakeland we still have the same values of excellent quality, value for money and exceptional customer care as we did when we first set up the company in the 1960s. Our products are carefully selected and rigorously tested to meet our high standards, so you can be assured that any product you purchase will be easy-to-use and highly durable.

Alongside statements promoting the company, a set of instructions, particularly for consumer goods, often starts by congratulating the user on their choice or purchase of that particular product, implying that the reader has exercised good judgement in choosing this product over others.

Later in the Bread Maker booklet, interspersed with procedural instructions, the ease of use of the machine is emphasized, thus also promoting the product and its functions. Examples are statements such as: *This will also show you how easy the Bread maker is to use*; *The electronic scales are very accurate and easy to use*; and *The Bread Maker will produce approx 450g jam or marmalade simply and easily*; and the prefacing of some instructions with *simply*, for example *To adjust the baking time simply press the TIME button and set your own baking time.*

Streamlined-step procedures

Farkas' (1999) analysis is of streamlined-step procedures in computer help systems, but this gives us a useful starting point for thinking about the typical or key components of instructions more generally. In the case of the streamlined steps of help systems, the steps themselves tend to be brief, made up of one or two action statements, sometimes followed by feedback statements about how the system will respond. Such steps can also be found in our Bread Maker text. Let's consider Excerpt 3.4, the components of which are then explained below.

EXCERPT 3.4

START/STOP

For starting and stopping the selected programme.
To START a programme, press the START/STOP button for approx. 2 seconds. A short beep will be heard and the two dots in the time display begin to flash. The programme will start.
To STOP a programme, press the START/STOP button for approx. 2 seconds until a beep confirms that the programme has been switched off.

Basic action statements

As is typical in English, the action statements in Excerpt 3.4 use an imperative verb form, *press*. Since there are two procedures in this section (starting and stopping the programme), the action statements are preceded by an infinitive clause, helping to make the goal or desired state of each procedure clear. It makes sense to cluster these two procedures together in one section, because they deal with closely related functions, performed in a very similar manner. Once you know how to do the first, you may simply require confirmation that the second is performed in a similar way. The action statements are followed by a modifying adverbial phrase. Farkas (1999: 47) calls these types of statements 'facilitating modifiers', because they typically give information relating to the location, time or manner of the action. In Excerpt 3.4 the information is about duration of the action (i.e. approximately 2 seconds).

Feedback statements

Both action statements are followed by sentences or clauses informing users of what they should expect to happen as a direct consequence of that action, that is, the result of the action. In this case they will receive visual or auditory feedback from the appliance to signal that they have achieved the desired state.

Headings, subheadings

The steps are streamlined in that there is relatively little information preceding them, other than the title *START/STOP* and a brief explanation, in the form of a subheading: *For starting and stopping the selected programme.* The heading (formatted in bold uppercase) and subheading perform the function of introducing the procedure but also enabling users to identify the procedure quickly and easily and decide whether it is relevant to their needs. The heading and subheading used here are formulated in ways which are very typical for English. Gerunds – *starting, stopping* – are often used and work well to designate processes. Other typical formulations for headings in English instructions are verb roots (as here, where the function designations are also the roots *STOP/START*), infinitives (e.g. 'to stop the programme') and noun phrases (e.g. 'termination of the programme'). Infinitives as headings are perhaps less flexible, because they require a set of steps to follow immediately, not allowing for the addition of conceptual information, described below.

We can see that procedures and sub-procedures are organized in a logical hierarchy using headings. If stepwise instructions were not organized in this way they could appear as a sequence of seemingly arbitrary steps which users might be able to follow, implement and to some extent remember, but the purpose of which may never be entirely clear.

More complex action procedures

The start/stop procedures presented above are very simple; many procedures will contain greater complexity, for example by encompassing variant goals or giving users options, as in Excerpt 3.5:

EXCERPT 3.5

Adding extra ingredients

You can do this in two ways (or a combination of both)

1. You can add extra ingredients to the bread pan with your basic ingredients. If added at the start of the programme they will be

> more finely distributed throughout the mixture and will not remain whole – they will however add flavour and colour to the dough.
> 2. Put the extra ingredients such as nuts, cranberries, raisins etc. in the auto dispenser – they will automatically be poured into the machine at the correct time and will remain whole.
> OR
> 3. If using the DOUGH programme you can knead extra ingredients in by hand before shaping and baking.

In other steps, users may be presented with conditions (often unwanted) to test for, with actions varying depending on the conditions found. Excerpt 3.6 illustrates a set of conditions and actions.

EXCERPT 3.6

POWER FAILURE BACKUP SYSTEM

The Bread maker is equipped with a power failure backup system or memory. If the power system is interrupted during the course of bread making, the process of making bread will be continued automatically within 10 minutes, even without pressing the START/STOP button. If the interruption time exceeds 10 minutes, the memory cannot be kept and you must discard the ingredients in the bread pan and start again. If the dough has not entered the rising phase when the power supply breaks off, you can press the START/STOP button directly to continue the programme from the beginning.

The conditions outlined in Excerpt 3.6 may not worry users too much, since they only need to be consulted in the event of power failure, which is likely to be quite rare in those environments where bread-making machines are commonly found. However, Farkas (1999: 48) notes that a preponderance of conditional and user option steps can be off-putting and disruptive, forcing users to perform more decision-making and troubleshooting than desirable, and suggesting deficiencies in the product and documentation.

Conceptual information

Other optional elements may be found in procedures, particularly when they are more complex. These include what Farkas (1999) calls a 'conceptual element', that is, further information to help the user to decide whether to perform the procedure. Excerpt 3.7 from another section of the Bread Maker text illustrates this. Some conceptual information follows the heading and subheading to explain the procedure further in the form of a concrete example.

EXCERPT 3.7

DELAY FUNCTION

TIME (This enables you to delay the start time)
   The maximum delay time is 13 hours. If you want to delay the start time so that the bread cooks overnight and is ready to eat in the morning:

Example:
   It is 8.30 pm and you want your bread ready at 7 am the following day – i.e. in 10 hours and 30 minutes.

• Select your programme, loaf size and colour.
• Press the TIME button to add the time until 10.30 appears on the display screen.
• Remember to include the operation time of your chosen programme.
• Press the START/STOP button to activate the delay function.
• The dots will flash and the numbers will count down to show you the remaining time.
• The bread will be ready for you at 7 am.

Adding functional information to instructions can help users to understand the device or system (Steehouder et al. 2000). In particular, research (ibid.) indicates that adding this information before the action statement, rather than after, can be more helpful to readers (compare *To turn light Y on, press button B* with *Press button B to turn light Y on*). By contrast, there seems to be little evidence to show that the addition of real-life references or situations contributes to meaningfulness of procedural instructions, although this technique is also used.

Safety notices

Actions which can lead to unwanted states usually appear before the step in question, often explicitly labelled, for example, as CAUTION or WARNING. As noted above, in the Bread Maker document, a preliminary section groups numerous safety cautions together, preceding all other procedures, as recommended by international standards guidance (British Standards Institution 2013). Within that section, one alert is preceded by *Warning* and another by *Caution*; examples are seen in Excerpt 3.8.

EXCERPT 3.8

WARNING: A cut off plug inserted into a 13 amp socket is a serious safety (shock) hazard.

[. . .]

CAUTION: The plastic bags used to wrap this appliance or the packaging may be dangerous. To avoid risk of suffocation, keep these bags out of reach of babies and children. These bags are not toys.

The *ISO/IEC Guide 37:2012 Instructions for use of products by consumers* (British Standards Institution 2013) recommends that instruction writers use a hierarchy of 'signal words' when alerting users to risks and unwanted states of various kinds. The *ISO Guide* suggests using DANGER, WARNING and CAUTION to alert users to high, medium and low risks respectively, though it also concedes that the distinctions might be too subtle to affect users' behaviour and it suggests the use of 'signal phrases' (e.g. DANGER OF DEATH or RISK OF BLINDING) where these might be more effective. The use of NOTE can also seen in some instruction texts, sometimes as a fourth, or lowest step in a hierarchy of alerts. Typical recommendations to technical authors are that they use the relevant signal word, then identify the hazard, say how to avoid it and say what consequences will follow if it is not avoided. It is also common practice (as codified, for example, in the international standard ISO 3864-2 *Graphical symbols – Safety colours and safety signs – Part2: Design principles for product safety labels* (British Standards Institution 2004) or the American ANSI Z353.4 counterpart) to reserve DANGER for hazardous situations which, if not avoided, will result in death or serious injury, CAUTION for those situations which may result in death or serious injury and WARNING for risks which may result in minor or moderate injury. NOTE or NOTICE, by contrast, usually does not relate to injury.

Taking the installation guide for the Mira Platinum shower as an example, we may note that the section entitled *Important Safety Information* is divided into two sub-sections, the first comprising a set of statements entitled *Warning!* and the second a set of statements entitled *Caution!* In addition to these headings, bold formatting and capitalization are used in some formulations for emphasis, for example in the *Warning!* section. Elsewhere among the procedural instructions for the Mira Platinum shower additional alert indicators are used (*Note!* and *Important!*), also in conjunction with bold formatting for added emphasis, but not related to the risk of injury, for example **Important! If supplied Slide Bar spacers are required,** *centre distance for hole will increase to 75 mm from wall* (p. 22, bold emphasis in original).

Rich-step and paragraph-format procedures

The streamlined-step procedure may be most straightforward and simplest, but instruction writers may use other formats, for example a rich-step procedure, in which multiple steps are clustered together, or a paragraph-format procedure (Farkas 1999), which is likely to include information types other than procedural (see next section). An example of an effective rich-step procedure can be seen in Excerpt 3.9 from the installation booklet for the HPS Hı-Velocity Air Purification System (ingenious-air.co.uk/wp-content/uploads/2014/04/HPS-Hi-Velocity-Air-Purification-System-Installation.pdf). This section explains how to reset the service lights when the filter or lamp has been changed in the air purification system. Here, we can note that several action statements (*bend, insert, push*), with facilitating modifiers (*into only the hole corresponding to; lightly until*), are combined in one procedure, which also combines the two variants of resetting the service light for the lamp and the service light for the filter. The action statements are preceded by highly relevant conceptual information to enable the user firstly to locate the reset holes and then to distinguish one from the other. The final element is a feedback statement, and the title, in gerund form, makes clear what the multi-step procedure aims to do.

EXCERPT 3.9

Resetting Service Lights

On the right side of the service panel, there are arrows pointing to two small holes marked reset. One is marked filter and one is marked lamp. Using a small paper clip, bend out one leg straight and insert the end of the paper clip into only the hole corresponding to the replaced component and push lightly until the service light returns to the green position. The computer is now reset.

Declarative and motivational information

Other types of information may also be present in instructions, generally described as declarative information and motivational information (in contrast to procedural). Declarative information may describe the workings of the equipment, device or system; this is also called operational information or system information in the technical writing literature. While it is thought that some information of that kind can improve users' mental representation of the system or device, much of the existing research is inconclusive as to its usefulness for users. Karreman and Steehouder (2004), for example, conclude from experiments that the inclusion of system information may have more negative than positive effects, in that it presents a higher cognitive load to users, causing users to judge the text (and potentially the appliance or device) as difficult to work with and leading to a decrease in users' self-efficacy ratings. Excerpt 3.10 presents an example of operational information from the user guide for the Zeiss Conquest HD Binoculars; and Excerpt 3.11 is from an instruction booklet for Bosch refrigerators.

EXCERPT 3.10

The effective protective coating for the lens surfaces noticeably reduces contamination of the lenses through a special smooth surface and the combined beading effect. All types of contamination adhere less and can be quickly and easily removed, smear-free.

EXCERPT 3.11

The more refrigerant an appliance contains, the larger the room must be. Leaking refrigerant can form a flammable gas–air mixture in rooms which are too small. The room must be at least 1 m^3 per 8g of refrigerant.

A further example can be seen in the installation instructions for Adore Touch UK (click-click) floor covering. A 6-page document contains some step instructions under headings of *General Guidelines* and *Installation*. However, more than three pages are devoted to sections giving detailed declarative explanation of various flooring conditions, effects of products which may or may not be used, construction principles and standards. These are intermingled with some procedural instructions on how to rectify certain conditions or how to act if particular conditions are encountered.

Motivational information is thought to help to engage readers, give users a sense of satisfaction or positive experience from using the instructions, or motivate them to persevere with the task if they encounter difficulties. In research to ascertain how users might benefit from motivational information in instructions, Karreman and Loorbach (2013) identified three motivational goals leading to user satisfaction: (i) users' attention should be stimulated and sustained; (ii) users should be convinced of the relevance to their situation or personal goals; (iii) users should have an appropriate level of confidence in their ability to perform the task. The *For Dummies* series of guide books is often cited as an example of how text and graphics, frequently humorous, are used to engage and motivate potentially reluctant users in these ways.

If the writer has consciously intermingled declarative and motivational information with procedural statements, it may be with the explicit aim of engaging readers and furnishing them with more elaborate conceptualizations of the product, system or action as they undertake the action. However, the intermingling of different types of information may also be indicative of poorly written instructions which would benefit from reformatting or rewriting in a more explicitly procedural manner.

Translating instructions

Many products are distributed internationally or nationally to different language communities. User instructions are often authored in one language and then translated into a range of other languages. The international standard, *EN 82079-1:2012 Preparation of instructions for use. Structuring, content and presentation. General principles and detailed requirements*, specifies how instructions for use should be produced and recognizes the need for translation, but does not say very much more about it. It specifies that 'expert translators or specialists shall be responsible for the translation including checking and proof reading' and that they should have 'basic competences in communication, particularly technical communication' as well as familiarity with the subject area and be fluent in source and target languages, being 'preferably native speakers in the target language'. The standard also recommends that 'colloquial expressions and untypical regional variations of names and product features should be avoided'. Finally it stipulates that the translations should be 'edited by qualified persons specializing in writing and translating for the target groups' (British Standards Institution 2012).

We noted above that the booklet or manual may contain sections other than the main set of instructions. If you are commissioned to translate the booklet or manual, your task will be to translate all of these sections. Therefore, while most of your work will involve technical procedures and technical concepts, a small part of it may require you to deal with legal terminology or phraseology too, if often rather formulaic, as in this example from a liability statement: *The Company shall not be liable for any indirect, exemplary, special, punitive, consequential or incidental damages in connection with or arising out of the use of products provided hereunder.* By consulting terms of business, warranty and liability statements in your two languages, you can become familiar with conventional forms of wording for such statements.

We will use an example of a short instruction booklet for the Lakeland Hand Mixer Set Model 13653 and its translations into German and Arabic to illustrate some points below. The English instructions are reproduced in Appendix 1, courtesy of Lakeland (www.lakeland.co.uk) and can also be found online. Other short examples are taken from a variety of sources to illustrate additional points. Some observations relate to a set of instructions for a more specialized technical document, the 160-page manual for the Mobotix FlexMount S15 thermal-imaging camera and accompanying software, available at www.mobotix.com/eng_GB/Products/Thermographic-Cameras/FlexMount-S15-Thermal/. This will be referred to as the Mobotix S15.

User background knowledge and expectations

Like the Bread Maker Plus instructions, the instructions for the Hand Mixer Set may also be considered typical of instructions aimed at non-specialist users of household appliances. Users can be expected to have some interest in the tasks performed with such appliances but are not expected to have specialist technical knowledge. An awareness of the difference between whisking, blending and chopping is presupposed in the English-language instructions. A similar skill set and background knowledge may be assumed for the users of the German and Arabic instructions.

As was the case for the Bread Maker Plus, the target readership for the English-language instructions is British. As such, the instructions contain some UK-related information. Translators into other languages, producing instructions for use in other countries, may need to question the usefulness of that information for their readership and modify or omit accordingly. For example, the English instructions conclude with a section on electrical connections, specifically a section on how to fit a new three-pin plug conforming to British standards. Presumably because this particular set of instructions would not be relevant, the German text simply omits any reference to electrical connections or plugs. However, the Arabic instructions include this full section. This may be an appropriate strategy, given that the Middle-Eastern countries in which Lakeland operates use three-pin plugs, among others, but it is unclear whether all the information, including the reference to British standards, is relevant for the target readership.

Other examples from the text might lead us to question whether sufficient attention has been given to intended readership by the translator into Arabic. The passage reproduced as Excerpt 3.12 is clearly for the benefit of UK consumers. Its reference to UK recycling points is not likely to be relevant to the Arab consumers. However, it has been translated in full in the Arabic instruction booklet. The German translation, by contrast, simply omits this section.

EXCERPT 3.12

RECYCLING YOUR ELECTRICALS

Along with many other high street retailers, Lakeland has joined a scheme whereby customers can take their unwanted electricals to recycling points set up around the country. Visit www.recycle-more.co.uk to find your nearest recycling point.

Similarly, consider point 14 from the list of safety precautions reproduced as Excerpt 3.13. In the second of the three sentences, there is a reference to a customer support helpline. The German version translates the other two sentences but omits the sentence about the helpline, since this UK-based, English-language service may not be particularly useful or relevant for a German consumer. The Arabic version includes that sentence and the telephone number, though this information is not likely to be of any use, particularly given that the phone number is not preceded by the relevant international dialling code. The Lakeland website for the Middle-Eastern region gives the telephone numbers of the stores in the region; if alerted to the inappropriateness of the UK phone number for Arab consumers, perhaps Lakeland, as client, could have considered whether the contact details of those stores could have been included here instead, as more useful to the Arab consumer, or whether the helpline information could have been omitted.

EXCERPT 3.13

14. Do not use the blender if the power cord or plug show any signs of damage, or if the appliance is dropped, damaged or working incorrectly. Call the helpline on 015394 88100 to arrange a repair by an authorised repairer, or a replacement. Never try to repair the blender yourself as this may cause electric shock.

Streamlined-step procedures

The English-language instruction booklet for the Bread Maker Plus consists, to a large extent, of streamlined-step procedures, and in the previous section we identified the various components of these, as well as noting additional declarative and motivational information. The instructions for the Hand Mixer Set can be characterized in a similar way. After the list of 14 safety precautions, the user is instructed on how to unpack and handle the appliance, and how to use for blending, whisking and chopping, as three separate sets of procedural instructions. The procedural steps are numbered and provide succinct and clear instruction, using imperative verb forms for the action statements, for each chronological stage in the process. Translating these streamlined-step procedures into other languages should be relatively straightforward, due to the logical structuring, use of headings, short sentences and uncomplicated syntax.

Languages may have various options when it comes to expressing directives. Frequently the second-person imperative form of the verb is used in English, as illustrated often in our example texts, such as in Excerpt 3.13: *do not use . . . , call . . . , never try to*. Other ways of expressing directives in English that figure in the example text include modal constructions, in passive or active voice; for example: *[c]hildren should be supervised to ensure they do not play with the blender*; and, from the instructions for a software installation: *At this point, you can create a new VM based on the newly-cloned-and-modified* [sic] *template*. Directives that might be more typical of a textbook than an instruction booklet include first-person imperatives (e.g. *let's . . .*) and performatives (e.g. *we note that . . .*). Other indirect forms could include formulations such as *it is recommended/advisable to*. Where different options are available when translating directives into a TL, translators can decide based on typical writing practice in similar streamlined-step instructions written in the TL. The prevalence of the passive voice in the English version of the Mobotix S15 instructions is striking and could be accounted for by the use of the passive in the German text; arguably the genre conventions could be better met by translating some of those instances using other constructions that are more typical of directives in English, like imperatives.

Similarly, every language has options and conventional patterns for formulating headings and subheadings. We noted that the English gerundial form is particularly effective for denoting processes. When translating into other languages, we can assess the options available and make choices based on our genre-related observations and analyses.

As we saw above, the combination of action statements is common in streamlined-step procedures, and these can be similarly effective when translated. However, it may be necessary to check that the combination of steps remains logical after translation decisions have been taken for individual action statements. For example, an English-language instruction from the Moulinex multilingual booklet for use of their kettles reads: *Before first use, rinse the inside of your kettle, and boil and empty it once or twice.* Previous experience may enable the user to realize that the kettle should also be filled with water before it is boiled, not simply rinsed (the French source text reads *Avant une première utilisation, rincez l'intérieur de votre bouilloire et réalisez 1 ou 2 ébullitions*). The scope and positioning of facilitating modifiers (modifying adverbial phrases) with action statements may also require attention, even in short, streamlined-step instructions, as illustrated by an example from the English instructions for the Swiss-made Solis plate warmer: *When the warm plates are taken out, after 15-20 minutes, it is imported* [sic] *to remove the plug at the same time.*

Finally, translators may have the scope to consider the level of explicitness and level of detail or granularity of stepwise procedures. Sometimes SL instructions can contain information which is likely to be regarded as superfluous, repetitive or redundant in the TL, and vice versa. This can prompt a discussion with the client about possible omissions or reorganization of the instructions, particularly if ST and translations are not being printed side by side in multilingual versions.

Declarative and motivational information

Each set of procedures in the Hand Mixer Set instructions is preceded by declarative statements of outcomes, making reference to likely situations of usage, that is, *soups, sauces, dips, mayonnaise, milkshakes and baby food can be blended in moments, the balloon whisk is suitable for whipping cream, egg whites, light sponge mixes and instant desserts* and *meat, cheese, onion, fresh herbs, garlic and nuts can all be successfully chopped using the chopping bowl and blade.* As noted above, some indication of the outcome can improve users' performance of the procedural task. Given that our experiences of food can vary across cultures, the translator might review these outcomes to ensure that they represent typical desired outcomes for the target reader and substitute other food products if necessary.

These statements motivate the user through use of adverbs like *easily* and *successfully*; the user of the TL text might be similarly motivated by lexical choices made by the translator. Even in the much more technical instructions for the Mobotix S15, we can also observe some attempts to motivate the user, such as on p. 15, for example mounting a particular module is described as *extrem einfach* (*extremely easy* in the English version), and, to emphasize the ease and motivate the user, the stepwise set of instructions that follow are concluded by an exclamation: *fertig!* (*You're done!* in the English version).

Promotional function

As in the case of the Bread Maker, the rhetorical function of selling the product and the company is performed by text on the first page. However, perhaps for reasons of space and brevity, the passage promoting the company and its values and strengths, which featured in the Bread Maker Plus booklet and in instruction booklets for numerous other Lakeland products, is not included on this shorter leaflet. Here the appliance is simply introduced in terms of its strengths, functions and usefulness, as seen in Excerpt 3.14.

EXCERPT 3.14

Thank you for choosing this stainless steel stick blender, complete with a range of accessories for blending, chopping and whisking. This powerful kitchen helper takes the time and effort out of many culinary tasks, and comes with a handy storage bag.

Translators may seek to maintain this promotional function through their lexical choices, thus encouraging a favourable attitude towards the product and the instructions. The German translator has done so in Excerpt 3.15 through the use of expressions such as *Reihe von Zubehör* (range of accessories), *leistungsstarker Küchenhilfer* (powerful kitchen helper), *handliche Aufbewahrungstasche* (handy storage bag) and the idiomatic expression 'zu einem Kinderspiel machen' – to make it child's play.

EXCERPT 3.15

Vielen Dank, dass Sie sich für diesen Edelstahl-Stabmixer von Lakeland entschieden haben, der mit einer Reihe von Zubehör zum Pürieren, Zerkleinern und Verquirlen ausgestattet ist. Dieser leistungsstarke Küchenhelfer macht viele Aufgaben in der Küche zu einem Kinderspiel und wird in einer handlichen Aufbewahrungstasche geliefert.

As we noted above, modifications have been made elsewhere to maintain an impression of credibility in the German text, notably by removing details which are not relevant to the German users. The Arabic text, on the other hand, preserves UK-specific details, which may arguably be detrimental to the Arabic users' impressions of reliability or usability of the instructions.

Terminology

On the first content page of the instructions booklet for the Hand Mixer Set, the appliance is depicted and its component parts numbered and labelled. These terms identify the main component parts (e.g. *balloon whisk, whisk collar, blender stick, speed selector*) and they are used consistently throughout the English text. A typical feature of instructions for consumer goods and other perhaps familiar items is that they use labels for components parts that are otherwise seldom referred to by users and may only ever be encountered by users in written instructions on use, maintenance, etc. For example, *whisk collar* may not be a term familiar to the users of hand blenders, though it should be readily understood with the help of the diagram and knowledge of the context. Translators into other languages may likewise not be immediately familiar with the terms for component parts of familiar items, so some research is necessary; other sets of instructions in the target language for similar products can be a useful source of terminology. Once translators have identified the corresponding TL terminology, they will seek to use it with the same degree of consistency (as can be observed, for example in the German translation of the Hand Mixer Set instructions).

It is important to note that some companies create or use terms for their products or product parts in a proprietary or company-specific way, as a way of distinguishing themselves and their products from competitors. If that is the case, it is useful for clients to provide translators with company glossaries to indicate their preferred or required terms. Without glossaries or information from the client, a study of any existing translations for the client's products may provide some terminological insight.

Other aspects of language usage discussed above concerned the use of signal words for hazardous situations. Since the use of a hand blender is not particularly hazardous in normal situations, the English text uses only *CAUTION* and *PLEASE NOTE*. Translators into other languages would normally employ lexical items denoting corresponding levels of seriousness, as conventionally used in instruction manuals, for example as can be seen in the use of *ACHTUNG* and *BITTE BEACHTEN SIE* in the German instructions for the Hand Mixer Set.

Completeness

A more technical product will often be accompanied by more extensive documentation, and this is the case for the Mobotix Flex Mount S15 thermal-imaging camera and accompanying software; the manual comprises 160 pages of text and image. As might be expected, the manual contains a substantial amount of declarative information about how the product works and how it can be used before getting to instructions on how to install and set up. It is clearly anticipated that the user should have an in-depth understanding of the product before starting to work with it. Some of the challenges of translating longer and more complex texts can be illustrated by means of this documentation. One risk is that translators and checkers can overlook parts of the text and an instance of this can be seen in section 2.2.7 of the S15 Mobotix S15 instructions. A text box, headed *Note*, contains two short paragraphs in English and one in German; clearly it was intended for the third paragraph to be in English too, but it has been overlooked in the translation process.

Consistency

Another general challenge for authors and translators of technical documentation alike is to achieve consistency between graphics and text referring to the graphics. This can be particularly problematic when translating instructions pertaining to software. For example, at several points in the Mobotix S15 manual (e.g. pp. 132 and 136), it is clear that the software interface for controlling the camera and its recordings is in German, so the menu items, buttons, dialog-box text, etc. that appear in the screenshots are in German. However, the software menu items, buttons, etc., when they occur in the instructions, have been translated into English. Therefore there is a lack of correspondence between the graphics, in German, and the instructions, in English.

This may not matter too much to the user when the buttons in the screenshot are labelled *Ja* and *Nein* and the instruction says *Click Yes*, assuming it has been explained to the user what they are agreeing to! However, more complex instructions and less familiar software functions will not be accessible to an English-language user if the software interface is in German and the screenshots display the German interface but the software functions have been translated into English in the written instructions. For example, is a user to know that *Anzeige-Modus* as a menu item in the software corresponds to *Display Mode* in the instructions? The question to be asked of the client before completing this translation is whether the interface has been or will be localized in English (or whatever the target language). If so, it would be necessary for you, as translator, to know what terms are to be used for menu items, for buttons and in dialog boxes in the interface and use them in the verbal instructions. Ideally the screenshots in the German manual would be replaced by a new set of screenshots from the English interface for the English version of the manual. If the interface of the supplied software is to remain in German, the screenshots in the English manual would benefit from some additional English-language labelling for non-German-speaking users, even if superimposed over existing images.

For any long document, it may also be challenging to achieve consistency across the document. Where instructions are detailed and some procedures are similar, it is common and generally advised to use similar or repeated or consistent forms of wording. The ISO/IEC GUIDE 37:2012 *Instructions for use of products by consumers* notes that repetition can help to reinforce key points of operation or safety:

> given that the understanding and memory of consumers can never be assumed to be perfect, there is a need for a degree of 'redundancy' (in engineering terms) to be incorporated into the design and communication of product instructions in order to improve their effectiveness.
>
> (British Standards Institution 2013: 5)

Some examples can be seen in the Mobotix S15 manual (e.g. p. 87), where the instructions for connecting the patch cable to the camera are very similar to the instructions for connecting the patch cable to an MX patch box, MX-NPA box or a standard network port, and both sets of instructions are more or less repeated in a later section (ibid. p. 98). The English translated text also repeats the formulations, showing that the translator had noticed the repetition and opted to reproduce it. When translating, repeated or similar segments in the ST can easily be identified with the help of translation memory tools (see Chapter 2), thus helping to ensure that the translator is, in turn, consistent in their wording of the TT.

Exercise 3.1: Consulting technical writing guidance

There are many guides available online and in print that set out to teach people how to write various kinds of technical documents, including procedural instructions. An accessible one that focuses on writing instruction manuals is the *Tech Writing Handbook* (Wiens and Bluff 2014) produced by Dozuki. Dozuki is a visual, online documentation platform that emerged from iFixIt, an online community of people producing and sharing their own repair manuals. The manual can be accessed at www.dozuki.com/tech_writing. Read it and extract five key messages about writing instructions that you think will also be relevant for translating instructions.

Exercise 3.2: Translating instructions for a consumer product

For a consumer product of your choice, find operating instructions in your source language and translate (all or sections) into your target language. If a set of instructions is already available, disregard them until you have completed your translation. You may then wish to compare your version with the published one, bearing in mind that the published one may have deficiencies. Discuss the ST, TT and the translation process, considering aspects such as:

- Communicative purposes of ST and TT;
- Likely profiles of target audiences for ST and TT;
- Usability of ST and TT;
- Key features of procedural discourse in ST and TT, for example formulation of title and subtitles, hierarchical or logical organization of procedures and sub-procedures, formulation of action statements and feedback statements;
- Use of declarative information, for example conceptual information about procedures, general principles of the device/system, depiction of real-life situations in which the product or system may be used;
- Use of motivational information;
- Use of technical terms and cultural references;
- Use of graphics and their relationship to the verbal elements of the text, for example positioning, layout, labelling, numbering, cross-referencing.

Exercise 3.3: Translating specialized technical instructions

For a technical product of your choice which is not familiar to you, find operating or installation instructions in your SL and translate (all or sections) into your TL. If a set of instructions is already available in your TL, disregard them until you have completed your translation. You may then wish to compare your version with the published one, bearing in mind that the published one may have deficiencies. Discuss the ST, TT and the translation process; consider aspects such as those listed in the previous task.

Exercise 3.4: Thinking about usability

Find a set of instructions for a particular procedure for which you need guidance (e.g. using a software feature or device with which you are not familiar). Using the instructions, complete the procedure, then reflect on the usability of the instructions, with reference to efficiency, effectiveness and user satisfaction, or the 5 Es, namely were the instructions effective, efficient, engaging, error tolerant and easy to learn? Can you identify any changes which might improve the instructions in terms of any of these criteria?

Exercise 3.5: Thinking about readability

Find two excerpts from technical documentation of any kind, one that you perceive to be quite difficult to read and one that is much easier, in your view. Try to identify some features of the texts that make them difficult or easy to read. Then, using an online readability test, such as the one found at www.read-able.com, test both text segments. Do the readability scores tally with your perceptions? If not, can you offer any possible explanations for the differences?

Taking a text that the readability score judged to be difficult, and knowing what you do about how readability scores work, edit the text in a deliberate attempt to achieve a better score, that is, a text that is more readable, according to the test metrics. What types of changes had most impact on the score? What kinds of impact might your changes have for readers of the text? How do the readability judgements relate to usability?

Exercise 3.6: Learning about technical communication research

Research on technical communication is published in a number of international journals, including those listed below. These are useful resources if you are interested in knowing about research on various aspects of technical communication, written and oral. Check whether you have access to any of the following journals and search them for any relevant contributions relating to translation or multilingual documentation production.

* *IEEE Transactions on Professional Communication*
* *Journal of Business and Technical Communication*
* *Journal of Technical Writing and Communication*
* *Technical Communication*
* *Technical Communication Quarterly.*

Further reading: Learning about technical translation research

Research on technical translation is relatively sparse in translation studies. Consult Olohan (2008, 2013) or Aixelá (2004) for an overview.

The *Journal of Specialized Translation, JoSTrans* (www.jostrans.org), is an open-access resource with some articles related to technical translation.

Key points from this chapter

- Instructions for use of products by consumers and specialists are produced in a variety of formats and forms and they are frequently translated between languages.
- Technical writers work to informal guidelines (as in the Dozuki Tech Writing Handbook) or more formal specifications (as in the ISO/IEC Guide 37: 2012) when producing instructions, and instructions can be judged in terms of their usability.
- A key purpose of instructions is to guide the reader through a set of procedures, but instructions can also perform informative and promotional functions, and procedural information can be accompanied by conceptual/declarative information and motivational information.
- Research comparing instructions in the SL and the TL will provide the translator with ample information about genre conventions, relating to aspects such as how directives are typically expressed and how procedures are organized in sections and logical progressions.
- Instructions may require cultural adaptation, not only in relation to cultural references, but also with regard to degree of explicitness and level of detail of stepwise instructions.

References

Aixelá, Javier Franco (2004) 'The Study of Technical and Scientific Translation: An Examination of Its Historical Development', *Journal of Specialised Translation* 1: 29–49, online at: www.jostrans.org/issue01/art_aixela.php (accessed 15 January 2015).

Alexander, Kara Poe (2013) 'The Usability of Print and Online Video Instructions', *Technical Communication Quarterly* 22(3): 237–59.

Amare, Nicole and Alan Manning (2008) 'A Language for Visuals: Design, Purpose, Usability', in *Professional Communication Conference (IPCC 2008) Proceedings*, pp. 1–9, online at: http://dx.doi.org/10.1109/IPCC.2008.4610192 (accessed 30 January 2015).

British Standards Institution (2004) *ISO 3864-2 Graphical Symbols – Safety Colours and Safety Signs. Part 2: Design Principles for Product Safety Labels*, London: British Standards Institution.

—— (2010) *EN ISO 9241-210:2010 Ergonomics of Human–System Interaction. Part 210: Human-Centred Design for Interactive Systems*, London: British Standards Institution.

—— (2012) *EN 82079-1:2012 Preparation of Instructions for Use. Structuring, Content and Presentation. General Principles and Detailed Requirements*, London: British Standards Institution.

—— (2013) *ISO/IEC Guide 37:2012 Instructions for Use of Products by Consumers*, London: British Standards Institution.

Byrne, Jody (2006) *Technical Translation: Usability Strategies for Translating Technical Documentation*, Dordrecht: Springer.

Cyr, Dianne, Milena Head and Hector Larios (2010) 'Colour Appeal in Website Design within and across Cultures: A Multi-method Evaluation', *International Journal of Human–Computer Studies* 68(1-2): 1–21.

Dell'Orletta, Felice, Simonetta Montemagni and Giulia Venturi (2011) 'READ-IT: Assessing Readability of Italian Texts with a View to Text Simplification', in *Proceedings of the Second Workshop on Speech and Language Processing for Assistive Technologies, SLPAT'11*, Stroudsburg, PA, USA: Association for Computational Linguistics, pp. 73–83.

Eiriksdottir, Elsa (2011) *The Role of Principles in Instructions for Procedural Tasks: Timing of Use, Method of Study, and Procedural Instruction Specificity*, unpublished PhD thesis, Atlanta, Georgia: Georgia Institute of Technology.

Eiriksdottir, Elsa and Richard Catrambone (2011) 'Procedural Instructions, Principles, and Examples How to Structure Instructions for Procedural Tasks to Enhance Performance, Learning, and Transfer', *Human Factors: The Journal of the Human Factors and Ergonomics Society* 53(6): 749–70.

Farkas, David K. (1999) 'The Logical and Rhetorical Construction of Procedural Discourse', *Technical Communication* 46(1): 42–54.

Ganier, Franck (2004) 'Factors Affecting the Processing of Procedural Instructions: Implications for Document Design', *IEEE Transactions on Professional Communication* 47(1): 15–26.

Hancke, Julia, Sowmya Vajjala and Detmar Meurers (2012) 'Readability Classification for German Using Lexical, Syntactic, and Morphological Features', *Proceedings of COLING 2012*: 1063–80.

Karreman, Joyce and Nicole Loorbach (2013) 'Use and Effect of Motivational Elements in User Instructions: What We Do and Don't Know', in *Professional Communication Conference (IPCC 2013) Proceedings*, pp. 1–6, online at: http://dx.doi.org/ 10.1109/IPCC.2013.6623940 (accessed 30 January 2015).

Karreman, Joyce and Michaël Steehouder (2004) 'Some Effects of System Information in Instructions for Use', *IEEE Transactions on Professional Communication* 47(1): 34–43.

Kress, Gunther and Theo van Leeuwen (2006) *Reading Images: Grammar of Visual Design*, 2nd ed., London: Routledge.

Olohan, Maeve (2008) 'Scientific and Technical Translation', in Mona Baker and Gabriela Saldanha (eds) *Routledge Encyclopedia of Translation Studies*, London and New York: Routledge, pp. 246–9.

—— (2013) 'Scientific and Technical Translation', in Carmen Millán Valera and Francesca Bartrina (eds) *The Routledge Handbook of Translation Studies*, London and New York: Routledge, pp. 425–37.

Quesenbery, Whitney (2003) 'The Five Dimensions of Usability', in Michael J. Albers and Mary Beth Mazur (eds) *Content and Complexity: Information Design in Technical Communication*, Mahwah, NJ: Routledge, pp. 81–102.

Steehouder, Michaël, Joyce Karreman and Nicole Ummelen (2000) 'Making Sense of Step-by-Step Procedures', in *Professional Communication Conference (IPCC 2000) Proceedings*, pp. 463–75, online at: http://dx.doi.org/ 10.1109/IPCC.2000.887303 (accessed 30 January 2015).

van der Meij, Hans and Mark Gellevij (2004) 'The Four Components of a Procedure', *IEEE Transactions on Professional Communication* 47(1): 5–14.

Wiens, Kyle and Julia Bluff (2014) *Tech Writing Handbook*, San Luis Obispo, California: Dozuki, online at: www.dozuki.com/tech_writing (accessed 15 January 2015).

4 Technical data sheets and technical brochures

This chapter focuses on the genres of technical datasheets and technical brochures. Both genres play an important role in the marketing and supply of technical products, and are frequently translated in the context of international trade and distribution of goods. We consider their communicative purposes and use examples to highlight their typical features, and we reflect on some ways in which you can prepare to translate them. Translation challenges are also addressed with reference to examples of translated texts.

Introducing technical datasheets and brochures

In the previous chapter we focused on a genre with a strong operative function. In this chapter our attention is directed at a genre whose primary function is to inform users about a technical product, the technical data sheet, or TDS. A TDS is often a short document, one or two pages, containing a summary of the key features of the product and a set of technical specifications or more detailed information about the product. The TDA enables expert users to understand the specific features of that product, for example so that they can compare it with alternative products. While TDS may vary in their degree of technicality, they usually address readers with some existing expertise on the product or its potential application. This is the reason for some of the distinctive features of the genre, as we will see below. In addition, it may be noted that the product information is important, but TDS often perform a promotional function too, specifically by highlighting the key features of the product as strengths or advantages. Thus, some features of marketing discourse will often appear in TDS too, as we will also see below. Most commercial organizations provide access to their TDS on their websites and many provide translations in a range of languages for international markets. This is a very frequently translated genre. TDS in multiple languages are usually published as separate documents, but can sometimes be seen in bilingual or multilingual formats; examples of bilingual English and German TDS can be found in the product information on the Thermokon website (www.thermokon.de/produkte/), while examples of TDS in five languages can be seen on the Zanardi Alternatori site (www.zanardialternatori.it).

Technical brochures are generally longer documents than TDS, often consisting of several data sheets, for example to represent an entire product range or series, or a set of products that share specific properties. Those data sheets are often prefaced by other text and images in the brochure with a strong promotional function. The brochure itself is therefore often a document with higher production values than the TDS. For the purposes of international trade and marketing, these brochures are also translated, though it is not uncommon to find that companies commission translations of their TDS, but not of some of their longer brochures.

TDS and their translation

In this section we examine closely a typical TDS in English, to become more familiar with some features of the genre, and we consider some of the decisions to be taken if we were to translate this material. Our example is the TDS for a product called 'HardieBacker 12mm cement board for walls'. HardieBacker is the brand name and this product, produced by James Hardie, is a cement board which can be fixed to a wall and onto which tiles or stone can be laid. On the product page of the company website (www.jameshardie.co.uk/hardiebacker-12mm-cement-board), HardieBacker 12mm is described as in Excerpt 4.1.

EXCERPT 4.1

HardieBacker 12mm is a water-resistant, cement backerboard for tile that fastens directly to the wooden frame of a wall. A good tile job begins with using the right materials, and when tiling onto a wall in a wet area, there are a few important things to consider.

HardieBacker cement backer board is impervious to water damage and will not rot, crack, or swell in the wettest conditions.

It contains MouldBlock Technology™, an anti-mould additive that prevents unseen mould growth behind the walls. It contains no paper facing, a food source for mould[,] or gypsum, which can disintegrate with continuous water exposure.

Unlike plasterboard, Hardie Backer board has a unique cement formulation providing a strong bond to all ceramic or natural stone tiles for applied weights of up to $100kg/m^2$.

It is non-combustible and carries an A1 fire rating. Hardie Backer 12mm can also be used on the floor when additional height is needed, behind a boiler, or even behind a multi-fuel or log burning stove.

This description highlights the key features of the product (is impervious to water, prevents mould growth, provides a strong bond for tiles, is non-combustible). In one statement it is compared explicitly to an alternative (*unlike plasterboard . . .*). Reference is made to compliance to fire regulations (*A1 fire rating*) and to propriety technology, the anti-mould additive called *MouldBlock Technology (TM)*. From this description non-specialist readers can understand the key features of this product and their attention is directed to the advantages offered by this product, as outlined in the text and as highlighted graphically alongside it by four green icons with slogans underneath them (*Water resistant, Mould resistant, Strongest on market, Easy to install*) and brief further explanation below each one which repeats the information in the text above (see www.jameshardie.co.uk/hardiebacker-12mm-cement-board).

The TDS for the product is available as a downloadable PDF from www.jameshardie.co.uk. It is a two-page document, available in English only. It is reproduced in Appendix 2, courtesy of James Hardie Building Products Ltd. Examining it more closely, we can identify some specific features which are also typical of TDS more generally.

Corporate and brand identity

In the banner at the top of p.1 of the HardieBacker TDS, the product name is given on the left-hand side, with the header *Technical Data Sheet* on the right-hand side announcing the document type very clearly. The company name, logo and website URL are displayed at the bottom of p. 1 of the TDS. The banner across the top of both pages of the TDS is in the green of the company logo. The company contact details are at the bottom of p. 2 of the TDS, alongside logos of certifying bodies (see below). The bottom of p. 2 features a trademarked company strapline or slogan: *DO IT ONCE, DO IT RIGHT*. The footer of both pages contains a statement, in a very small font size, pertaining to copyright, trademarks and additional information:

> © *May 2012. James HardieTechology Ltd. All rights reserved.* ™ *and* ® *denote trademarks or registered trademarks of James Hardie Technology Ltd. Additional installation information, warranties and warnings are available at www.jameshardie.co.uk.*

These features are very typically found in the TDS; as a document presenting a company's product, the TDS is likely to display the company or corporate brand and identity prominently, using product brand names, logos, slogans and straplines, as well as names, contact information and website addresses. Many companies use a template for their TDS, with these elements set up as standing items to ensure consistency of layout and presentation across an entire product range. Logos of external certifying bodies or partners lend credibility to the company and, by extension, to the product.

It is generally expected that the look and feel of the document, which may include the overall layout and the use of colour and graphics, will be recreated in the translated text, given the important attention-attracting and unifying functions these elements perform. If translating from English, it is not uncommon to leave logos and slogans in the SL, but there are also circumstances in which slogans and perhaps product names may be transliterated and/or translated. It is important to consider the probable effectiveness of these strategies for your particular target readership and to take note of existing translation practices for your language combination. For example, slogans and product names in English would typically not be translated into German; indeed companies operating in German-speaking countries sometimes create their own slogans in English rather than in German. The Swiss company Autoform provides an example of this. Autoform produces software for die-making and sheet metal forming. It uses the English-language slogan *Forming reality*, incorporated as part of its logo. This English-language logo is reproduced throughout all of its documentation in numerous other languages, including German, Chinese, Korean, Japanese and Russian. Autoform does not transliterate the company name, but reproduces it in Roman script, even in languages that use other scripts or writing systems. Autoform product names are also reproduced in Roman script only for the most part, though an explanation or 'gloss' is added in brackets to the Chinese text, as this page header illustrates: Auto Form-Process Planner plus 工艺规划. This is not uncommon practice and is also a useful approach for proper nouns designating proprietary technology. Similarly Dyson's Airblade Tap hand dryer is marketed in Japanese as Dyson Airblade Tap ハンドドライヤー and in Russian as Сушилка для рук Dyson Airblade Tap (where the Japanese and Russian text indicate that it is a hand dryer but the English product name is used).

An example from a JCB brochure, to be discussed further in the next section, is the reference to *our Efficient Design philosophy* in the English text, which is translated in a FR brochure, with gloss, as *notre philosophie Efficient Design (conception efficiente)*, thus preserving the brand identity while providing further explanation of the concept in the TL. Finally, as noted by Wang (2012), it is not uncommon for brand names to be transliterated in Chinese, preserving the sound of the original, as in 克里斯第安迪奥, a transliteration of Christian Dior. It can be a further challenge, in transliterating brand names into

Chinese, to try to establish this phonetic resemblance to the SL while choosing words or phrases that also convey some of the positive attributes of the product. Wang (ibid.) presents the example of Peak Sport's running shoes, with Peak transliterated as 匹克, two characters that also figure in the Chinese word for Olympic, 奥林匹克, thus constituting an apt name for a sports brand. Similar transliteration considerations can come into play when translating in the other direction; Kum et al. (2011), for example, explore users' preferences for transliteration, translation or what they call 'phonosemantic translation' of brand names from Chinese to English.

Footers are often used to present legal or administrative information, including disclaimers, and such statements often appear in small print on TDS. Despite their unobtrusive appearance, they usually include some text which needs to be translated. The contact details given in the ST may be reproduced in the TT but they might need to be replaced or added to by the client, for example if there are local offices or distributors. Telephone numbers may need to be adjusted, for example by adding an international country code, and it is useful for the clients to consider what services they can or cannot offer non-SL speakers through their website, email addresses and telephone lines.

Graphical elements

Apart from the banner noted above, the green icons summarizing key characteristics of Hardiebacker which we saw on the product web page also appear here, in a vertical configuration on the left-hand side of p. 1. Some TDS contain images of the product itself in a prominent position on p. 1, though this is not the case here. At the bottom of p. 1. there is a restatement of the key advantages of the product, in uppercase letters and a larger font size, coloured green for additional eye-catching appeal (*PREVENTS MOISTURE DAMAGE[,] MOULD GROWTH & TILE FAILURE*). The TDS contains three tables with technical specifications, and the final section on installation shows three colour diagrams with components labelled, to provide guidance on installing.

Graphical elements which incorporate text, such as the green icons and the installation diagrams, may present practical difficulties for translation when the text within the graphics has to be translated, depending on the file formats that are made available to the translator and the expectations of the client. One possible scenario is that the TDS is made available in its native file format, that is, the format in which it was originally produced, thus allowing the text and graphics to be edited. In that case, the SL text in the graphic will be replaced by text in the target language(s). This may be relatively straightforward but can sometimes entail adjustments to spacing and sizing of text to make sure that the TL text (which may be longer or shorter than the SL text) fits comfortably and appropriately in the space available. If DTP software is being used to produce a publication, the translator (via an LSP) may pass text on to a DTP specialist to incorporate into the graphics. An alternative scenario may involve the translator having to work with graphics that are not fully editable. In those cases superimposing text boxes onto existing graphics can be a solution, though this may not be ideal.

Promotional function

As in this TDS, the product description is usually featured towards the top of the first page of a TDS. This, along with the document heading, makes it clear what product is being specified, and what its key features are, perhaps distinguishing it clearly from other similar products in a range. You may also find a set of key strengths or advantages of the product, either as part of the description or as a separate list, often presented as a bulleted list. For example, the list of features of the Horstmann ChannelPlus XL Series 2 electronic programmers is prefaced on the TDS by: *Electronic programmers that offer up to four independent channels and feature a clearly read display and ease of programming.* Excerpt 4.2, from the TDS of the Flymo Power Trim 500 XT grass trimmer, provides another example of marketing discourse in the TDS.

EXCERPT 4.2

Powerful electric grass trimmer and lawn edger. The quick and easy way to trim and edge contours of your lawn.

Twin Autofeed cutting line: Automatic double line feed for easy use and fast trimming.

Plant Guard: Plant guard preserves line and protects plants and shrubs.

Shrubbing: Trim difficult to access places.

In line edging: Unique roller for easy edging.

Technical data

As the name suggests, a TDS is highly likely to contain arrays or tables of technical data, often product specifications which include numerical values, as in the HardieBacker example. These can make up a large part of the TDS. In the HardieBacker TDS they are presented as a small table under the 'Physical Properties' heading and two tables under the 'Health and Safety' heading, one for the

6-mm backerboard and one for the 12-mm backerboard. Each table lists a set of material properties grouped into categories of physical attributes, durability, fire, thermal and weight capacity. For each property, the following are given: a test method (reference to an international standard), the unit or characteristic being tested or measured, the test requirement and the result of the test for this product (e.g. for some tests simply *Pass*, but for others a specific measure, score or category).

Units of measurement

Given the focus on technical specifications, TDAs often include units of measurement. SI (Système International) metric units are widely used internationally, though not universally. The USA continues to use US customary units, though dual-labelling (metric and customary units) is mandatory on consumer goods and both systems can be found in use in technical industrial sectors. The UK operates only a partial metric system alongside imperial units, but metric units are generally accepted in technical documentation. EU regulations continue to permit the use of non-SI units for specific uses, thus allowing the pint of beer or milk, for example. It is also useful to note that occasionally metric and imperial are used together, as in tyre sizing. A 235/55 R17 tyre means the type is 235mm wide, has a profile which is 55 per cent of the width, and is for wheels with an inner-rim diameter of 17 inches.

This TDS contains data expressed in SI base units of length (millimetres, mm) and weight (kilograms, kg) and in SI-derived units of pressure or stress (mega-pascal, MPa), area density (kilograms per square metre, kg/m^2), thermal conductivity (watts per metre-kelvin, $W/(m \cdot K)$) and thermal resistance (square-metre-kelvin per watt, $(m^2 \cdot K)/W$). If translating this TDS, we can therefore use the same abbreviations in translations in Roman scripts and the standardized equivalent words or abbreviations in other languages.

One issue in translation of technical specification data is the use of the comma or point as the decimal marker, and to a lesser extent the comma or point as the thousands separator. To avoid confusion with the thousands separator, SI specifications recommend use of the space as the thousands separator, but decimal markers are either the comma or point, depending on language, and translators often need to convert them from one to the other marker. Given that this is a relatively straightforward conversion, it is surprisingly common to see translated TDS data where no conversion has been done, perhaps because the client has not commissioned a translation of the numerical data but has simply reused a data table or figure from the ST. At the time of writing, examples could be seen in the German, French and Italian

TDS for various solar panel modules, translated from English for the Indian solar energy company Moser Baer Solar (www.moserbaersolar.com/products-downloads-datasheets.asp).

It may be noted that the Moser Baer Solar TDS translations also provide examples of graphs whose captions and axis labels have been removed in translation, presumably unintentionally, since it is no longer possible to know what the graph depicts. They also contain figures where text has not been translated at all, which may be less than ideal for readers. We are not singling out this company's documentation for particular criticism; rather the example is given to highlight the fact that these are not uncommon problems in the commercial world, but can be avoided by translators, and indeed clients, with appropriate awareness. Decimal marker conversion (along with conversions of other relatively fixed formats, like dates) can be done automatically and/or checked by translation memory software, thus helping translators not to overlook those details without having to spend too much time on them.

Reference to standards, certifications, regulations

The manufacture and use of many products are governed by legislation or standards, often to ensure safety. There are several explicit references to such matters in this TDS.

In the 'Approved Products' section of the TDS, we learn that this product has been evaluated and approved by the British Board of Agrément (BBA; see the section on abbreviations below). The certificate number thus attained is given, which means that the evaluation could be checked or verified if necessary. The BBA certification logo is also displayed at the bottom of p. 2 of the TDS.

The product is stated as meeting the European standard for fire cement EN12467. Its reaction to fire is given as a rating in accordance with another European standard EN13501, and the rating attained is A1, S1-d0. We may note that reference was made to the product carrying 'an A1 fire rating' in the webpage description, but without any reference to specific standards. Moreover, only the A1 part of the rating was given, which will nonetheless signal a high/favourable rating, even for those with no knowledge of these classifications. The additional details given in the TDS refer to smoke production and burning droplets or particles; S1 is the lowest rating for smoke product and d0 is the lowest rating for burning droplets or particles.

The two technical specification tables show the measurements, characteristics and test results of numerous properties of the material. Each row of the table makes reference to the European (prefixed with EN) or American (prefixed with ASTM) standards which specify the test method for those properties.

Where standards referred to are international, their inclusion in translations poses less of a problem than when standards and regulations are national. In the latter cases, a disclaimer may be added to translations. For example, in its translation into English of its TDS for various construction components, German company Knauf Gips AG adds a note at the top of the first page of the TDS to say that the document is a translation of the technical data sheet valid in Germany and that 'all stated details and properties are in compliance with the regulations of the German standards and building regulations'. It also 'denies any liability for applications outside of Germany as this requires changes acc. to the respective national standards and building regulations' (see examples from a range of datasheets available at www.knauf.de/profi/tools-services/dokumenten-center/).

Abbreviations

The TDS readers are expected to be familiar with a range of abbreviations, most of which are given in their abbreviated form only. Apart from those denoting units of measurement, already mentioned, two abbreviations in this TDS relate to a particular technology and a type of documentation: HEPA stands for high-efficiency particulate air and is a type of filter or vacuum; MSDS stands for material safety data sheet (see next section).

The other abbreviations refer to international standards and certifying bodies: EN stands for European Standard (developed by the CEN, Comité Européen de Normalisation); ASTM refers to what was formerly the American Society for Testing and Materials; SDI is explained as Smoke Development Index; and, as mentioned above, BBA stands for British Board of Agrément, an independent authority that certifies products, systems and procedures for use in the construction industry.

Particularly when translating from English and when a technical abbreviation is a short form of a term for a technology, process, component, piece of equipment, etc., the English-language abbreviation is often reproduced in many TLs, alongside the corresponding TL term, as seen in Excerpt 4.3 (from the JCB brochure that will be discussed in the next section).

EXCERPT 4.3

English ST: A hose burst check valve (HBCV) on the boom, together with an audio warning alarm, are included.
Spanish TT: Incluye una válvula de seguridad de presión de mangueras (HBCV) en la pluma y una alarma sonora.

However, the decision whether to use the SL abbreviation as well as the gloss or TL term may be linked to the extent to which the term or abbreviation is used in the document. The abbreviation in Excerpt 4.3 occurs only twice in the ST (the second time without the long form). This is perhaps why the German translator uses the German term, without English abbreviation, on both occasions, as in Excerpt 4.4.

EXCERPT 4.4

English ST: A hose burst check valve (HBCV) on the boom, together with an audio warning alarm, are included.
German TT: Zur Ausstattung gehören ein Schlauchbruchsicher-ungsventil und eine akustische Warnanlage.

Assumed technical knowledge and terminology

Given the intended use of the TDS, we might expect the information conveyed in it, even in general description sections, to be more techni-cal than, for example the description offered on product websites. This is indeed the case here, as is illustrated in Excerpt 4.5 from the Description section of the TDS:

EXCERPT 4.5

Hardie Backer® Cement Backerboard for tile and stone is a unique, cement based water resistant tile backerboard that can be used on walls, floors and countertops. HardieBacker® has high flexural and compressive strength, resulting in a superior tile bonding surface whilst adding value with its Mouldblock™ Technology.

Comparing this with the description on the product webpage (Excerpt 4.1 above), we can note, firstly, that the webpage draws attention to the possibility of fastening the backerboard directly onto the wall (or other surface). This point is omitted from this description in the TDS, reflecting the fact that the technical user knows what backerboard is and how it is generally fixed. Secondly, the range of uses is extended in the TDS, from fixing onto the wall in a wet or heated area to use on floors and countertops too. Finally, the strength, bonding ability and mould resistance are referred to in the TDS, but in much more succinct form than on the website. Detail is added on the nature of the strength, and noun phrases and technical terms are used to condense the information into a single sentence: *high flexural*

and compressive strength, resulting in a superior tile bonding surface.
In Chapter 6 we will look in more detail at how this increased information density is achieved through a process called grammatical
metaphor (Halliday 2004). Information is also condensed here
through the use of the four adjectives preceding the noun in the first
sentence: *unique, cement-based, water-resistant, tile.*

Also reflecting the TDS user's level of technical knowledge, numerous terms related to construction materials and properties of materials are used throughout the TDS. Apart from those already mentioned
above (units of measurement and abbreviations), the terms in use here
can be loosely classified as:

- Materials: Portland cement, sand, cellulose, asbestos, gypsum,
  glass fibre, formaldehyde, crystalline silica, fibre cement, tile, stone
- Properties of materials: dimensions, dimensional tolerance, weight,
  flexural strength, compressive strength, apparent density, water
  impermeability, durability, warm water resistance, heat/rain resistance, freeze/thaw resistance, soak/dry resistance, surface burning,
  combustibility, tile weight carrying capacity, cement-based, water-
  resistant, non-combustible, respirable, high-strength, gap-filling
- Construction components: internal substrate, water-resistant board,
  reference plate, lining sheet, fire protection board, bonding surface,
  screw, tile adhesive, tile, wooden substrate, bead, cartridge adhesive, masonry anchors, self-embedding head, stud
- Techniques: score and snap technique, wet cleanup method
- Equipment: HEPA vacuum, domestic boiler, multi-fuel stove, log
  burning stove
- Proper nouns, including product and trade names: JamesHardie,
  HardieBacker, EZ Grid, Mouldblock Technology, BBA, Smoke
  Development Index, Flames Droplets Index.

If translating this TDS, research on construction materials and
their characteristics would therefore be required to enable us to gain
an understanding of this product and its characteristics and to find
terminological correspondences in our TL. An ideal way to start
would be to identify products of a similar nature produced in the target culture and consult data sheets for similar products in the target
language. For this particular product, for example, some similar
characteristics and applications can be seen in a German-manufactured
product called Aquapanel, produced by Knauf (ww.aquapanel.com).
TDS for this product are available in various languages, including
German, English, Greek, Spanish, Brazilian Portuguese, Chinese and
Turkish.

To illustrate the usefulness of this approach to research, we can
immediately recognize some terms used in the Knauf TDS in German

that could be relevant for our translation if we were translating into German:

- Fliesenuntergrund für den Innenausbau (internal tile substrate)
- Portlandzement (Portland cement)
- Zuschlagstoffe (additives)
- 100% wasserbeständig (100% water impermeable)
- Widerstandsfähig gegen Schimmelpilzbefall (mould-resistance)
- Dicke (thickness)
- Länge (length)
- Breite (width)
- Gewicht (weight)
- Dichte (density)
- Wärmefähigkeit (thermal conductivity)
- Biegfestigkeit (flexural strength)
- nichtbrennbar (non-combustible)
- bearbeitbar durch Ritzen und Brechen (can be worked by scoring and snapping).

Further research of this kind would be likely to provide further potential terminological correspondences. It is often not essential for the comparison products to be as similar as in this case. For example, consulting multilingual information about a product called Jackoboard, which is not a cement board so therefore somewhat different from HardieBacker, nonetheless produces terms in several languages for some of the material properties that are also specified for HardieBacker.

Safety data sheets

Products or materials containing hazardous, dangerous or toxic substances must be supplied with information about the hazardous substances in the form of a safety data sheet (SDS) or material safety data sheet (MSDS). These documents describe the hazards, thus allowing those handling the products to assess the risks to them in their workplace and to enable them to handle the products safely. They are referred to both as MSDS and SDS, but ongoing work to harmonize systems of classifying and labelling chemicals should result in just one term being used for these documents, the safety data sheet. In 2002 the UN introduced the Globally Harmonized System of Classification and Labelling of Chemicals (GHS), designed to provide a basis for harmonization of rules and regulations on chemicals throughout the world. Since its introduction, and through subsequent revisions, it has been adopted into national regulations in many countries of the world (see www.unece.org/trans/danger/publi/ghs/implementation_e.html

for more details of country-by-country implementation). The GHS includes recommendations for a harmonized hazard communication system, encompassing labelling and SDS. The provisions of GHS have also been integrated into EU regulations applicable to EU member states.

The EU regulation system that incorporates the GHS is called REACH (Registration, Evaluation, Authorization and Restriction of Chemicals). Apart from the requirement to provide SDS for chemical substances, EU regulation also makes it necessary for SDS to be translated: the SDS 'must be supplied in an official language of the member state where the substance or mixture is placed on the market' (European Chemicals Agency 2014). The GHS and REACH requirements prescribe the structure and format of the SDS, outlined below by means of the required section headings. Details of subsection and section contents can be consulted in the guidance offered by the European Chemicals Agency (ECHA), or UN documentation on GHS or other national standards, for example, China's GB/T 17519–2013.

- Section 1: Identification of the substance/mixture and of the company/undertaking
- Section 2: Hazards identification
- Section 3: Composition/information on ingredients
- Section 4: First aid measures
- Section 5: Firefighting measures
- Section 6: Accidental release measures
- Section 7: Handling and storage
- Section 8: Exposure controls/personal protection
- Section 9: Physical and chemical properties
- Section 10: Stability and reactivity
- Section 11: Toxicological information
- Section 12: Ecological information
- Section 13: Disposal considerations
- Section 14: Transport information
- Section 15: Regulatory information
- Section 16: Other information.

ECHA-term

If working with EU languages, the ECHA's termbase, ECHA-term (n.d.; http://echa-term.echa.europa.eu), is immensely useful for the translation of SDS. It provides validated terms in 23 EU languages; the EU's 24th language, Croatian, is included in the termbase, but Irish is not. A full term entry includes the term in your chosen source and target languages, a definition, contextual example for the TL terms, note on usage, acronym if applicable, reliability value and creation date. Entries include many names of chemical substances and descriptions of their properties. The termbase also includes recurrent precautionary phrases and their translations (e.g. *IF SWALLOWED: rinse mouth. Do NOT induce vomiting* or *Store in a well-ventilated place. Keep container tightly closed*) and other terms and phrases from the regulation of chemical substances that you may encounter in SDS. It is worth noting that some terms and phrases that occur in SDS are also used in TDS and in operating or installation instructions, so this termbase may be useful to you when translating those documents too. The full termbase or part of it can be downloaded for your own use.

Technical brochures and their translation

In addition to publishing TDS for the products they distribute, a commercial company may produce technical brochures. These tend to be longer documents, sometimes covering a range or series of products rather than just one. They often contain the TDS for the products, preceded by other textual and graphical material serving a strong promotional function for the product range and the company. In other words, these technical brochures contain all available technical data on the products but this is pushed to the background by more overtly marketing-focused discourse. In this section we use an example of a technical brochure and its translations to help us to identify particular features of technical brochures.

These brochures, perhaps due to their importance as a marketing tool, often have high design and production values, produced as glossy magazines replete with high-quality images and a professionally designed and executed layout. As you will see from reading TDS, some TDS share these qualities but many are less polished in terms of layout and production. The more low-tech approach that some companies take to their TDS is practical; it allows them to make updates in-house rather than having to engage a graphic designer or communications agency each time a change is made. The same deliberations on practicality might apply to productions of the translations of TDS. Most brochures, by contrast, have substantial design input from advertising, marketing or communication specialists and are professionally produced.

Since brochures are professionally designed and substantial documents with a strong marketing function, it can be costly for companies to get them translated, since additional costs are also incurred in producing the translated version to the same professional standard. Perhaps for this reason, many companies will content themselves with translating their TDS and their websites, but offering their brochures in one language only. For example, Autoform, the Swiss company mentioned previously, produces quite detailed information on its products in several languages on its website, but makes available its product brochures almost exclusively in English only.

To see when and how brochures are translated, we can turn our attention to larger companies benefiting from strong international markets for their products. One such example is JCB, a manufacturer of construction equipment, exporting its products to 150 countries around the world (www.jcb.com). Clearly the localization of marketing materials is important for JCB and they offer websites, brochures and TDS in a range of languages. JCB has produced websites for numerous locales, with readers invited to choose their region and country. As with many websites, the apparently large set of options when countries are listed does not mean that each has a localized website. For example, while there is a Brazilian Portuguese website, readers choosing Portugal as their country are brought to the English-language website, and the same is true for choices of many other European and some Latin American countries. A website has been produced for the Middle East, but in English. A North American website caters for the USA and Canada and promotes a specific range of models for that market. A website for readers in Africa offers information in English or French, depending on the choice of country.

The products section of each website contains a page for each product where the key characteristics and strengths are outlined. From these pages, readers may access TDS and brochures, if available. By way of illustration we will focus on one product, the backhoe loader, which comes in several ranges and models. JCB produces a brochure promoting the entire backhoe loader range but also brochures for specific models. We will take as an example the product brochure that encompasses two models, the 3CX and 4CX ECO. In English this is a 24-page document, described in more detail below. Translations of this brochure are available from the JCB websites in German, Italian, Spanish and Russian. A French product brochure is also available but with a somewhat different design. In addition, some information on these machines is available on JCB websites in Dutch, Czech and Chinese, with links to the English-language brochure. A brochure is available in Brazilian Portuguese for the whole range of backhoe loaders, not for these specific products, though their TDS are available in Brazilian Portuguese. Interestingly, the Brazilian Portuguese TDS for this model is prefaced with a highlighted *FABRICADA NO BRASIL*, potentially an important selling point in that market.

Brochure organization and layout

The brochure cover shows a full-page photograph of the backhoe on a building site transporting a palette of bricks to a bricklayer at work, featuring the product name prominently below it: *BACKHOE LOADER | 3CX/4CX ECO* and the JCB logo. A brief summary of the machine's capability is given in smaller font size below the product name: *Gross Power: 55kW (74hp) – 81kW (109hp) Maximum Dig Depth: 4m – 6.14m Maximum Shovel Capacity: 1.0m³–1.3m³*. Pages 2–15, the main body of the brochure, contain information about the model, organized in one-page or two-page sections by area of strength or selling point. In English these sections are headed: *Cost of ownership and efficiency; Quality, reliability and durability; Productivity and performance; Comfort and ease of use; Security and serviceability; The options list; Livelink, work smarter; Value added*. Below each heading is a highlighted paragraph summarizing the distinctive feature, then a set of bullet points going into more detail, with numbered references tying the text of bullet points to one of several images on each page, mostly photographs. These sections are followed by 7 pages of technical specifications accompanied by drawings. The inside back cover shows another full-page image of a backhoe in action on a building site, and the back cover contains 15 tiled images of different JCB machines, the product name and brief description as on the front cover, JCB Sales contact details, space for the dealer's contact details, a legal disclaimer, the JCB logo and the slogan: *one company, over 300 machines*. As noted above, this is a high-production publication, with a very professional appearance.

Distinctive features

Apart from layout, length and use of images, as outlined above, the brochure can be distinguished from the TDS in its use of language. Certainly we can identify the features previously observed in the TDS: terms (e.g. *variable flow pump, kingpost hose, cat tail weld*); abbreviations (e.g. *DPF, SCR, HBCV*); units of measurements (e.g. *kg, kW, hp, bar, l/min*); technical drawings; references to international standards or benchmarks (e.g. *EHTMA Class C tool operation standards*); and proper nouns to designate proprietary technology (e.g. *EcoMAX engine, TorqueLock system, SmoothRide System*). However, to fulfil the additional promotional function of the brochure, language is also used in ways not previously observed in the TDS. Some examples are outlined below.

Interpersonal reference and direct address

The reader is directly addressed on numerous occasions (33 instances of *you* or *your*), and *we* (15 occurrences) and *our* (26) are used to refer to JCB, appealing to the reader's direct experience, needs and expectations, with JCB taking personal responsibility for its design and manufacturing decisions and offering the user a dedicated solution, service or response. Excerpts 4.6 and 4.7 show two examples and their translations in the German-language brochure.

EXCERPT 4.6

English ST: The latest 3CX and 4CX backhoes don't just provide you with the power to get things done; they also offer you countless features to ensure that performance is efficient, and ownership costs are reduced.
German TT: Die neuen Baggerlader 3CX und 4CX zeichnen sich neben der herausragenden Leistung durch zahlreiche Merkmale aus, die Effizienz gewährleisten und die Betriebskosten senken.

EXCERPT 4.7

English ST: Irrespective of what you opt for, our maintenance teams around the world charge competitive labour rates, and offer non-obligation quotations as well as fast, efficient insurance repair work.
German TT: Unabhängig vom gewählten Paket berechnen Ihnen unsere Wartungsteams rund um den Globus extrem günstige Stundentarife, unterbreiten Ihnen unverbindliche Angebote und führen Service-oder Wartungsarbeiten schnell und effizient durch.

Other language versions may not employ as much interpersonal reference, though a glance at several versions shows that they all use it to some extent. The German translation addresses the reader a little less (29 instances of *Sie* and *Ihnen*) and refers to JCB using first-person plural pronouns substantially less (21 instances of *wir* and all inflected forms of *unser*). The German translations in Excerpts 4.6 and 4.7 provide a good illustration of how these interpersonal references are handled in German. The German sentence in Excerpt 4.6 uses an impersonal construction, thus avoiding reference to the reader. In Excerpt 4.7 the nominal construction of 'the chosen package' (BT) rather than *what you opt for* also removes a pronominal reference. However, in the rest of the sentence, two pronouns (*Ihnen*) are added where there were none in the English: 'charge you' and 'offer you' (BT).

There is an interesting tension when it comes to the addressee in the ST. At times the brochure addresses the person who might be deciding on the purchase of this machine, and the operator of the backhoe is described in the third person. However, the potential operator is also sometimes addressed, as in Excerpt 4.8. The Spanish and Italian versions also address the operator directly here, with the Italian selling this option further by referring to the operator's relaxation during their well-earned break. The German text, by contrast, uses an impersonal construction (BT: 'it is possible to prepare a cup of hot coffee or tea') and the French refers to the operator in the third person. Note also how these two translations reorder the drinks, perhaps to reflect better the drinking habits of their respective markets.

EXCERPT 4.8

English ST: Exclusive to JCB backhoe loader, we have integrated a hot drinks machine option into the cab to provide you with a delicious cup of hot tea or coffee throughout the day.

Italian TT: In esclusiva per le sole terne JCB, abbiamo inserito in cabina un distributore di bevande calde opzionale che vi consente di prepararvi una deliziosa tazza di tè o caffè caldo nel corso della giornata, rendendo la vostra meritata pausa ancora più rilassante. [making your well-earned break more relaxing].

Spanish TT: En exclusiva en las retrocargadoras JCB, hemos integrado una opción de máquina de bebidas calientes en la cabina para que pueda disfrutar de una deliciosa taza de té o café durante su jornada de trabajo.

German TT: Nur JCB Baggerlader sind mit der Möglichkeit ausgestattet, jederzeit eine Tasse heißen Kaffee oder Tee zubereiten zu können.

French TT [new-format brochure, not a translation of the English brochure]: Le distributeur de boissons chaudes permet à l'opérateur d'apprécier un café ou un thé bien chaud pendant sa journée de travail.

Colloquial lexis and contractions

Technical description is juxtaposed in this brochure with a small number of colloquial expressions. In addition, contractions (*we'll, we've*) are used throughout the document. Some examples are given in Excerpts 4.9, 4.10 and 4.11. These options serve to strengthen reader–writer interaction in English (similar issues are discussed in terms of metadiscourse in Chapter 6 and proximity in Chapter 7). The contraction, in particular, cannot be used in the same way in written German; thus these informal forms are standardized in the German translation, which also uses fewer modifiers and boosters (i.e. no equivalent for *all-day* or *extremely*).

EXCERPT 4.9

English ST: In order to help you reap the maximum benefit of the 3CX and 4CX's superior performance, we've designed these machines to be all-day comfy, ergonomic and extremely intuitive for operators to use.

German TT: Damit Sie das Beste aus der überragenden Leistung des 3CX und des 4CX herausholen können, sind die Maschinen komfortabel, ergonomisch und intuitiv bedienbar.

EXCERPT 4.10

English ST: There's storage aplenty in our 3CX and 4CX cabs.
German TT: Die Kabine des 3CX und des 4CX bietet reichlich Stauraum.

EXCERPT 4.11

English ST: All the materials with which we construct our backhoe loaders are tested to the very max.

German TT: Alle Materialien der Baggerlader werden bis zur Belastungsgrenze getestet.

Evaluative lexis for promotional purposes

The English brochure abounds with evaluative language. On the one hand, the machine and its performance is described in glowing terms using comparatives, superlatives, evaluatively loaded adjectives and boosters, alongside nouns with positive connotations (e.g. *efficiency, productivity, asset, versatility*) or more neutral nouns inscribed with positive evaluation based on their frequent collocations, a phenomenon known as positive semantic prosody (see Partington 2004). For example, *performance* can be *poor, worse, disappointing*, etc., but is much more likely to be *good, better, best, outstanding, impressive, excellent, superb, brilliant* or even *improving* or *improved*. The instances of *performance* with positive semantic prosody outweigh the negative by 3 to 1 in the British National Corpus. The list below gives some examples of evaluative epithets and other phrases used in the brochure.

- excellent excavator performance; ultimate performance; even greater traction and performance; unparalleled power, performance and versatility

- ultimate efficiency; ultra efficiency
- easily resalable; proven to excel; ultra reliable
- legendary productivity; exceptional on-site productivity; maximum productivity
- ultimate backhoe loader; largest, most productive backhoe model; ideal machine
- great asset
- superb build quality
- easier control
- lighter lever effort
- only the finest materials and processes
- added rigidity
- ultimate fuel-injection system protection
- innovative hydraulics

On the other hand, the machine is described as overcoming or helping the operator to overcome problems or challenges. These ideas are expressed using a selection of verbs such as *to reduce, stop, improve* alongside a negatively connoted object, where evaluative lexical items and boosters are also employed: e.g. *inevitable rigours of site life; impact damage; perils of trenchwork; debris; stress concentrations; viscous drag; massive shock loads; tyre wear; extreme temperatures; the most hostile conditions; the toughest applications and environments.* All of these negative experiences can be overcome with the help of the backhoe loader.

In many cases, it will be possible for translators to choose similarly evaluative lexical items to help fulfil the strongly promotional function of the text. Torresi (2010) coins a term, the 'information-to-persuasion ratio', which may be a helpful concept when considering texts such as this. She proposes that texts with a higher information-to-persuasion ratio requires closer translation than a text with a lower ratio, where some rewriting may serve to enhance the text's persuasiveness.

Production values

The way in which a text is written and produced can help to establish the credibility of a company or brand. We noted that the JCB brochures are high-production value publications with a professional appearance. This impression is maintained for the reader through consistency of terminology and other linguistic choices. However, even with such professional document production, minor mistakes can be made. At least two typos can be spotted in the English brochure (Excerpts 4.12 and 4.13), but neither causes any problems for translators.

EXCERPT 4.12

English ST: This allows you to dig in areas simply not possible with a conventional backhoe, such as around objects like tress[*sic*], telegraph poles or lamp posts.

German TT: . . .Hindernisse wie Bäume, Telegrafenmasten oder Laternenmasten.

Italian TT: . . .ostacoli quali, alberi, pali del telegrafo o pali della luce.

Spanish TT: . . .objetos como árboles, postes telegráficos y postes de iluminación.

EXCERPT 4.13

The 3CX and 4CX have optional LSD to stop wheelspin in difficult ground conditions, inturn [*sic*] reducing tyre wear.

While a professional approach has clearly been taken with the translations too, these are also not immune from typos. Excerpt 4.14 makes reference to the unit of measurement for flow as *l/min*, an abbreviation of litres per minute. This unit appears in all translations as *l/min* except the Italian one, where it erroneously becomes *giri/min*, that is, revolutions per minute.

EXCERPT 4.14

English ST: The hose reel meets EHTMA Class C tool operation standards and features low back pressures, 138 bar pressure and a 20 l/min flow rate.

Italian TT: L'avvolgitore è conforme agli standard di funzionamento EHTMA degli utensili di classe C e presenta basse contropressioni, pressione max di lavoro pari a 138 bar e 20 giri/min di portata.

A second example that evaded checking can be seen in the Brazilian Portuguese brochure for the backhoe loader range. Here the JCB slogan, *one company, over 300 machines* is rendered as *uma máquina, mais de 300 máquinas* [one machine, over 300 machines] instead of the version seen in some of the other brochures: *uma empresa, mais de 300 modelos de máquinas* [one company, more than 300 models of machines]. A final remark in relation to the translation of this slogan is that other language versions use an expression corresponding to 'over' or 'more than' in *over 300* (e.g. in Spanish, *una empresa, más de 300 máquinas*; in Italian, *un'azienda, oltre 300 macchine*; and, in French, *un constructeur, plus de 300 modeles*). Only the German translator removes the hedging – *ein Unternehmen, 300 Modelle* – we can only assume, to produce a punchier slogan.

Exercise 4.1: Familiarizing yourself with TDS in your languages

For a product of your choice, find a technical datasheet in your source and target language, ideally where one is likely to be a translation of the other. You could start your search at the websites for regional/national subsidiaries of a global group (like Daiken, air-conditioning and refrigeration specialists, www.daiken.com). If you cannot find a text and its translation, look for a technical datasheet in each language for a very similar product. Compare the two documents and identify similarities and differences in the following aspects:

- Overall layout and use of colour: How many pages? Monochrome or multicoloured? Which colours are used and how?
- Corporate and brand identity: What use of logos, straplines, slogans? Product name? Company contact details?
- Legal information: Any disclaimer? Copyright statement? Other text with particular legal significance?
- Textual organization: Section headings/subheadings used? Bulleted lists? Paragraph structure? Ordering of section? Tables, figures, graphs?
- Communicative purposes: Promotional or operative as well as informational?

Exercise 4.2: Researching SDS in your languages

First consult the ECHA's (2014) *Guidance on the Compilation of Safety Data Sheets* for a detailed account of SDS stipulations. Then find websites of a paint manufacturer (or similar) based in countries where your languages are used. Access the safety data sheets (SDS) for one product on each website, choosing similar products if possible, for example primer, emulsion, gloss, wood stain (examples for English can be found at www.duluxtradepaintexpert.co.uk/products/datasheets). Compare the two SDS, drawing correspondences for SDS headings, terms and phrases, particularly precautionary notices. Make a note of these in a bilingual glossary for reuse.

Exercise 4.3: Using data from the ECHA termbase

Access ECHA-term, the ECHA's termbase, at http://echa-term.echa. europa.eu and familiarize yourself with the online search facility, including a closer look at the more detailed information that is available for terms (e.g. context, status indicator). Click on the 'Download data' link at the top of the screen. From this page you can export data from ECHA-term for your own use, either as an Excel file or in TBX format (see Chapter 2). Export the termbase data you require for your languages and import it into your terminology management software or save as a spreadsheet for offline use as a glossary.

Exercise 4.4: Preparing to translate a technical brochure

Examine the excerpt below from the JCB brochure for the 3CX/4CX ECO backhoe loader, reproduced courtesy of JCB. (The text is pp. 6–7 from the brochure that can be downloaded from www.jcb. co.uk/Products/Machines/Backhoe-Loaders/4CX-ECO/, where you will also find photos showing parts referred to in the description.) Highlight all evaluative lexical items and any other aspect of language use that seems to contribute to the promotional function. Think about the challenges of translating this text into another language. Disregard your terminological gaps for the moment but think about some of the choices you could make to fulfil that promotional function in your target language. Then, if you work with Russian, German, French, Spanish or Italian, consult the product brochure in that language on the JCB relevant website to see what solutions are offered by those translations. If you work with Dutch, Czech, Chinese or Brazilian Portuguese, consult the product information on the website; this may cover some similar ground. Do you find the target texts persuasive? Justify your answer. Now turn your attention to the terminology. Using resources from the JCB website and from other manufacturers and distributors of backhoe loaders, prepare a bilingual glossary of the terms used in this text.

Productivity and performance.

JCB Backhoes have always led the way in power and performance, and our latest 3CX and 4CX models are no exception. In every respect – from digging to lifting and manoeuvring – these machines will maximise your productivity.

A productive drivetrain.

Choose from three engines to suit your requirements – with 55kW, 68kW and 81kW options, you can balance ultra efficiency against ultimate performance.

To give your 3CX or 4CX even greater traction and performance, as well as reduced tyre wear, opt for our automatic limited slip differentials.

Innovative hydraulics.

There's more tractive effort at the pile than ever, thanks to new variable flow pump power management combined with our new EcoMAX engine.

The 3CX Contractor and 4CX's heavy-duty lift rams provide 3.87 tonnes of force for improved lifting performance.

Digging further.

A 3CX or 4CX ECO's 4-ram self-levelling loader automatically adjusts the shovel on both raise and lower cycles without any need for manual adjustment. It also provides unhindered front shovel visibility, especially when loading at height.

The JCB return-to-dig feature means operators can quickly reset the shovel to dig.

To ensure an extra 1.2m dig depth and reach – and to minimise repositioning – the 3CX and 4CX are fitted with our inner box design Extradig feature.

Both the 3CX and 4CX ECO boast high ground clearances of up to 370mm, together with 20° departure angles. This means operators can work easily on steep slopes and uneven ground at maximum productivity.

JCB 4CX: the ultimate backhoe loader.

As the largest, most productive backhoe model we produce, boasting unparalleled power, peformance and versatility, the JCB 4CX ECO is the ideal machine for just about any application, from road-building to house-building, waste recycling and landscaping.

The 4CX ECO's large optional 1.3m³ shovel capacity along with 3 steering modes provide exceptional on-site productivity.

Exercise 4.5: Translating a TDS

For a product and sector of your choice, identify a TDS that you will translate, hypothesizing that the company in question is aiming to distribute its products in a market in which your target language is spoken. Consider your translation brief, do your preparatory research and produce a translation for publication purposes. Discuss your translation process and product.

Exercise 4.6: Debating ethical issues

An interesting question for discussion is whether there are TDS and brochures for sectors, companies or products that you would have reservations or objections translating, on ethical or ideological grounds. Examples that could be considered might include material promoting military equipment used in war zones, or equipment used for exploitation of sensitive environmental sites. Consider whether or how the translation of texts like this (or other examples that you can think of) can raise ethical issues for translators or project managers. Discuss various ways in which you might react to and handle those kinds of situations.

Key points from this chapter

- Technical data sheets inform specialist users about specifications and other details of technical products, and are often translated into multiple languages, in line with international sales and distribution strategies.
- Although companies have some freedom regarding format, layout and content, typical features of TDS include technical product descriptions, quantitative data and company information, with elements of promotional marketing discourse also possible. Translations of TDS generally follow a similar structure and format to the ST, and accuracy and consistency of technical data are prioritized in the translation process.
- Safety data sheets are strictly regulated in terms of format and content, and translators can make use of existing termbases and documentation to access standardized terminology and phraseology.
- Technical brochures typically employ rhetorical strategies to promote the product and persuade the readership of its merits, while also conveying the technical information of TDS. Translators generally seek to achieve similar promotional functions in their translations, drawing on their knowledge of genre conventions and making use of appropriate TL resources to deal with the combination of information and promotion.

References

ECHA-term (n.d.) European Chemicals Agency, online at: http://echa-term.
echa.europa.eu (accessed 15 January 2015).

European Chemicals Agency (2014) *Guidance on the Compilation of Safety Data Sheets*, Helsinki: European Chemicals Agency.

Halliday, M.A.K. (2004) *The Language of Science*, Jonathan J. Webster (ed) London and New York: Continuum.

Kum, Doreen, YihHwai Lee and Cheng Qiu (2011) 'Testing to Prevent Bad Translation: Brand Name Conversions in Chinese–English Contexts', *Journal of Business Research* 64(6): 594–600.

Partington, Alan (2004) '"Utterly Content in Each Other's Company": Semantic Prosody and Semantic Preference', *International Journal of Corpus Linguistics* 9(1): 131–56.

Torresi, Ira (2010) *Translating Promotional and Advertising Texts*, Manchester: St Jerome Publishing.

Wang, Fade (2012) 'An Approach to the Translation of Brand Names', *Theory and Practice in Language Studies* 2(9): 1945–49.

5 Patents

This chapter focuses on a genre with specific relevance for the design and manufacturing stages of product development, namely the patent application or specification. It gives you an understanding of the purpose of patents and the procedures by which they are applied for and granted. We analyse a patent application to gain an understanding of the ways in which language is used to fulfil the specific purposes of the application. We then examine the international dimension of patenting by focusing on the work of the European Patent Office (EPO) and the World Intellectual Property Organization (WIPO) and the role of translation and machine translation (MT) in those settings. We conclude by discussing approaches typically taken by patent translators in their work.

Introducing patents

A patent is a legal document describing an invention, highlighting the original aspects of it and granting the inventor some rights or protection over that invention. An inventor (or a patent agent or attorney acting on their behalf) chooses to apply for a patent because the patent will give legal protection for their invention, stopping others from copying or manufacturing the invention without the patent holder's permission. If an invention is protected, it is also possible for the inventor to make money from manufacturing the product, selling invention and intellectual property (IP) rights or licensing the invention. It should be noted here that a patent application requires the applicant to disclose publicly all details pertaining to their invention; in return for that disclosure, they hope to be granted protection for that invention and enforceable patent rights.

To obtain a patent, the applicant must submit a patent application to the relevant patent office for approval. The application is examined against specific criteria. If the criteria are met, the patent is granted; if not, the patent is refused. If granted, the text of the application becomes the text of the granted patent, or the patent specification, and is published as such.

As stipulated by the UK Intellectual Property Office (www.gov.uk/intellectual-property/patents), for a patent to be granted, an invention must be new; it must involve an inventive step that is not obvious to someone with knowledge and experience in the subject. It therefore should not be a simple adaptation or combination of existing products. Finally it must be capable of being made or used in some kind of industry.

In some countries, for example the USA, a distinction is made between utility patents and two other patent types. In the USA, **utility patents** are granted for inventions (or improvements) of processes, machines, articles of manufacture and compositions of matter, while **design patents** are granted for new designs of articles of manufacture, and **plant patents** for new varieties of plants (USPTO 2014a). In many other countries, (industrial) designs are protected through registration or copyright, rather than by patent law, and under the European Patent Convention it is not possible to patent plant or animal varieties (EPO 2014c). Some countries (e.g. Germany, Austria, Japan) make use of utility models, alongside patents, to offer easier access to IP protection, particularly for inventions involving small improvements to existing technologies. These may have other labels in other systems; for example in Australia they are distinguished from standard patents and are called innovation patents.

The remainder of this chapter focuses on the standard or prototypical patent, granted for inventions related to processes and products that can be made or used in some kind of industry, whether mechanical, electronic, biological, chemical, pharmaceutical, etc. We will not address design or plant patents explicitly, though they are subject to application and granting procedures similar to those outlined below. The patenting of genes or genetic material is a controversial topic and has been the subject of much debate. Some countries (e.g. USA, Australia) allow for patents to be granted for biological substances themselves (as well as techniques or procedures to manufacture or process them) if they can be isolated from their naturally occurring states, so patentability discussion revolved around the extent to which the substances occur in nature or are made by humans. In 2013 the US Supreme Court ruled that genes could not be patented; this ruling marked a clear distinguishing line between genes, as products of nature, and the synthetic creation of genetic material (e.g. DNA) in the laboratory, which can be patented (Liptak 2013).

Patent as genre

Like other genres examined so far, the patent application is a communicative event embodying communicative purposes. These are realized within the social context of the patent system and manufacturing industry. As noted by Bazerman (1994: 84), the patent application and the patent specification are classic examples of speech acts and each can be seen as having a dominant illocutionary force; the application is a directive (requesting) and the patent specification is a declaration (granting of protection).

Patent application

Various components of the patent application have to be present and meet certain conditions for the application to be successful and for its overall illocutionary force to be met.

The first component is the novel idea to be patented, the invention. This is represented through a **title** and **summary description** of the invention. The patent application is then expected to give a **full and detailed description** of the invention, usually with illustrations or drawings. This typically focuses on describing the invention, its component parts, operation, use or construction. It is worth remembering that this is a representation or depiction of a product which may not have been produced to that specification as yet.

The application must also contain a set of **claims** made by the applicant defining the invention. The claims state explicitly how the invention meets the condition of novelty and detail the specific features or capabilities of the invention which form the basis for those claims. Although these claims (like the rest of the application) are written before the patent is granted, they are nonetheless written in a form which presupposes that the patent will be granted.

As noted by guidance issued by the United States Patent and Trademark Office (USPTO), the application must contain "a full and clear disclosure of the invention", explaining that "[t]he requirement for an adequate disclosure ensures that the public receives something in return for the exclusionary rights that are granted to the inventor by a patent" (USPTO 2014b).

Patent searches and examination

The **patent examiner** evaluates these representations of the invention, requiring them to be accurate, clear and specific. The examiner then carries out searches of the **prior art**, defined as

> everything which has been made available to the public anywhere in the world by means of written disclosure (including drawings and other illustrations) and which is capable of being of assistance in determining that the claimed invention is or is not new and that it does or does not involve an inventive step (i.e., that it is or is not

obvious), provided that the making available to the public occurred prior to the international filing date.

(WIPO 2014c)

Through the searches, based on documentation, especially existing patents, the examiner compares the invention with the prior art to ascertain the invention's patentability on the grounds of being novel and involving an inventive step. As the definition of prior art implies, it may be necessary to consult translations during research into prior art (before an application is prepared or during examination after submission). Overall, the patent examination is not designed to check whether the idea is workable or whether the product which might ensue is useful or marketable. It is merely an examination of the potential of the idea, as represented in the patent application, and its patentability.

The EPO (see next section for more details), for example, describes the job of patent examiner as involving "searching in online databases, analysing documents, communicating orally and in writing with patent applicants and their attorneys, and then taking decisions on the grant of patents" (www.epo.org/about-us/jobs/vacancies/examiners.html). More detail on each part of the search and examination process can be consulted on the EPO website, along with profiles of examiners.

Searches carried out before the application is made can help potential patentees to establish patentability. As we will see later, patent applications and specifications are published so it is possible for a member of the public to perform research on prior art. However, this is also a service offered by **patent attorneys** and **patent agents**. Thorough searches before applying can help to avoid problems relating to patent infringement and challenges. Translation can form an important part of that search process.

Patent infringement and litigation

Some scholars suggest that it is the threat of litigation, rather than litigation itself, that is the main value of patenting (Helmers and McDonagh 2012: 2,4). A patent therefore acts as a deterrent. Monitoring possible infringements can be a costly process, and a patent holder must decide whether to do so and, if possible infringements are detected, whether to take the matter further and initiate legal proceedings. This decision is often a complex one, based on calculations of losses and benefits accrued by either course of action, and it means that most patent disputes do not end up in court (ibid.: 3). Where litigation is embarked upon, it may be to stop the infringer from using a patented technology or with a view to selling licences for the patent right or obtaining a settlement payment from the infringer/competitor.

A high-profile example of a patent war which has been played out in courtrooms in the USA and Korea is the case of Apple and Samsung, two companies who are seldom out of the business headlines due to ongoing patent disputes in relation to various smartphone inventions (see Kane 2014). As noted by Kane (2014), initial attempts at imposing licensing fees failed in this case.

Helmers and McDonagh's investigation of UK court cases relating to patents between 2000 and 2008 showed that around 43 per cent of cases were filed alleging infringement, whereas around 31 per cent of cases sought to have a patent revoked, but only about half of cases proceeded to final judgement (ibid.: 5). Costs of litigation in the UK are high, with total costs of between £1million and £6million for those cases studied (ibid.). The low number of cases brought to court in the UK can be compared with the EPO's procedures for opposing a granted patent; latest statistics for 2013 show that only 4.5 per cent of patents were opposed in that year (of those patents where the deadline for opposition had not lapsed). Where court proceedings take place and have an international dimension, it is common for the translation of documents to be required, not just of patents but also of other court documents, correspondence, expert witness statements, etc.

A closer look at patents and their makeup

Like many speech acts which are formalized and which occur in institutional settings, and perhaps especially for those with specific legal status, like marriage declarations or business contracts, some of the language used in patents is conventionalized, to the point of being formulaic.

This section will focus on a patent specification, *EP 0916952 B1: Conveyor system for clinical test apparatus*, the text of which is reproduced in Appendix 3 (see the online version to consult the diagrams too). It can be consulted online via Espacenet, the EPO's patent database, introduced in the next section. Go to http://worldwide.espacenet.com and search for the application by number, that is, *EP 0916952*. The *B1* designation indicates that it is a granted patent. The French and German titles made available in translation by the EPO are *Fördersystem für Gerät für klinische Tests* and *Système de transport pour dispositif pour essais cliniques*.

In the following sections we will describe the structure and components of this patent specification.

Header

The header comprises several elements, each labelled with a number in parenthesis. These numbers are internationally standardized codes – **INID codes,** or Internationally agreed Numbers for the Identification of [bibliographic] Data. The list of INID codes can be found in Appendix 1 of the WIPO (2013c) standard ST.9: *Recommendation concerning Bibliographic Data on and relating to Patents and SPCs.*

The codes used in this patent's header and their significations are outlined below:

- **(19) Identification of the office publishing the document**
  In this case, the EPO logo is depicted.
- **(11) Number of the patent document**
- **(12) Plain-language designation of the kind of document**
  In this case it is "European Patent Specification". In the case of patent applications this designation would read "European Patent Application".
- **(45) Date of publication and mention of the grant of the patent**
  This patent was granted on 1 January 2014, and was published in the EPO's *Bulletin* issue dated January 2014.
- **(21) Number assigned to the application**
- **(22) Date of filing the application**
  This application was filed in 1998.
- **(51) International Patent Classification**
  In this case, two numbers are given, G01N 35/04 and G01N 35/02, designating the specific technical fields to which the invention belongs. The specificity of the classification can be seen if we present the superordinate classes to which these belong, as well as the description of these classes:
  - G: Physics – instruments
  - G01: Measuring; testing
  - G01N: Investigating chemical or physical properties of materials
  - G01N 35: *Automatic analysis not limited to methods or materials provided for in a single one of the preceding groups; handling materials therefor*
  - G01N 35/02: *Using a plurality of sample containers moved by a conveyor system past one or more treatment or analysis stations*
  - G01N 35/04: *Details of the conveyer system.*
- **(54) Title of the invention**
  In EPO patent specifications, the title is given in the three official languages, English, French and German.
- **(84) Designated contracting states**
  In this case, 18 of the EPO member states are listed.
- **(30) Data related to priority**

Information (in this case a date and a number) about a priority application. In this case reference is made to a US application from 1997 and its filing date is given.

- **(43) Date on which the unexamined patent document is made available to the public**

  This document was published in the 20th issue of the *Bulletin* in 1999. This is an unusually long gap between filing and granting of the patent. Many EPO patents are granted within 4 years of filing, but there is a long tail of applications that take a lot longer, for various reasons (see Knowles 2012 for a patent attorney's perspective on this). It is possible to compare the granted patent with earlier versions of the application and to note some changes, including ownership and claims; so it might be assumed that such changes were partly responsible for the delay.

- **(73) Name of proprietor**

  This is the grantee or holder of the patent, in this case a company division, Siemens Healthcare Diagnostics Inc.

- **(72) Name of inventor**

  Four US-based inventors are listed here.

- **(74) Name of attorney or agent representing the applicant**

  This is the name and address of a patent attorney or agent, in this case an attorney employed by Siemens AG in Germany

- **(56) References cited**

  A list of prior art documents: a US patent, an Austrian patent (prefaced AT), and two WIPO patent applications.

Finally the header contains a remark indicating that the file contains some technical information which was submitted after the application was filed which is not included in the specification. This might be related to the delay noted above between filing and granting. The remainder of the document contains the description, claims and drawings, which we will examine in greater detail.

Description

This particular description is divided into subsections: background of the invention (9 paragraphs); objects and summary of the invention (23 paragraphs); description of the drawings (2 paragraphs); and detailed description of the invention (67 paragraphs). In all patent applications or specifications, paragraphs are numbered in this way, though there is some flexibility in the use of subsections for the description part of the document.

Paragraph [0001] contains a general description of the invention, that is, a conveyer system that will move containers containing biological material (e.g. blood or urine samples) along a main conveyor belt, with gates which divert specific groups of container samples into sidebar lanes leading to the appropriate clinical test apparatus for that sample. Paragraph [0002] explains what is meant by clinical testing and how important it is for diagnostic evaluation and surgical decision-making. [0003] notes the desirability of reducing the costs of such clinical testing while benefiting from the expansion of available tests. [0004] suggests that costs can be reduced by performing the tests automatically and gives a brief explanation of known testing systems, which are usually dedicated to a specific test. [0005] argues that those systems require separate sets of personnel to oversee the separate clinical test apparatus and a lot of space. [0006] announces the development of a common transport system to deliver test material containers automatically to a variety of unrelated and independent clinical test apparatus, via a conveyer with different clinical test apparatus along the travel path of the conveyor. Paragraph [0007] notes that known systems are usually custom built and require dedicated installations of power, plumbing, vacuum and pressure services, and are therefore inflexible once installed. [0008] refers to a prior patent which discloses a conveyor system with a main and a spur line; however, it is not possible to attach further auxiliary conveyors to the main line. [0009] concludes that is therefore desirable to provide a conveyor system for clinical testing which can be constructed with modular stations for each clinical test apparatus, with simplified installations for electricity, plumbing and other services, without requiring ground, wall or ceiling installation.

Up to this point, the text and language of the description is relatively straightforward to process and understand. We may note some recurrent phrases: *The/this invention relates to* . . . and the use of the word *known* to refer to existing systems or prior knowledge. This section is structured very deliberately to summarize the invention, to explain the circumstances in which it is required, to highlight the deficiencies in existing systems and to conclude that the invention as disclosed is therefore desirable.

The next section of the description provides more detail, focusing on the novel nature of the invention. The first paragraph of this is reproduced as Excerpt 5.1.

EXCERPT 5.1

[0010] Among the several objects of the invention may be noted the provision of a novel conveyor system for clinical test apparatus, a novel conveyor system that has a main transport lane and one or more auxiliary lanes corresponding to each clinical apparatus, a novel

> conveyor system for clinical test apparatus wherein auxiliary trans-
> port lanes are provided alongside main transport lanes for side by
> side movement of sample tubes on a main transport lane and on an
> auxiliary transport lane, a novel conveyor system for clinical test
> apparatus including a main transport conveyor and a plurality of sep-
> arately run auxiliary conveyors, and wherein each auxiliary conveyor
> is associated with a separate clinical test apparatus, a novel conveyor
> system wherein each auxiliary conveyor is provided with traffic con-
> trol gates including a diverter gate and an interface gate wherein the
> diverter gate selectively diverts sample tubes from the main transport
> conveyor to the auxiliary conveyor and the interface gate controls
> return of the diverted sample tubes to the main transport conveyor, a
> novel conveyor system for clinical test apparatus that also carries its
> own utility service lines such as electrical, plumbing, pressure and
> vacuum lines, a novel system for supporting the utility service lines, a
> novel conveyor system for clinical test apparatus wherein the main
> transport conveyor is separately driven by one motor while the auxil-
> iary transport conveyors are each driven by separate motors, and
> novel gates for directing sample tubes to selected clinical apparatus
> for testing or other functional purpose.

The most obvious point to make about this paragraph is that it is, in fact, a single sentence of 248 words. A first reading highlights the degree of lexical repetition. Emphasizing the novelty of the invention, this sentence/paragraph contains nine instances of *novel*. Key terms are also repeated; thus we note seven occurrences of *conveyor system*, six occurrences of *clinical test apparatus* and two of *clinical appara-tus*, five occurrences of *transport conveyor* or *transport conveyors*, and other recurring items, including *main (transport) lane(s)*, *auxil-iary (transport) lane(s)*, *auxiliary conveyor*, *diverter gate*, *interface gate* and *sample tubes*.

The almost complete absence of pronouns and pronominal reference is striking when compared with descriptive passages that we might encounter in other documents. This lexical repetition is, however, a key characteristic of patents, as an ambiguity-reducing strategy.

Wherein is used five times to link clauses; this word choice may strike readers as somewhat legalistic but it is a very characteristic way of including and elaborating detail in patents. Similar usage seen else-where, for example *hereinafter referred to as . . .* or *as used herein the term sample tube 106 is generally intended to include ... .*

The subsequent paragraphs of that section go into more detail on the functioning and structure of the system, with similar lexical rep-etition. Verbs typical of such descriptions recur here: X *defines* Y; X *permits* Y; X *is associated with* Y; X *cooperates with* Y; X *includes*; X *is provided*; X *maintains*, and fairly regular use of the simple 'X *has*'.

Drawings

The paragraphs of the next section introduce the 24 figures. The detailed description of the invention then makes detailed reference to those figures, each of which depicts component parts, labelled with numbers between 10 and 455, though not all numbers in this range are used. As is typical in patents, and unlike the figures that we usually find in instruction booklets or manuals, there is no numbered list of parts that can be consulted. Therefore, it is only by reading the patent description that the components and their numerical designations can be discerned; the drawings support the description and are difficult to decipher alone. The drawings usually appear as the last item in the documentation. They are usually black and white line drawings, with numbers, either printed or handwritten, as is mostly the case here.

Claims

The claims section follows the description. In some respects the claim section is the most important part in that it specifies precisely what it is about the invention that is patentable. This is the section that the EPO provides translations of, so that it is available in the three official languages of the EPO, English, French and German. There are six claims listed. Claim 1, with its eight subsections, is reproduced as Excerpt 5.2 so that we can examine it further.

EXCERPT 5.2

1. A conveyor system for clinical test apparatus comprising:

   a) a main transport conveyor defining a closed circuit path of travel in a generally horizontal plane, the closed circuit path of travel permitting objects on the conveyor to repeat the path of travel when the conveyor is moving in one direction, the closed circuit path of travel including a straight line path and a curved path,

   b) a plurality of auxiliary conveyor modules, each comprising an auxiliary conveyor defining a straight line path of travel in a generally horizontal plane, the straight line path of travel permitting objects on the conveyor to move from one point to another without retracing any point of travel when the conveyor is moving in said one direction, said auxiliary conveyor having an upstream end and a downstream end relative to said one direction of movement,

   c) said auxiliary conveyor being positioned alongside the straight line path of travel of said first transport conveyor to run in the same direction as said first conveyor,

d) segregation means between the straight line path of said main transport conveyor and said auxiliary conveyor for normally preventing objects from said transport conveyor from moving onto said auxiliary conveyor and vice versa,

e) said segregation means including first and second openings spaced a predetermined linear distance from each other along said straight line path,

f) a divert gate device provided at one of said openings proximate an upstream end of said auxiliary conveyor, said divert gate device having diversion means for diverting movement of objects on said main transport conveyor through said one of said openings in said segregation means to said auxiliary conveyor,

g) an interface gate provided downstream of said one opening and upstream of said other opening in said segregation means, and

h) said other opening providing a flow path that leads directly from said auxiliary conveyor to said main transport conveyor, said conveyor system including first motor means for moving said main transport conveyor and second motor means independently operable of said first motor means for moving said auxiliary conveyor of said auxiliary conveyor modules said auxiliary conveyor modules being detachably fastened to said main transport conveyor.

The first claim of a set of claims is usually of the broadest scope, with subsequent claims becoming increasingly restrictive. We can note that this first claim begins conventionally with a **preamble** comprising a general description of the device: *a conveyor system for clinical test apparatus*. It continues with *comprising* as a means of introducing the specific components or features which are integral to the system and on which patentability rests. Other common formulations in English-language patents to link the preamble to the elements or steps which are new or improved are 'including', 'characterized by' or variations such as 'characterized in that it comprises'.

Claim 1 and its subsections encompass the main transport conveyor, the auxiliary conveyor modules, the diverter gate and the functioning of these components in relation to one another. This claim, like all claims, is written as a single sentence, with punctuation and numbering used to separate specific parts of the 360-word sentence, but a full stop used only at the end of the claim.

In addition to the lexical repetition noted earlier, repetition of another element is evident here and throughout the claims, that of the lexical item *said*, repeated 67 times in this claims section, to refer to something previously mentioned.

Subsequent claims often build on previous ones, so, for example, in this patent Claims 2–6 are **dependent claims**, in that they refer to

Claim 1 and extend from it with more specific claims about specified components. The opening phrases of each claim are reproduced as Excerpt 5.3. This prolific use of *said*, which would be judged excessive in many other genres, is indispensable in a patent to refer anaphorically to previously mentioned claims, components, functions, etc.

EXCERPT 5.3

2. The conveyor system as claimed in claim 1 wherein said divert gate . . .
3. The conveyor system as claimed in claim 1 wherein said diversion . . .
4. The conveyor system as claimed in claim 1 said plurality of said auxiliary conveyor modules . . .
5. The conveyor system as claimed in claim 1 including support means . . .
6. The conveyor system as claimed in claim 5 wherein said support . . . .

As can be seen from the French and German versions of these claims in the EPO patent specification (in Appendix 3), other languages have similarly conventionalized formulations; for example: in French, *Système de convoyeur suivant la revendication 1, dans lequel;* and in German, *Förderanlage nach Anspruch 1, wobei.*

Likewise the linking phrases noted above, like *characterized in that it comprises*, have relatively fixed formulations in other languages too; for example *caractérisé en ce qu'il comprend* and *dadurch gekennzeichnet, dass es [. . .] umfasst.*

Another observation from this set of claims which would also apply to many other patent specifications is that the claims, though specifying components and functions, are expressed in terms which are previously used in the description. However, the wording seems somewhat circular and rather vague. Take, for example, the claim in 1f, which relates to a *divert gate device*, which is described in rather a circular formulation as having *diversion means for diverting movement of objects*. The use of *divert gate device* rather than another term, *like diverter gate*, may appear to be less specific. *Divert gate device* perhaps leaves open many of the characteristics of that *device*. Likewise saying that a device *[has] diversion means* does not tell us much about those means other than their intended function. *Diverting movement of objects* is also quite vague. Claims 2 and 3 give us more detail but remain vague in their designations: the divert gate has a *hold back means*, and the diversion means includes a *diversion member*. Likewise, segregation is achieved using *segregation means*, support is provided by *support means* and the conveyor has *openings*. Wording of this kind is somewhat less specific than that of the detailed description, where generic vocabulary such as *device, means, opening, wall* and *portion* were often modified for greater specificity, for example *sidebar exit opening, sidebar entrance opening, edge wall, ledge portion.*

These observations tally with advice given to patent applicants by the UK's Intellectual Property Office (IPO), which states that applications should "avoid using terms that are too restrictive in meaning" (Intellectual Property Office 2010). Quoting the example of an invention which is described as using a hook on which to hang coats, it is recommended that "you should not necessarily call it a hook in your claim. Instead, consider whether you should call it simply 'a support for clothes'" (ibid.). We will examine these particular lexical choices in more detail later, when considering approaches to translation.

Abstract

Patent applications to most patent offices must be accompanied by an abstract. Abstracts are not formally part of the specification. However, abstracts, along with titles, are frequently translated, to facilitate public searches, as we will see in the following section. It is therefore useful to highlight their key features here.

Summarized from the *USPTO Manual of Patenting Examining Procedure* (2014b), the abstract should enable readers, regardless of familiarity with patents, to determine the gist of the invention and its novelty, quickly and from a cursory inspection, enabling them to decide whether they need to consult the full text. It should not refer to the prior art or to speculative applications of the invention, but it should include whatever is new or improved in the invention, without containing extensive technical or design details. It should avoid the legal phraseology often used in patent claims (e.g. 'said') or implied information, for example 'the disclosure defined by this invention' or information given in the title, for reasons of conciseness. Most applications specify a length of up to 150 words for the abstract. The abstract for the patent above can be accessed via Patentscope (see next section) and is reproduced as Excerpt 5.4.

EXCERPT 5.4

The conveyor system for clinical test apparatus includes a main transport conveyor and a plurality of auxiliary conveyors located alongside the main transport conveyor. The auxiliary conveyors define straight line paths of travel parallel to the straight line paths of travel of the main conveyor. Each of the auxiliary conveyors is operated by drive means separate from the main transport conveyor. Two crossover points are provided between the main transport conveyor and the auxiliary conveyor. One crossover point is an entrance from the main transport conveyor to the auxiliary conveyor and the other crossover point is an exit from the auxiliary conveyor to the main transport conveyor. Each crossover point is controlled by a gate. One of the gates is a divert gate which can be actuated to block the main transport path thereby diverting puck traffic onto the auxiliary conveyor. The other gate is an interface gate which is used primarily to read information on a sample tube before it is introduced into a test apparatus and also functions as a load and unload station for the clinical test apparatus. The conveyor system also has a main unload and load system wherein tubes that have been completely tested are removed from pucks and reloaded with new tubes that are to be tested.

In the following section we will discuss some specific circumstances in which patents are translated.

Patents and translation

Patent applications may be submitted to and granted by national patent offices or IPOs. In the UK, for example this is the IPO. However, in the context of international trade, a patent that is valid only in one country may be of little value, and to make a separate patent application in every country in which protection is sought is increasingly impractical. For this reason numerous international initiatives exist to streamline the international processing and administration of patents. The international dimension of patenting also represents one area for which translation is visible and relevant.

This section outlines the work of some key international patent offices and their use of human and machine translation. Some statistics on present-day international patenting activity serve to give you a sense of recent geopolitical and economic shifts in IP which also have an impact on current and future translation needs.

The EPO

The EPO, headquartered in Munich, handles patent applications from its 38 member states. Membership covers the European Union but extends beyond it, including also Norway, Iceland, Switzerland and Turkey, among others. Applications to the EPO are required to be in the format typical of patent applications worldwide, encompassing abstract, description, drawings and claims. The EPO completes the search and examination process prior to granting a patent. A European patent that is granted by the EPO then has to be validated in the states for which protection is sought, with translations into national languages required in some cases, at the patentee's expense (see discussion of the London Agreement below).

The working languages of the EPO are English, French and German. As we saw in the example of the patent for the conveyor system for clinical test apparatus in the previous section, the EPO publishes the claims sections for patent specifications in those three languages, using translation to do so. At the time of writing, the EPO's Language Service employs 34 permanent staff, including 24 translators and editors. In addition, it works with approximately 140 freelance interpreters and 40 freelance translators, so this is one way in which skilled linguists may become involved in patent translation.

Espacenet

Espacenet, www.epo.org/espacenet, is the EPO's patent database, containing some 80 million patent documents from around the world, searchable in various ways. **Smart search** is the default mode, allowing you to perform single-word or multi-word searches or to search by patent document number, or to perform advanced searches using a query language (CQL, Contextual Query Language). Various search terms can be combined in the Advanced search mode. Finally the classification search is a tool used in professional patent searching, enabling all publications related to a particular technical area to be retrieved.

PatentTranslate

For languages other than the EPO's three working ones, and for parts of patent specifications or applications other than abstracts, which are also accessible by the public via the Espacenet interface but for which a human translation is not provided, an MT system is available. The EPO's MT service, called PatentTranslate, is the result of collaboration between the EPO and Google. Google trained its statistical MT engine using "millions of official, human-translated patent documents" provided by the EPO (EPO 2012). Training an MT engine with texts and translations of a specific genre and subject domain should improve the overall quality of the MT output.

The MT service launched in February 2012, for translation into and out of English and six other languages: French, German, Italian, Spanish, Portuguese, Swedish. More languages were added in October 2012 and the project was completed in December 2013, offering MT between English and 31 languages, and between French and German and 27 languages. It therefore covers all 28 languages of the EPO member states, plus Russian, Chinese, Korean and Japanese.

As stated on the PatentTranslate website, the purpose of the MT is to "give you the gist of any patent or patent-related document, and help you to determine whether it is relevant. You might decide on this basis whether you need to invest in a human translation of the document. Please note that the engine cannot provide legally binding translations" (EPO 2012).

Other regional patenting bodies

Like the EPO, the African Regional Intellectual Property Organization (ARIPO), the Organisation Africaine de la Propriété Intellectuelle or African Intellectual Property Organization (OAPI) and the Eurasian Patent Organization (EAPO) and its executive body, the Eurasian Patent Office, deal with patent applications in their respective regions.

WIPO and the Patent Cooperation Treaty

Moving beyond the national and regional dimensions, there have also been considerable efforts to establish international procedures for handling the protection of IP more widely. The Patent Cooperation Treaty (PCT), which came into effect in 1978, established an international patent application system. This system is administered by WIPO, a specialized agency of the United Nations, based in Switzerland. An international application can be filed in any of the 148 PCT contracting states or with any of the regional patent offices above (i.e. only one application in one language is required). It then undergoes an international search and receives the resultant report on prior art and patentability. On that basis, applicants may choose to withdraw the application or proceed to its publication on WIPO's patent database, Patentscope (see below). They may also request an optional supplementary international search or an international preliminary examination of their application.

Note that the PCT does not grant an international patent, but rather facilitates international applications; the granting of the patents ultimately remains the responsibility of the national and regional patenting bodies. However, this international filing and searching gives applicants more time and more information about likelihood of patentability before they continue to the next stage of seeking protection from national or regional patenting bodies. The PCT's international patent filing route therefore enables applicants to postpone the incurring of national/regional patenting costs, while helping them to decide on patentability and potential commercialization and allowing them to publicize their invention internationally. It is also designed to reduce duplication of work by different patent offices.

The growth in popularity of the PCT application route (as well as the growth in worldwide patenting activity) can be seen in the fact that it took 26 years (1978–2004) to reach one million PCT applications, but then only 7 years (2004–2011) to reach two million.

The 2014 report on PCT applications highlights how the top ten countries of origin accounted for 87 per cent of applications in 2013. These were (in order of applications) the USA, Japan, China, Germany, South Korea, France, the UK, Switzerland, the Netherlands and Sweden (WIPO 2014b: 32). Moreover, 20 per cent of applicants account for over 80 per cent of applications (ibid.: 36), and the largest number of applications came from the field of electrical machinery, followed by computer technology, electrical engineering and medical technology (ibid.: 42).

Patentscope

Patentscope is WIPO's patent database containing more than 43 million patent documents. 2.5 million of these are international applications submitted under the PCT. The remainder are documents from national patent offices. In 2014 the national patent collections of 37 countries could be accessed. Patentscope also includes documents from the regional patent offices of the EPO and the Eurasian Patent Office.

A simple search enables you to look for patent documents by keyword, ID number, name, etc. You can choose the type of search that will be done, that is, a search of the front page of the patent application, a search of any fields of the document, the full text of the document, the English text, ID numbers, International Patent Classification (IPC) codes or names of inventors, applicants, companies or dates.

PCT and translation

As noted above, PCT applications may be filed in any contracting country or region and can therefore be accepted in any language of the receiving office. However, they must be published in one of the ten official/publication languages, which are English, Japanese, Chinese, German, Korean, French, Spanish, Russian, Portuguese and Arabic.

The latest statistics on languages used for filing, available at the time of writing, were estimates for 2013 (WIPO 2014b: 60). According to these, 51 per cent (some 104,100 PCT applications) were filed in English, 20 per cent (41,254) in Japanese, 9.5 per cent (16,531) in Chinese, 8.1 per cent (16,531) in German, 5 per cent (10,229) in Korean, 3 per cent (6,158) in French, 0.9 per cent (1,848) in Italian, 0.8 per cent (1,647) in Spanish, 0.5 per cent (1,031) in Russian and 0.3 per cent (555) in Portuguese.

WIPO's International Bureau deals with the publication and translation of PCT applications. Translation is done to ensure that all titles and abstracts are available in English and French, and that all international search reports (ISR) and reports from the preliminary examination (International Preliminary Reports on Patentability, IPRP) are available in English. This represents a substantial translation effort, which, in recent times, has increased year on year, mostly due to increased demand for translation from Japanese, Chinese and Korean (WIPO 2014b: 61). In 2013 280,820 abstracts and 93,459 reports were translated. Most of this translation work was outsourced – almost 90 per cent of abstracts and almost 96 per cent of reports – while the remainder was done by the in-house PCT Translation Service. The unit cost of translation is also increasing, as Asian languages assume a higher proportion of demand (WIPO 2013b: 5). WIPO budgeted approximately 50 million Swiss francs for PCT translation in 2014–2015 (WIPO 2013b: 25), which was a hefty increase of around 10 million francs from the 2012–2013 period.

The International Bureau uses a translation-quality indicator to measure the quality of translations produced by both in-house translators and external suppliers, based on random sampling of documents. The result is a rating of 'acceptable' or 'not acceptable'. The proportion of acceptable translations was 87.1 per cent for 2013, and this rate has been relatively stable over the previous 5-year period (WIPO 2013b: 63). Contracts with external suppliers whose quality rate falls consistently below 80 per cent are discontinued (ibid.: 232).

If you are interested in gaining professional experience in this area, you might wish to apply for the annual internship programme at WIPO's PCT Translation Service, called the Translation/Terminology Fellowship Programme. It is aimed at giving recent graduates of translation or terminology programmes some experience as assistant translators, terminologists or technical specialists. Those who are awarded a place on the programme may be involved in translating abstracts and patent examination reports or in helping to develop translation tools, including terminology work, for example extracting scientific and technical terms from documentary sources or creating or validating termbase entries.

WIPO Pearl termbase

WIPO Pearl (n.d.) is a multilingual termbase for the 10 PCT publication languages. It is developed and maintained by the PCT Language Service, which also validates the content. Since autumn 2014 WIPO Pearl has been publicly accessible via the WIPO website: www.wipo.int/wipopearl/.

At the time of writing, the termbase contained 91,152 terms and 14,951 concepts, but is being added to all the time. You may find this a very useful resource for your own translation work. You can search it by term (linguistic search) or by concept or subject field (concept search). To illustrate with a brief example, my linguistic search for *wireless communication system* produced validated translations as follows:

- English: wireless communication system
- Spanish: sistema de comunicación inalámbrico
- French: système de communication sans fil
- Japanese: 無線通信システム and ワイヤレス通信システム
- Korean: 무선 통신 시스템
- Chinese: 无线通信系统

and then three MT-generated (so not validated) suggestions:

- German: Drahtloses kommunikations (missing 'system' after 'Kommunikations', which should also be capitalized). However, links to Patentscope bring me useful alternatives, for example 'System zur drahtlosen Kommunikation'
- Portuguese: sistema de comunicação sem fio
- Russian: системе беспроводной связи

A contextual example is available for each of the validated terms, and there are direct links from all terms to Patentscope to view patent documentation containing those terms. From the Patentscope results we can also access the documentation for each of the patents if we wish.

A direct link to the conceptual map is also available from the search results page. Alternatively a concept system search can be carried out separately. This produces a graphical display of the relations between concepts, depicting associative, generic or partitive relations between concepts. For example, the concept map for *wireless communication system* shows a generic/partitive relation with three concepts: *wireless network*, *communications system*, and *wireless communication*, and an associative relation with *wired communication system*.

Cross Lingual Information Retrieval

Cross Lingual Information Retrieval (CLIR) is one of the search modes available via the Advanced Search in Patentscope and it is likely to be useful to you in your translation practice. It is a search facility which enables you to search patents for terms and possible translations of those terms in Chinese, Dutch, English, French,

German, Italian, Japanese, Korean, Portuguese, Russian, Spanish or Swedish. You enter your search term or terms in one language and the system proposes potentially equivalent search terms in the other languages. These suggestions are based on bilingual dictionaries extracted statistically from corpora of patents.

Start by entering your query in the search box. Then select the language of the query and select your desired expansion mode ('supervised' means that you can choose the subject domains for the search, 'automatic' means that these are decided by the system). You then have the option to move the slider to prioritize precision (roughly understood as 'exactness of results') or recall ('completeness of results'). If you prioritize precision the system will try to give you the most relevant results, with the risk of missing some, while recall will maximize the quantity of results, therefore including a higher proportion of irrelevant ones. In supervised mode, the next step is to choose the subject domains for the search. In the next stage, the system proposes search term variants that can be added to your initial query. Add as required. Click on 'Translate selected terms' to have translations of those variants. By proceeding from here, a multilingual search of the patent database is carried out.

As an example of how this functions we could take a key term from our previous patent example, *conveyor system*. When I search for this, the system suggests that two subject domains are most relevant. These are [MANU] Manufacturing & Materials Handling Tech and [PACK] Packaging & Distribution of Goods. I can add others or remove these if I disagree. Since they seem relevant, I accept them and I am then presented with several possible variant terms for *conveyor system*. These include *transport system, conveyance facility* and several others. Choosing only *conveying system*, alongside my original query of *conveyor system*, the system proposes numerous terms in each of 11 languages being proposed by the system for my search. As examples, the French and Chinese variants proposed are given below:

- French suggested variants: "système de convoyeur" OR "système de transport" OR "système transporteur" OR "système convoyeur" OR "installation de transport" OR "système de transporteur" OR "systèmeconvoyeur" OR "transporteur" OR "chemin de transport" OR "convoyeur"
- Chinese suggested variants: "用于控制输送" OR "控制输送" OR "传送系统及" OR "式设备非恒定" OR "在输送系统中" OR "传送系统中" OR "及传送" OR "输送及系统的使用" OR "输送及" OR "输送机构" OR "来在输送" OR "及其输送"

I can then proceed to do a search of the patent database using all or some of the suggested terms, for all or some of the languages in question. If I limit my search to one target language, the search effectively becomes a simple search, bringing me back to the simple search screen, but with the generated TL search terms already entered.

Once patent results are retrieved in languages other than English, an MT facility is offered on the results page, using either TAPTA (see below) to translate titles and abstracts or Google Translate for other parts of the patent documentation. Consult the Patentscope user's guide (WIPO 2013a) for a more detailed version of these instructions.

TAPTA

WIPO also offers an MT tool, called TAPTA, to provide gist translations of titles and abstracts between English and a small set of languages, namely French, German, Japanese and Chinese. It can be accessed at https://www3.wipo.int/patentscope/translate/translate.jsf.

TAPTA is a statistical MT system, using a Moses engine trained on human translations of patent titles and abstracts. In addition to producing a gist translation, the system gives users the possibility of choosing between translation variants and of editing the MT output. For more information about how TAPTA works, consult the TAPTA user manual (WIPO 2014a) or Pouliquen and Mazenc (2011) or Pouliquen et al. (2011).

Developments affecting translation activities

One development which will be immediately obvious from the outline above is that patent organizations are turning to technology, specifically statistical MT, to help them to meet translation demands and/or reduce translation costs. The notion of **gist translation** is a common one in this context. Given that people generally search patent databases to find out about prior art, there is a rationale for using MT to provide gist translations of titles and abstracts, if these translations give sufficient information to enable the user to decide whether they need to read more. When documents are found which are relevant to the search or examination, human translation of descriptions and claims may then be needed and undertaken.

Initiatives have been developed previously by the EPO and other bodies to limit translation efforts. For example, the **London Agreement**, which took effect in 2008, dispensed with some previous requirements for patents to be supplied to the EPO in national languages as well as EPO languages. What is stipulated depends on the national status of EPO languages and on whether states have prescribed English. See EPO (2014a) or van Pottelsberghe de la Potterie and Mejer (2010) for more details.

An ongoing initiative with implications for translation is the setting up of a unitary European patent (more precisely put, a **European patent with unitary effect**) and of a **Unified Patent Court**. After many previous attempts, agreement was finally reached, and regulations to offer a unitary patent entered into force in January 2013, though do not yet apply. Twenty-five EU member states are participating in the scheme. The unitary patent will be a European patent granted by the EPO, to which unitary effect for the territory of the 25 participating states can be given if the patentee requests it (and subject to payment of fees not yet agreed).

It will be possible for the single unitary patent to be enforced by a single infringement action across all the participating states and to be revoked for all those states in a single action. The Unified Patent Court will be a specialized patent court which will handle all litigation relating to European patents and European patents with unitary effect. Ratification of the agreement concerning the court is ongoing at the time of writing; you can find the latest news on the EPO website (EPO 2014b).

The regulations for the unitary patent include specific arrangements for translation; ultimately these reduce the requirement for human translation of patents, except in the case of disputes, although a transitional period of 12 years has been agreed prolonging the use of translation. During the transition period a translation into English is required for patents processed in French or German, and a translation into another (any) official EU language is required for patents processed in English. However, it will no longer be necessary for patentees to commission translations for individual member states in which patent protection is sought, thus representing a cost saving for some.

Patent translation outside of institutional contexts

Apart from in-house and freelance work done by translators for patent offices like those detailed above, there are many other sources of patent translation work for freelance translators. These include the translation of documentation in preparation for submission of a patent application, and the translation of documentation in relation to patent disputes or litigation. In these cases, patent searches may be required, and documents pertaining to prior art may need to be translated so that inventors, agents or attorneys can make judgements about the novelty and patentability of their invention. As we saw above, WIPO's and the EPO's MT systems help to give those conducting searches access to information produced in languages foreign to them, but for many purposes this is simply insufficient. For example, translation may be needed between languages not covered by the MT systems. In the case of WIPO's system, translation of a title and abstract will not be sufficient if the patent is relevant to the case. In those instances, agents or attorneys will require translation of claims and descriptions too. The quality of MT systems, even when trained on patent documentation, may simply not suffice for an in-depth understanding of a detailed description of a complex technical product or process.

Freelance translators can be hired directly by attorneys, or translations are commissioned via LSPs. Numerous LSPs advertise specializations in patent translation, often emphasizing the experience which their translators have in specialist subject areas and in patent matters. Some LSPs have associated arms which specialize in IP matters, so that they can offer international search services by professional searchers and patent application filing services (also for foreign patent offices), including checks by in-country attorneys. Translation is then also embedded in these other procedures and activities. Among the documents for which translations may be required are parts of patent documents, in particular abstracts and claims, but also other documents pertaining to prior art, the patent application itself, and documents pertaining to patent litigation.

Principles and practices of translating patents

Based on what we now know about the function of patents as part of the apparatus of IP protection, as well as the way in which patent applications are prepared and processed and typical features of the genre, we can formulate some general principles of assistance to you in your translation practice.

Client expectations and documentary translation

For many of the circumstances in which patents are translated, as outlined above, the translation will generally be visible and used alongside the source text. While it might only be read in one language by any one reader, the fact that it is a translation will be evident to many users of the translation, and in some cases, for example opposition or litigation, the translation may assume particularly significant status, not just as a means of informing readers about a technical invention, but indeed as evidence to be used in constructing arguments pertaining to infringements or challenges.

It is therefore useful to understand patent translation as an example of what Nord calls **documentary translation** (Nord 1997: 47; 2005: 80–1). This is translation that documents the communication between the ST author and the ST receiver. The TT reader is placed in the position of observing the ST communicative situation. Documentary translation is contrasted to instrumental translation, which fulfils a communicative purpose in its own right in the target culture. Of course the translation of a patent has a communicative purpose, but this is closely linked to the ST; its purpose is to document the ST, to communicate, as clearly and unambiguously as possible, what claims and descriptions were put forward in the ST, in the source context of the source author (inventor or agent) seeking to patent the invention represented in the ST.

For that reason, documentary translation often focuses on certain ST features to highlight them for the TT reader, for example, a syntactically close translation might be done to enable a TL reader to appreciate those aspects of the ST in a linguistic or literary analysis. In patent translation and other cases of documentary translation, for example translation of official documents such as birth, death or marriage certificates, passports, school or university transcripts, there is an expectation of 'literalness' or closeness to the source text, to represent (or document) as closely as possible the claims and descriptions of the ST.

Clients are unlikely to be familiar with the term 'documentary translation', but they may ask for a literal translation, although they may not always be able to specify what they mean by this. In general, what is meant in patent translation is that the ST structures and lexis are mirrored where it is feasible to do so, even if this produces a slightly awkward, though comprehensible TT. Depending on language combination, the client will often expect to be able to trace the ST sentence structures as they read the TT. In concrete terms this approach generally means that translators avoid merging or splitting sentences, they follow punctuation patterns of the ST where possible and they may opt for cognate forms in their choice of lexis, where this is a viable option.

Consistency and ST deficiencies

Given the circumstances of patent searches or patent challenges, for which translations are prepared, and the attention to detail that may be crucial in those circumstances, it is important for translators to focus on consistency in their translations of patent documents. The involves checking and double-checking all details, including numbering, cross-references and references to diagrams. Due to their close scrutiny, translators may spot inconsistencies in patent source texts. Given the frequent complexity of drawings and descriptions, it is certainly possible for the source author to have made mistakes, for example by introducing some mislabelling or inconsistencies between the written text and the drawings. If you find apparent inconsistencies or errors in the ST, keep the inconsistency or error in the TT but add a translator's note to explain it. Your note enables those using the TT for their purposes, for example the patent searcher, examiner or attorney, to decide on the significance of the error or inconsistency. Adding a translator's note might be deemed inappropriate in other translation situations, but is appropriate and common practice in many forms of documentary translation, including patent translation. In our example text, an inconsistency in use of terms can be seen in paragraph [0010], where *diverter gate* is used (twice only), while all other instances throughout the text refer to *divert gate*. As with any other document, there may be typos too, as in Excerpt 5.5 from our example. In these cases the meaning is not obscured or misrepresented, and the typos do not pose a problem for translators.

EXCERPT 5.5

- [0028] Robots (not shown) at the station 40 remove tested sample tubes 106 from the conveyor 30.
- [0034] As most clearly sown [*sic*] in Fig. 4 and replaces [*sic*] them with new sample tubes 106 to be tested.

Terminology, lexis and phraseology

Patent applications use elements of legal language and style, including some formulaic expressions which appear in all or most patents. We noted above some phrases which often occur in claims, for example *characterized by* and variants. Other examples of recurrent phrases from our text include:

- is associated with
- one/another/a further embodiment of the invention
- as claimed in claim
- in a known manner/in the/a (same/similar) manner (as) previously described/shown

We noted also the use of legalistic adverbs such as *wherein, thereof, herein, hereinafter, thereinafter*. Patents also reuse other phrases that serve the purpose of organizing the discourse; examples from our text include: *as shown in Fig.* and *indicated by the reference number*. If you are translating patents, it is useful to identify sets of these regular and recurrent formulations in your SLs and TLs and familiarize yourself with them so that you can use them in your translations.

Extracting keywords and term candidates from our text (see Chapter 2), the single-word and multi-word terms listed as Excerpt 5.6 emerge as key:

EXCERPT 5.6

- *conveyor system, main transport conveyor, main transport lane, auxiliary conveyor (module), conveyor belt, sidebar lane, straight line travel path, closed circuit travel path, exit opening, (sidebar) entrance opening, crossover point*
- *sample tube, clinical test apparatus, tube recess*
- *puck, puck rotating mechanism, puck rotating collar, (sidebar) plunger device, gate housing, traffic control gate, divert gate, diverter gate, divert gate device, divert head, interface gate, star wheel device, biasing unit*
- *load/unload station, singulator device, label check station, bar code label, label reader device*
- *schematic plan view, sectional view.*

As noted earlier, patents, and claims in particular, show a tendency towards generalized description which contrasts with practices in many other technical genres, where every component is designated by a specific term. It is possible that a patent application introduces novel technical concepts for which no term has been coined as yet. However, this tendency to describe some technical components or processes in more general terms also serves a useful and practical purpose in the patent application. Often these components have not yet been physically created, produced or realized, and some aspects of their composition or form may still be unknown or undecided. In our text, the description and claims indeed tend to foreground the function of the component, and this is sufficient for the purposes of the description and the claims. We can see this clearly in our example, as shown in Excerpt 5.6, where many components of this invention are denoted by means of modified nouns *device, means, mechanism, system or member.* Following this practice, patent translators tend to resist the temptation to disambiguate or clarify further the precise nature of these concepts. This means that it may not be helpful to research and assign terms from other technical contexts, used for technologies which are already manufactured and in use. Instead, it is helpful for translators to identify general lexis, corresponding to means, *device, system*, etc. that can be used throughout the translation to preserve the functional description without assigning further characteristics to the concept. The generic nature of the description is also maintained through reference to range of generic mechanical parts or components (e.g. *housing, segment, plate, portion, pin*), also listed in Excerpt 5.7.

EXCERPT 5.7

Means: *hold-back means, biasing means, control means, diversion means, drive means, motor means, segregation means, separation means, support means.*
Device: *conveyor device, functional device, divert gate device, gate device, interface gate device, motor device, plunger device, label reader device, reader device, label reading device, robotic device, label scanner device, scanner device, sensor device, singulator device, solenoid device, star wheel device.*
Mechanism: *puck rotating mechanism, rotating mechanism, singulator mechanism.*
System: *(novel) conveyor system, unload and load system, utility support system, transport system.*
Member: *bracket member, column member, deflector member, diversion member, joining member, securement member.*
Nouns denoting generic mechanical parts: *pulley, fastener, housing, cantilever, valving, switch, bracket, cabinetry, segment, guide pin, plate, portion, sensor, motor, edge wall, column, stanchion, container, pan, finger, member, slot, sleeve.*

In addition to the above observations, a comparison with a reference corpus reveals other patterns of language use in our text. Organized by part of speech in Excerpt 5.8, we can note a strong tendency towards recurrent nominalizations to designate processes, and derived adjectives and adverbs, some rather novel, to designate capabilities. This abstraction of processes and qualities to act as entities (designated by nouns) is a typical feature of technical and scientific English and is discussed further in Chapter 6 under the heading of Grammatical metaphor (Halliday 2004). A limited set of recurrent verbs can also be identified, many denoting functional movement of the apparatus. Lexical variation for purely stylistic purposes is not recommended for patents (whether in the source text or the translation); thus, the degree of repetition noted in our ST will normally be reproduced in the TT.

EXCERPT 5.8

Nouns: *singulation, extrusion, drippage, intersection, diversion, inclusion, alignment, protraction, confinement, retraction, separation, installation.*
Adjectives and adverbs: *singulated, rotatable, retractable, protracted, detachably, pneumatically, proximate, sectional, protractible,*

counterclockwise, elevational, operable, fragmentary, slidable, rotatably, non-singulated, engagable, actuatable, robotically, coplanar, hematological, spaced.
Verbs: *retract, rotate, divert, predetermine, load, unload, protract, actuate, singulate, retrace, travel, space, bypass, transport, activate, include, define.*

Exercise 5.1: Familiarizing yourself with the components and language of patents in your SL and TL

Using the links to patent databases (e.g. Patentscope), select some patent documents written in your languages to become more familiar with the component parts (title, abstract, description, claims, diagrams, etc.). Then focus on the use of language and identify recurrent terms and phrases. Make a bilingual list of legal phraseology used in your source and target languages. What other observations can you make about the use of the SL and the TL?

Exercise 5.2: Translating a title and abstract

Imagine a hypothetical situation where you are translating the title and abstract of a patent application for inclusion on a patent database like Espacenet. If you are translating out of English, you may wish to work on one of the abstracts below. You can use the patent ID number to locate the full document. Alternatively, choose a source text in an appropriate language from a patent database. Carry out the necessary preparatory research, using the WIPO Pearl termbase, where appropriate. Reflect on the main translation challenges and discuss your translation choices.

EP 1993910 – METHOD FOR SEALING A LIDSTOCK TO A CONTAINER

The invention relates to a method for heat sealing a lidstock (9) to a container (1) for a blister package, the container having a top surface comprising a substantially flat sealing flange (3) surrounding a blister (2) and a lip (4) having at least one raised surface (6), the method comprising the steps of a) locating the lidstock on the top surface; b) providing a first seal between the lidstock and the at least one raised surface of the lip with a first heat sealing tool (11); c) providing a second hermetic seal between the lidstock and the sealing flange surrounding the blister with a second heat sealing tool. The invention also relates to a package for storing a hydrophilic contact lens comprising a lip having at least one raised surface and a removable lidstock sealed to a sealing flange and to the at least one raised surface. Also disclosed is an apparatus for heat sealing the lidstock to the container.

US 20080236621 – INTEGRATED WASHER AND STERILIZER

A method and apparatus provides for cleaning and sterilizing a device in one machine. The method comprises the steps of: a) placing the device into a container; b) placing the container into a washing/sterilization apparatus; c) the washing/sterilization apparatus washing the device by applying a washing fluid to an interior of the container to wash the device; d) after washing the device, and without removing the device from the washing/sterilization apparatus, the washing/sterilization apparatus packaging the device in a bacteria impermeable package; e) the washing/sterilization apparatus sterilizing the device by exposing the device to a sterilizing vapor; and f) removing the device while it remains in the package whereby to preserve its sterility until use.

Exercise 5.3: Translating a claims section

Choose a patent application or specification, in your SL, from a technical area that interests you. Imagine that you are being commissioned by a patent attorney to translate the claims. Carry out the necessary research. Reflect on the main translation challenges and discuss your choices.

Exercise 5.4: Exploring PatentTranslate

For a patent of your choice, found on Espacenet (EP), generate an MT using PatentTranslate. Consider the usefulness of the MT for (i) an inventor preparing to submit a similar invention and (ii) a patent attorney involved in a patent dispute.

Further reading: Consulting advice from patent translators

For interesting insights into patent translation from practitioners, read the *Translating Patents* blog (Cross, n.d., http://patenttranslations. wordpress.com) and *Patenttranslator's Blog* (Vitek, n.d., http://patent-translator.wordpress.com).

> **Key points from this chapter**
>
> - Patent applications and specifications are key genres in the context of IP protection in the commercial world.
> - The distinctive features of the genre relate to the nature of the patenting process and the need for patentability criteria to be met, as well as the potential for patents to be challenged. Abstracts, titles, descriptions, claims and drawings are standard components of patent applications and specification, with conventionalized structures, organization and use of linguistic resources.
> - Translation, by humans and machines, plays an important part at various stages of the patenting process, in preparing patent applications, in processing of applications by international organizations involved in the patenting process and in patent litigation, as well as in ensuring that patent information is disclosed to the public.
> - Patent translation can be understood as a form of documentary translation and, as a result, involves translation strategies and practices that are distinct from those of many other technical genres.

References

Bazerman, Charles (1994) 'Systems of Genres and the Enactment of Social Intentions', in Aviva Freedman and Peter Medway (eds) *Genre and the New Rhetoric*, London: Taylor & Francis, pp. 79–101.

Cross, Martin (n.d.) *Translating Patents* blog, online at: http://patenttranslations.wordpress.com (accessed 30 January 2015).

EPO (2012) 'Patent Translate Service – FAQ', European Patent Office, online at: www.epo.org/searching/free/patent-translate/faq.html (accessed 15 January 2015).

—— (2014a) 'Key Points', European Patent Office, online at: www.epo.org/law-practice/legal-texts/london-agreement/key-points.html (accessed 15 January 2015).

—— (2014b) 'Unitary Patent', European Patent Office, online at: www.epo.org/law-practice/unitary/unitary-patent.html (accessed 15 January 2015).

—— (2014c) 'The European Patent Convention', European Patent Office, online at: www.epo.org/law-practice/legal-texts/html/epc/2013/e/ar53.html (accessed 15 January 2015).

Halliday, M.A.K. (2004) *The Language of Science*, Jonathan J. Webster (ed) London and New York: Continuum.

Helmers, Christian and Luke McDonagh (2012) *Patent Litigation in the UK*, London: London School of Economics, online at: www.lse.ac.uk/collections/law/wps/wps.htm (accessed 15 January 2015).

Intellectual Property Office (2010) 'Patent Factsheet: Claims', online at: www.gov.uk/government/uploads/system/uploads/attachment_data/file/330278/factclaims.pdf (accessed 15 January 2015).

Kane, Yukari Iwatani (2014) 'How Apple Tried to Avert a War With Samsung', *Re/code*, online at: http://recode.net/2014/04/01/how-apple-tried-to-avert-a-war-with-samsung/ (accessed 12 January 2015).

Knowles, James (2012) 'How Long until a European Patent Is Granted?', *Patentia* online at: http://patentia.co.uk/index.php/how-long-until-a-european-patent-is-granted/ (accessed 12 January 2015).

Liptak, Adam (2013) 'Justices, 9-0, Bar Patenting Human Genes', *The New York Times*, 13 June 2013, online at: www.nytimes.com/2013/06/14/us/supreme-court-rules-human-genes-may-not-be-patented.html (accessed 30 January 2015).

Nord, Christiane (1997) *Translating as a Purposeful Activity: Functionalist Approaches Explained*, Manchester: St Jerome Publishing.

—— (2005) *Text Analysis in Translation: Theory, Methodology, and Didactic Application of a Model for Translation-Oriented Text Analysis*, 2nd ed., trans. by Christiane Nord and Penelope Sparrow Amsterdam: Rodopi.

Pouliquen, Bruno and Christophe Mazenc (2011) 'COPPA, CLIR and TAPTA: Three Tools to Assist in Overcoming the Patent Language Barrier at WIPO', *Proceedings of the 13th Machine Translation Summit*, pp. 24–30.

Pouliquen, Bruno, Christophe Mazenc and Aldo Iorio (2011) 'Tapta: A User-Driven Translation System for Patent Documents Based on Domain-Aware Statistical Machine Translation', in *Proceedings of the 15th International Conference of the European Association for Machine Translation (EAMT)*, pp. 5–12.

USPTO (2014a) 'General Information Concerning Patents', United States Patent and Trademark Office, online at: www.uspto.gov/patents-getting-started/general-information-concerning-patents (accessed 15 January 2015).

USPTO (2014b) *USPTO Manual of Patenting Examining Procedure*, United States Patent and Trademark Office, online at: www.uspto.gov/web/offices/pac/mpep/ (accessed 15 January 2015).

van Pottelsberghe de la Potterie, Bruno and Malwina Mejer (2010) 'The London Agreement and the Cost of Patenting in Europe', *European Journal of Law and Economics* 29(2): 211–37.

Vitek, Steve (n.d.) *Patenttranslator's Blog*, online at: http://patenttranslator.wordpress.com (accessed 30 January 2015).

WIPO (2013a) 'Patentscope Search: The User's Guide', online at: www.wipo.int/edocs/pubdocs/en/patents/434/wipo_pub_l434_08.pdf (accessed 15 January 2015).

—— (2013b) *WIPO Program and Budget for the 2014/15 Biennium*, Geneva: World Intellectual Property Organization.

—— (2013c) *ST.9: Recommendation Concerning Bibliographic Data on and Relating to Patents and SPCs*, online at: www.wipo.int/export/sites/www/standards/en/pdf/03-09-01.pdf. (accessed 15 January 2015).

—— (2014a) 'TAPTA Translation Assistant for Patent Titles and Abstracts', online at: www3.wipo.int/patentscope/translate/wtapta-user-manual-en.pdf (accessed 15 January 2015).

—— (2014b) *Patent Cooperation Treaty: Yearly Review*, Geneva: World Intellectual Property Organization.

—— (2014c) 'Regulations under the Patent Cooperation Treaty', online at: www.wipo.int/pct/en/texts/rules/rtoc1.htm (accessed 15 January 2015).

WIPO Pearl (n.d.) World Intellectual Property Organization, online at: www.wipo.int/wipopearl/ (accessed 15 January 2015).

6 Scientific research articles and abstracts

This chapter focuses on communication between professional scientists through the genres of research articles and abstracts of research articles. We examine the typical circumstances in which research articles are translated, situating translation against the backdrop of the use of English as a scientific lingua franca. We then focus on a number of specific features of the genre of the research article and the research article abstract, namely academic vocabulary, rhetorical moves, metadiscourse and grammatical metaphor. An in-depth understanding of the conventions of these genres and an ability to compare and contrast anglophone and other language conventions is essential for translators wishing to specialize in the translation of scientific research.

Introducing professional scientific discourse

In this chapter we shift our attention towards the domain of professional science, examining two genres that are key to scientific communication among specialists and that are often translated. These are research articles and research article abstracts. Reading, understanding and translating scientific research articles can be a real challenge. They are written by specialists, for specialists, and their linguistic and textual choices usually mean that non-specialist readers will feel excluded in the first instance. The authors assume that their readers are familiar with the existing body of knowledge in their field and they write accordingly. They may therefore have no need to explain complex ideas or concepts, leaving the uninitiated reader in the dark. Translators, even very experienced ones, will seldom have the level of expertise of the professional scientist who is research-active in that field. It is worth remembering that a scientist reading a research article is likely to be doing so because it relates directly or indirectly to their own research or teaching. The relevance of the research article to their own interests may be high, and so too their motivation to read and understand the specific contribution made by the article. To fulfil their role in the scientific community of practice, they may also need to take a stance in support of or against the claims made in the article, which again necessitates careful reading and thorough understanding.

As with other genres already discussed, it is crucial that you gain an understanding of the subject and content of the text you are going to translate. This will inevitably involve paying a lot of attention to concepts and terms. You can make use of the strategies you have developed, including corpus-based analyses (see Chapter 2), to carry out terminological and conceptual research to familiarize yourself with the key concepts of the subject domain and the terms employed in the text. However, this chapter is devoted to other important aspects of the genre. We will start by reflecting on the nature of academic vocabulary and move on to examine the rhetorical and metadiscursive functions of the research article and the research article abstract in anglophone contexts.

The challenges facing the translator of scientific research articles and abstracts are strongly linked to the communicative events corresponding to these genres. For this reason, the next section directs your attention to the nature of scientific publishing and the communicative purposes fulfilled by publications written by scientists, beyond the perhaps obvious one of communicating research findings. As Hyland (2010: 116) notes, research publications are also sites in which scientists 'negotiate a credible account of themselves and their work by claiming solidarity with readers, appraising ideas and acknowledging alternative views'. As well as considering how scientists, as authors, negotiate social relationships, this chapter also prompts you, as translator, to reflect on your own social role in the machineries of knowledge.

English as the language of science

Just as Greek, Latin, Arabic, French and German have held the status of lingua franca of science over the centuries, much international exchange of scientific knowledge today happens through English (see Montgomery 2009). Many international science journals publish exclusively in English, and scientists throughout the world work towards submitting their research, written in English, to those leading journals, to ensure international dissemination, reach and impact. The traditional model of scientific journal publishing works as follows: authors submit their hitherto unpublished research in the form of an article; the article is reviewed by two or more academic peers; and, on the basis of reports and recommendations written by the reviewers, the editor(s) of the journal will accept or reject the article. The evaluation usually hinges on the extent to which the research makes a novel or useful contribution to knowledge, but also the robustness of the methods used to do so. Acceptance is usually conditional, that is, the author is obliged, or at the very least encouraged, to make certain changes to improve the quality of the article before it is published. Where there may be too many serious deficiencies, articles are rejected and resubmission may not be encouraged. Given these practices, journal editors, but also reviewers, are often referred to as the gatekeepers for their discipline, admitting research that they deem to meet certain quality standards, but keeping other contributions out. Although current developments in open-access academic publishing look set to change this model significantly, in ways which are not yet fully known or understood, the traditional model remains powerful and widely followed. Moreover, researchers' ability to achieve publication in leading international journals remains a benchmark against which they are often judged, institutionally, nationally or internationally.

Since we are interested in translating, one of our first questions might be: if the journals acknowledged as the leading ones in most scientific fields are published in English, is there any need or demand for translation of scientific articles? The answer is yes, and sections below outline some of those translation scenarios, focusing on translation into and out of English. However, before looking at those specific examples of translation activity, we reflect on the relationship between the dominance or hegemony of the anglophone academic writing model and translation.

Epistemicide

In 1997 Swales referred to English as *Tyrannosaurus rex*, 'a powerful carnivore gobbling up the other denizens of the academic linguistic grazing grounds' (1997: 374). He discusses some of the implications of English as the world's main medium of international professional communication, with a particular focus on the teaching of English for Academic Purposes (EAP). He argues that one of the roles of EAP teachers is to resist the 'triumphalism' of English, and he outlines his own attempts to educate his students in different academic traditions and to make them more aware of the consequences for discourse communities around the world of the unrelenting dominance of English.

Bennett (2007) raises similar issues but with a specific focus on translation. She notes how the anglophone writing conventions, characterized by a focus on precision, concision and clarity, run counter to rhetorical traditions in many other parts of the world. She discusses the relationship between writing conventions and epistemologies, that is, ways of organizing knowledge. By suppressing the distinctive rhetoric of a Portuguese academic when we translate their article into English conforming to anglophone academic discourse conventions, Bennett argues, we are not only performing a shift in rhetorical style. Rather we are undermining the very systems of knowledge of the Portuguese discourse community, which are different from those underlying the anglophone academic discourse model. She adopts the term 'epistemicide' from sociology to refer to this epistemological destruction performed by translators in particular.

While this is an important issue in translation into English, Bennett also argues (2013) that translators commit epistemicide when they translate from English into other languages too, if they preserve the English discoursal conventions in the other language instead of rewriting to fit with existing genre conventions of that target language and discourse community. Thus, English is allowed to dominate in both cases and the traditional discourse is eroded or obliterated.

Bennett (2007, 2013) calls on translators to resist the hegemony of English academic discourse, although she recognizes, to some extent, the difficulties of doing so. The client is the academic author who wants a translation, into English, that will make it through the gate-keeping mechanisms outlined above and succeed in being published in an anglophone journal. The last thing the author wants to hear is that his/her article has been rejected because the translation did not conform to anglophone genre conventions. And if that is what happens, the translator may well be judged by the client to be incompetent. Bennett (2013) suggests that translators need to be able to raise awareness of this issue among authors, editors and publishers, to negotiate and act as cultural consultants, to work towards a gradual change in the system as a whole. Translators also need to have a finely honed understanding of the epistemologies and genres at stake, so that they can subvert the hegemonic discourse where they have the opportunity to do so (Bennett 2013: 186).

A final point worth noting is that some scholars believe that the anglophone domination might be starting to be replaced by ELF (English as lingua franca) rhetorical patterns, and they therefore propose that translator training and research could also focus on the challenges of translating from and into ELF (see Taviano 2013; Pisanski Peterlin 2013).

There is also some resistance to the dominance of English in some national scientific communities. In Germany, for instance, the Arbeitskreis Deutsch als Wissenschaftssprache (ADAWIS), which the association translates as Association for the Maintenance of German in Academia, was formed in 2007. It acknowledges and accepts the role of English in international communication, but campaigns for the continued use of German and languages other than English in teaching and research in domestic contexts.

Translation and scientific publishing

The sections below outline some of the situations in which scientific translation forms part of the professional science publishing system.

In the vast majority of cases, this is translation work which is undertaken because of the dominance of English, and which, as just noted, is likely to reinforce that dominance.

Translating into English

Many scientists who are not native speakers of English write academic science in English to a standard which meets journal editors' expectations. However, it is also the case that others, who may or may not have some proficiency in English, experience difficulty producing articles deemed acceptable by those English-language journals and their gatekeeping editors. Scientists in the second group may make use of translation services or rely on bilingual colleagues to help them. Root-Bernstein and Ladle (2014), in a short article extolling the virtues of scientific translation, see shortcomings in both courses of action; they note that private translation services may not have sufficient understanding of the science and technical language or the structure of scientific articles, and that academic colleagues' time could be better employed on activities other than translating, editing or proofreading. They suggest a number of alternative solutions. For example, university departments could hire professional scientific translators, or they could hire English-speaking researchers with the specific remit of helping colleagues who need assistance or journals could provide translation services for free, to widen the range of submissions and the journals' readership. Mur Dueñas (2012) offers an interesting ethnographic account of the experiences of some Spanish researchers, writing in English, in their attempts, both failed and successful, to have their articles accepted for publication in international journals.

The kinds of measures suggested above are quite rarely implemented in practice. Universities and academics tend to outsource their translation work to translation agencies or seek voluntary help from colleagues, and publishers do not often commission translations of articles for publication. However, we can cite here some examples of other scenarios in which translators are quite closely involved in the scientific publishing processes.

The Forschungszentrum Jülich, Germany, provides us with an example of how scientific translation can be integrated institutionally. This is one of Europe's largest interdisciplinary research centres, employing over 5,000 people across nine research institutions. It also employs scientific translators, to work predominantly from German to English as part of a small language services team. These translators translate challenging professional scientific and technical texts as well as popular science texts and corporate communications. A particular feature of their work is that they collaborate with some of the Centre's scientific authors on copy-editing papers intended for publication in leading international journals which are written by non-native speakers of English.

The Institut de l'Information Scientifique et Technique (INIST) is an organization providing resources and facilities to French researchers. In addition to document supply, information portals, bibliographic databases, etc., INIST offers help with scientific publishing, including translation, with the aim of improving the visibility of French research. INIST also offers help producing research papers in English, through translation from French or editing of documents drafted in English. INIST is overseen by the CNRS, Centre Nationale de la Recherche Scientifique, whose translation department produces scientific and institutional documentation from French to English.

To facilitate publication by non-native speakers of English, publishers may provide translation and editing services to potential non-anglophone authors who are seeking to be published in anglophone journals. Elsevier, one of the world's largest scientific publishers, offers translation between British or American English and 14 other languages. Unlike most LSPs, Elsevier publish their prices online, perhaps hoping to win business through this level of transparency as well as their scientific publishing expertise. Taylor & Francis, likewise, have recently added translation to their services offered to prospective authors.

These are just a few examples of specific situations, beyond the usual scenario of commissioning a translation from a non-specialist LSP, in which translators work with non-anglophone researchers wishing to publish their research in English.

Multilingual scientific publishing

From the perspective of scientists at universities in anglophone countries, Root-Bernstein and Ladle (2014) also see an important role for translators and translations out of English. They argue that translations of research into Mandarin, Spanish, French, Russian and Portuguese, in particular, could increase readership, and they suggest that journals could provide those translations as part of its online provision, particularly under new pay-to-publish open-access publishing models. While Root-Bernstein and Ladle discuss impact predominantly from the perspective of citation metrics, they also mention the putative benefit of increased sharing of ideas and 'more rapid accumulation of support/refutation of hypotheses' (ibid.) if more scientific research were translated into other languages.

This represents a publishing model which is not seen often in anglophone countries, but which is sometimes implemented elsewhere. For example, *InfoAmérica: Iberoamerican Communication Review*,

based in Malaga, Spain, publishes translations of previously published research articles on Latin American studies. Its translations are
mostly, though not exclusively, from English to Spanish. On the website, translators are credited alongside editors, reviewers and editorial
assistants, though translators are not named on specific texts.

Sometimes journals undertake to publish all content in two languages, and use translation to achieve this bilingual coverage. The
Brazilian scientific publishing scene offers ample illustration of this
practice. For example, the *Arquivos Brasileiros de Cardiologia*, the
journal of the Brazilian Society of Cardiology, undertakes to provide
an English translation of any article which is not submitted in English,
without cost to the author. Likewise, the *Revista Brasileira de
Reumatologia/Brazilian Journal of Rheumatology*, the official news
outlet of the Brazilian Society of Rheumatology, has been published
in bilingual format since 2009. Not all journals are so generous, however. *Química Nova*, a journal of the Brazilian Chemical Society is
typical of many; it accepts articles in English, Portuguese or Spanish
and does not translate, but publishes a large number of articles in
Portuguese. Not all Brazilian science adopts a multilingual approach.
A counter-example is offered by the *Revista Brasileira de Psiquiatria*,
which serves as the official publication of the Brazilian Association of
Psychiatry, and which requires submitted papers to be in English only.

A useful snapshot of multilingual journal use in Brazil can be seen
on the SCIELO website (www.scielo.br), which lists over 300 Brazilian
academic journals, with access figures for each journal calculated by
language. This reveals that Portuguese articles, when they are available, are generally accessed much more frequently than their English or
Spanish counterparts or translations. Thus, despite the status of
English as the lingua franca of science and other academic disciplines,
non-native speakers of English often opt to read in languages other
than English if they have a choice.

A non-Brazilian example of translation of scientific content can be
seen in Turkey's *Acta Orthopaedica et Traumatologica Turcica*.
English is this journal's official language, but it arranges for translation of all content into Turkish and makes both English and Turkish
versions of papers available on its website. Some scientific translation
is also done by journals based in anglophone contexts. For example,
Nature publishes Chinese, Korean and Japanese editions, and the professional science magazines in the *Science* stable (i.e. *Science, Science
Signaling* and *Science: Translational Medicine*) publish Japanese
versions.

An alternative bilingual or multilingual model is represented by
journals that accept submissions in two or more languages, one of
which will usually be English. For example, numerous Canadian
journals publish in French and English. Some, like the *Revue des*

Sciences de l'Eau/Journal of Water Science, publish extensively in French, while others, like the *Canadian Journal of Chemistry*, present papers almost exclusively in English. Examples can also be seen in other countries. In some cases languages other than English dominate, for example Polish in *Przegląd Elektrotechniczny*, while other journals permitting submission in several languages nonetheless tend to carry mostly English-language articles. For example, the Swedish journal, *Konsthistorisk tidskrift/Journal of Art History*, accepts submissions in Swedish, Norwegian, Danish, French, German and English, but the vast majority of its published articles are in English.

Translation of abstracts

Journals which undertake to translate articles remain in the minority when considered globally, however. A more prevalent practice is for journals to publish abstracts of articles in a second or third language. Authors are usually expected to supply these, which are usually translations of the abstract that was written in the language of publication. In many cases where abstracts are translated, so too are titles and keywords. Examples, among many that we could cite, include the *Zeitschrift für Geologische Wissenschaften – Journal for the Geological Sciences*, based in Berlin, which publishes articles either in English or in German but provides an abstract in both. The Slovak journal *Filozofia* publishes articles in Slovak, Czech or English, and provides an English abstract for those articles in the other two languages. The *Arabian Journal for Science and Engineering* publishes papers in English but abstracts in Arabic and English. Many Chinese academic journals publish in either Chinese or English but frequently include abstracts in both languages. In North America, Canadian language policy is unsurprisingly reflected in the publication of abstracts in English and French in Canadian science journals. However, a bilingual approach can also be observed in the USA, where some journals publish titles and abstracts in Spanish; an example is *Conservation Biology*. Likewise, the *British Journal of Surgery* publishes abstracts in Spanish; and editor summaries of research articles in *Nature* are translated into Arabic.

Translation of scientific papers in other contexts

We can conclude this section by mentioning that scientific research articles and abstracts may also be translated in non-publishing contexts. For example, a researcher, research group or organization might need to consult a paper that has already been published but in a language that they cannot access; a translation could be commissioned for information purposes or for internal circulation rather than publication. In addition, many national and international organizations and institutions, both governmental and non-governmental, do not conduct scientific research themselves but rely on being informed about research, and may therefore commission translations to provide them with the information they need.

The remainder of this chapter will focus firstly on the nature of present-day anglophone academic discourse more generally. We will then examine the abstract and the research article as two scientific genres that are translated, as in the scenarios above, and which you could therefore be commissioned to translate. In each case, we will describe and characterize key features of the genres. It is important to stress that our focus will be on English as used for these academic and scientific communicative purposes. This awareness and familiarity will provide you with the understanding you need to make decisions about how they might be translated, whether your aim is to conform to or resist the dominance of English-language discourses, genre conventions and epistemologies.

Academic vocabulary

In acquiring English for Specific Purposes (ESP) or EAP, learners often make use of academic vocabulary or word lists, for example, Coxhead's Academic Word List (2000). These lists are designed to present the vocabulary which is relatively frequent in academic discourse but less common in other discourses. Examples in English are nouns such as *study, process, research, model* and *result*, or verbs such as *include, indicate, support* or *represent*. The idea behind such lists is that there is a core academic vocabulary which provides the 'framework for description and evaluation of the actions and processes necessary to report the experiences of science and technology' (Martínez et al. 2009: 185). Previously used labels for this notion of academic vocabulary include 'subtechnical vocabulary' or 'semi-technical vocabulary', but more recent work refers to it as academic vocabulary.

Increasingly the usefulness of such word lists has been questioned, both because of the way in which the lists are compiled and the way in which they might be used. Let's deal firstly with the issue of how the lists are constituted. The most widely used list, Coxhead's Academic Word List, groups words into word families. A word family consists of a stem or headword and all inflections and derivations. However, using the example of the word family for *react* as illustration, Gardner and Davies (2014: 307) point out the problems with this kind of grouping. In this case *react* is the headword and the family contains some words which share the core meaning of *react* (e.g. *reacted, reacts, reacting, reaction, reactions*), but also words which have rather different primary meanings (e.g. *reactionary, reactivate, reactor*). A solution to this compilation issue is offered by Gardner and Davies, who argue that using lemmas rather than word families would separate out words which are clearly different in meaning. A **lemma** represents words which are related by inflection (but not by derivation) and come from the same part of speech. Taking the lemma approach, *proceed* (verb, to continue), *proceeds* (profits), *procedure* (technique) and *proceedings* (minutes/records) would all be listed separately, with their inflected forms (e.g. noun plurals or different verb forms), rather than together in one single word family that includes both inflectional and derivational forms, as is the case in Coxhead's Academic Word List.

The second criticism of academic word lists is based on evidence that some academic vocabulary is domain specific (see Hyland and Tse 2007). This means that a learner may find that such word lists cover much more vocabulary than they need for their specific field, but may also lack some vocabulary which is more widely used in their field. It is also possible for words to behave differently, semantically and phraseologically, in different domains, taking on meanings which are specific to that discourse community and also combining in different collocations. Martínez et al. (2009) cite the example of *strategy* collocating with *learning* in applied linguistics, *coping* in sociology and *marketing* in economics. They also illustrate differences in meanings in different domains by contrasting the meanings of *volume* in social sciences and in natural sciences (ibid.: 185).

Compiling a corpus of research articles from agriculture and analysing its vocabulary, Martínez et al. (2009) showed that there was some overlap between the vocabulary of their corpus and the word lists and studies of vocabulary in other domains; for example, words such as *data, analysis* and *similar* figure prominently in both. However, many other words seemed to be more specific to the agricultural domain, for example: *site, region, area, stress, environments, culture*. Returning to the issue of collocations, and comparing with the example of *strategy* above, the main collocations of *strategy* in the agricultural corpus were *control strategies, management strategies* and *adaptation strategy* (ibid.: 191–2). The study also highlighted word clusters used academically in the agriculture corpus, for example: *had no effect on, had little effect on, a significant effect on, had no significant effect, to determine the effect*. Another example is the clusters of *control*, where there is homography; *control* is used to refer to a standard of comparison in analysis, for example: *the untreated control, the control plots, the control plants, compared to control*. However, it is also used to mean restrain or check, for example, *for weed control, of pest control* (ibid.). This corpus analysis also serves to show academic preferences among synonyms; for example, *study/studies*

Table 6.1 Top 30 nouns, top 15 verbs and adjectives, and top 5 adverbs from the AVL organized by lemma (Gardner and Davies 2014: 317; and www. academicwords.info)

Nouns	*study, group, system, research, level, result, process, use, development, data, information, effect, change, table, policy, university, model, experience, activity, history, relationship, value, role, difference, analysis, practice, society, control, form, rate*
Verbs	*provide, include, develop, suggest, require, report, base, describe, indicate, produce, identify, support, increase, note, represent*
Adjectives	*social, important, human, economic, low, significant, international, individual, environmental, cultural, likely, general, similar, common, current*
Adverbs	*however, both, thus, therefore, particularly*

was used approximately 6 times more often than *research*, and *result(s)* was used 100 times more frequently than *outcome(s)*.

To try to overcome those problems associated with previous academic word lists, Gardner and Davies (2014) have compiled a new Academic Vocabulary List (AVL) for English, which uses lemmas and is statistically derived from large, representative contemporary corpora. It tries to distinguish between 'academic core words' that appear in most academic disciplines (e.g. *process, analysis, indicate, establish, significant, critical, highly, moreover*) from 'general high-frequency words' that are frequent in most discourses (e.g. *way, part, take, know, small, good, never, very*) and 'academic technical words' which appear in a narrow range of academic disciplines (e.g. *assessment, regime, oscillate, rhetorical, lunar, semantically, psychologically*) (ibid.: 312, 315). They use 120 million words of academic text from the Corpus of Contemporary American English, composed of texts from nine broad discipline areas: education; humanities; history; social science; philosophy, religion and psychology; science and technology; medicine and health; and business and finance. For further details of materials and sizes of different components, see Gardner and Davies (2014). The AVL is available for you to use online at www. academicwords.info and can also be downloaded in various formats for offline use. To illustrate the data, Table 6.1 presents the top 30 nouns, the top 15 verbs and adjectives, and the top 5 adverbs from the AVL organized by lemma (Gardner and Davies 2014: 317).

Lexical bundles

Similar corpus-based analyses show that some of this academic vocabulary is used in academic discourse as part of lexical bundles, that is, 'strings of words which follow each other more frequently than expected by chance' (Hyland and Tse 2007: 119). Hyland and

Tse see these bundles as an important part of the discourse of a discipline, used with ease by competent members of the discipline but coming less naturally to novices. They analyse 4-word lexical bundles (introduced in Chapter 2 as 4-grams) in a range of genres from eight science, engineering and social science disciplines. Some bundles were common to all disciplines, for example: *on the other hand*, *in the case of*, *as well as the*, and *the end of the*. However over half of the items in each list did not occur in any other discipline (ibid.: 122), thus indicating that disciplines present information and construct arguments in diverse ways.

The lexical bundles of that study were classified into three categories: (1) research-oriented, (2) text-oriented, and (3) participant-oriented. Research-oriented bundles help writers to structure their activities and experiences (Hyland and Tse 2009: 122). They are expressions related to location (*at the start of*), procedure (*the purpose of the*), quantification (*a wide range of*), description (*the size of the*) and topic (*the currency board system*). Text-oriented bundles are concerned with the organization of the text (ibid.: 123). They signal transitions (*in contrast to the*), results (*it was found that*), structure (*in the next section*) and framing (*on the basis of*). Participant-oriented bundles are focused on the reader or writer, for example, conveying stance or evaluation (*are likely to be*) and engagement (*it should be noted*).

By comparing across disciplines, Hyland and Tse (2009: 123) were able to conclude that the texts from the natural sciences used a greater proportion of research-oriented bundles, whereas the applied linguistics and business studies corpora employed more text-oriented bundles. These differences reflect different ways of making claims for new knowledge. In the science disciplines hypotheses are tested, and empirical evidence is the primary means of presenting new knowledge and convincing readers. In those other fields, knowledge is more likely to be constructed and readers convinced by the author framing arguments and presenting plausible reasoning. The reluctance of writers to commit to a proposition was particularly prevalent through the hedging of the participant-oriented stance bundles in the social sciences. Engagement bundles, by contrast, were mostly to be found in the hard sciences, as directives telling readers how to note or interpret findings.

This work on academic vocabulary and phraseology shows us that, in addition to researching the highly specialized terminology of the domain, translators need to pay attention to the academic core vocabulary in the SL and TL, that is, those lexical items and phrases that are typical of research reporting among academics. There may be some common ground between neighbouring disciplines, as well as some divergence across discourse communities, in line with the different ways in which knowledge is generated, constructed, communicated, challenged and accepted in that community. Familiarity with discipline-specific discourses is therefore a key part of the translator's toolkit, as well as familiarity with the corresponding discourse practices of communities who communicate in languages other than English.

Scientific research articles

The research article is the most prestigious genre for most academic disciplines, although some humanities disciplines also value the book or monograph as the epitome of scholarly achievement, and others (e.g. computer science) regard conference proceedings as very important (Van Bonn and Swales 2007). It is beyond the scope of this chapter to trace the historical development of the anglophone research article to its present format. However, it provides a very good illustration of the dynamic nature of genres. Its evolution over the past few centuries is interesting, because changes in the form and content of articles reflect changes in how scientific research is done. Science has shifted from an amateur, individual occupation for gentlemen, who had the means and inclination, to a global industry pursued by highly trained teams of specialists, heavily funded by governments and corporations. In line with these developments, research articles, in anglophone contexts in particular, have become more abstract, more densely packed with information, more focused in their argumentation, and more centred on the research than the researcher. For detailed analysis of these historical developments of the genre, see Bazerman (1988) and Swales (2004). We will be examining some of those features of present-day scientific articles below, relating them to the ways in which scientists work and communicate within their scientific discourse communities. Translation, though challenging due to the specialized nature of the communication, is facilitated by this enhanced understanding of the functions and characteristics of the genre.

Analysing moves in research articles

Due to its significance, the research article, as a genre, has been studied widely, particularly in English but also in some cross-cultural comparisons, though usually such comparisons also revolve around their conformance or non-conformance with English conventions. One of the most influential approaches has been genre analysis, following the pioneering work of Swales (1990, 2004). In this research, the textual organization of research articles is analysed by identifying a series of **moves**. A move is defined as 'a discoursal or rhetorical unit that performs a coherent communicative function in a written or spoken discourse' (Swales 2004: 228). Thus, various communicative functions are performed by identifiable text segments, contributing towards the overall function of the text. Moves are often broken down into sub-moves, or in Swales' terminology, **steps**. Moves may occur in a linear order, but alternatively may be cyclical, and combinations of moves can also recur.

A research article, particularly in scientific fields and in anglophone publications, is typically presented in sections entitled or consisting of Introduction, Methods, Results and Discussion. This structure is denoted by the abbreviation IMRAD. Many analyses of research articles have focused on the moves of one of these specific sections, for example, the introduction, though more recent studies also try to widen the scope to consider the whole article rather than parts in isolation (Kanoksilapatham 2015). In this section we will take the example of the introduction to illustrate how genre analysis is performed.

Introductions have been studied extensively, drawing on the CARS (Create a Research Space) model developed by Swales (1990, 2004). The CARS model accounts for the moves usually fulfilled by the text of introductions, based on what Swales observed by studying a set of published research articles from the field of TESOL (teaching English to speakers of other languages). To help us to understand CARS, we can ask ourselves what academic authors are trying to achieve when they write a research article in the competitive anglophone publishing space. They are competing (against other academics) for the opportunity to put their research forward in published form and they are seeking to ensure that other specialists notice their work and are persuaded of its merits. In the introduction to the article, therefore, they generally wish to show how their area of research is important and identify where there might be a gap in knowledge that their research fills, or where they might have scope to add to or challenge existing knowledge. Having identified the potential gap, they then announce their present research and outline how it is intended to fill the gap or add to knowledge. Those three main moves identified by Swales are described as (1) establishing a territory; (2) establishing a niche; and (3) occupying the niche. These moves are realized through a series of obligatory or optional steps (sub-units of moves), which are presented in Table 6.2 (Swales 2004).

It is not practical here to conduct a moves analysis for an entire article, but we can use the Introduction section to illustrate the approach. Excerpt 6.1 is the introduction to an article about research estimating the quantity of plastic in the world's oceans (Eriksen et al. 2014) reproduced from *PLOS ONE* in accordance with the Creative Commons Attribution Licence (CC BY 2.5). The territory is established (move 1) in paragraphs 1 and 2 through description of the

Table 6.2 CARS model of rhetorical moves and steps (Swales 2004)

Move 1: Establishing a territory	Making topic generalization(s) of increasing specificity (citations required)
Move 2: Establishing a niche	Step 1A: indicating a gap or Step 1B: adding to what is known Step 2: presenting positive justification (optional) (citations possible)
Move 3: Occupying the niche	Step 1: announcing present research Step 2: presenting research questions or hypotheses (optional) Step 3: definitional clarifications (optional) Step 4: summarizing methods (optional) Step 5: announcing principal outcomes (some fields) Step 6: stating value of present research (some fields) Step 7: outlining structure of paper (some fields)

global distribution, fragmentation and dispersal of plastic in the oceans and some of the impacts of this. Twenty-three citations are given to previous work in the area, thus strengthening the impression that we are dealing with recognized and researched territory. Other signals for this move include: *have led some researchers to claim that* and *are well documented*.

In the first sentence of paragraph 3, the niche is established (move 2) when the authors perform step 1A of indicating a gap, that is, by telling us that previous models have been limited to microplastics of less than 5mm, with citations provided to studies of that kind. The shortcoming of that research is signalled by the concessive preposition *despite* and the verb choice *have been limited to*. Positive justification for monitoring the distribution of plastics (step 2) generally has already been provided in paragraph 2.

In the second sentence of paragraph 3, the researchers begin to occupy the niche (move 3), performing step 1 by announcing their research, to construct a model to estimate the distribution and quantities of plastic pollution of a range of sizes, from small microplastics to macroplastics: *we populated; the dataset used is; we also compared*. The novelty of the contribution is signalled by the reference to *new data*. The remainder of paragraph 3 performs step 4 by summarizing the methods of the research, with some definitional clarification (step 3) on variables and size classes. Other optional steps of presenting research questions, announcing outcomes and outlining the structure of the paper are not performed here. As might be expected, there are no citations from the point when the researchers announce their own research, *we populated an oceanographic model [. . .] to estimate [. . .]*, since they are now focusing on their own contribution, having already situated it against the backdrop of what had been done previously.

EXCERPT 6.1

Plastic pollution is globally distributed across all oceans due to its properties of buoyancy and durability, and the sorption of toxicants to plastic while traveling through the environment [1], [2], have led some researchers to claim that synthetic polymers in the ocean should be regarded as hazardous waste [3]. Through photodegradation and other weathering processes, plastics fragment and disperse in the ocean [4], [5], converging in the subtropical gyres [6]–[9]. Generation and accumulation of plastic pollution also occurs in closed bays, gulfs and seas surrounded by densely populated coastlines and watersheds [10]–[13].

The impact of plastic pollution through ingestion and entanglement of marine fauna, ranging from zooplankton to cetaceans, seabirds and marine reptiles, are well documented [14]. Adsorption of persistent organic pollutants onto plastic and their transfer into the tissues and organs through ingestion [15] is impacting marine megafauna [16], as well as lower trophic-level organisms [17], [18] and their predators [19], [20]. These impacts are further exacerbated by the persistence of floating plastics, ranging from resin pellets to large derelict nets, docks and boats that float across oceans and transport microbial communities [21], algae, invertebrates, and fish [22] to non-native regions [23], providing further rationale to monitor (and take steps to mitigate) the global distribution and abundance of plastic pollution.

Despite oceanographic model predictions of where debris might converge [24] estimates of regional and global abundance and weight of floating plastics have been limited to microplastics <5 mm [19], [25]. Using extensive published and new data, particularly from the Southern Hemisphere subtropical gyres and marine areas adjacent to populated regions [7], [10], [13], [26], corrected for wind-driven vertical mixing [27], we populated an oceanographic model of debris distribution [28] to estimate global distribution and count and weight densities of plastic pollution in all sampled size classes. The oceanographic model assumes that amounts of plastic entering the ocean depend on three principal variables: watershed outfalls, population density and maritime activity. The dataset used in this model is based on expeditions from 2007–2013 (Table S1), surveying all five sub-tropical gyres (North Pacific, North Atlantic, South Pacific, South Atlantic, Indian Ocean) and extensive coastal regions and enclosed seas (Bay of Bengal, Australian coasts and the Mediterranean Sea), and include surface net tows (N = 680) and visual survey transects for large plastic debris (N = 891) totaling 1571 locations in all oceans (Fig 1). We also compared plastic pollution levels between oceans and across four size classes: 0.33–1.00 mm (small microplastics), 1.01–4.75 mm (large microplastics), 4.76–200 mm (mesoplastic), and >200 mm (macroplastic) (Fig. 1).

We could contrast those moves with another article on a similar topic examining the spatial distribution of plastic debris in the oceans (Goldstein et al. 2013). The introduction comprises four paragraphs. The first two outline what is known about how plastic debris pollutes the oceans, then the third paragraph tells us about the factors that are known to influence its spatial distribution. Thus the majority of the Introduction is concerned with move 1, with only the final, short paragraph performing moves 2 and 3. The final paragraph of the Introduction by Goldstein et al. 2013 is presented as Excerpt 6.2, reproduced from *PLOS ONE* in accordance with Creative Commons Attribution Licence (CC BY 2.5). The first sentence performs step 2 of move 2, by presenting positive justification of the research, signalling this lexically with *important* and *significance*. The second sentence announces the research (move 3, step 1): *our objective in this study was*, using the adverbial *therefore* to link the previous positive justification to the study. The third sentence presents the research questions (move 3, step 2), explicitly given in question format. None of the other optional steps (3–7) are performed. It could be posited that introductions in scientific research articles are less likely to indicate outcomes, because many journals now display a bulleted list of highlights in addition to the abstract (where outcomes are usually also noted). Moreover, an outline of the article's structure may be redundant in articles that follow a prescribed IMRAD structure, more typical of science than humanities research. It can also be noted that, although our examples are linear in their progression through the moves, this does not have to be the case; longer and more detailed introductions and introductions pertaining to research where there is little consensus on the existing body of knowledge may perform the same moves but in a cyclical pattern (Brett 1994).

EXCERPT 6.2

Assessing the spatial distribution of debris is important to understanding its environmental significance. Therefore, our objective in this study was to examine the abundance and variability of debris during two cruises in the eastern North Pacific. To this end, we asked the following questions: 1) What is the spatial abundance and distribution of pelagic microplastic in comparison to biophysical variables? 2) What is the size-frequency spectrum of oceanic plastic, and how does methodology affect estimates of its abundance?

In the IMRAD model, the methods section follows the introduction. There is some variation in how methods sections are entitled, for example 'Methods' or 'Methods and materials', but they serve the function of detailing how the research was conducted. They can vary in length and by discipline, and the amount of detail supplied may also reflect the extent to which methodological rigour is or is not taken for granted in some discourse communities. Emerging discourse communities may be more explicit about methods. In addition, methods that are unfamiliar or controversial within a discipline may require lengthier justification and explanation. The principal moves in the methods sections of chemistry articles have been characterized as (1) describing materials; (2) describing experimental methods; and (3) describing numerical methods (Stoller and Robinson 2013). Within these moves, and in other disciplines, sub-moves or steps may also be identified for example, justifying procedures or describing research sites (see Kanoksilapatham 2015).

Similarly, the moves of the results section have been characterized as (1) reminding readers how results were obtained and (2) presenting results (Stoller and Robinson 2013). In a study of chemistry articles, these two moves are found to be repeated, cyclically, for each set of results. The discussion section then performs the moves of (1) interpreting the results and (2) summarizing the study and presenting the implications of the work. Stoller and Robinson (ibid.) note that these moves comprise steps, for example, comparing results with previously published work or highlighting unexpected results. Kanoksilapatham (2015), studying research articles from three engineering sub-disciplines, provides a detailed set of steps for each of these moves, adding also a third move to the results section, that is: (1) summarizing procedures, (2) reporting results, and (3) commenting on results.

Just as the communicative functions of the introduction are performed via various lexical and grammatical choices and citation patterns, the same can be said of moves and steps in the other sections of the research articles. Thus, for example, findings may be presented using expressions such as *Table 2 shows* . . ., while comparative and superlative adjectives with verbs of change in the past tense (e.g. *increased, declined*) may prevail in the comparison of results. Modal verbs (e.g. *may, could*) and other verbs that express the author's mode of knowing, for example *suggest, indicate*, reflect the tentative, qualified way in which claims may be made in the explanation of results.

It is important to note that there is some variation in textual organization and in the moves performed in research articles across disciplines, even within the anglophone publishing world. Although more and more disciplines are tending towards the IMRAD model, much research publishing in the humanities diverges considerably from that model. Science is also not unitary; rather, branches of science vary in their 'epistemic cultures' (Knorr Cetina 1999). What this means is that different disciplines have different ways of producing knowledge, establishing claims, etc. Those differences are reflected in some of the observable features of the research article genre, for example as seen in Kanoksilapatham's (2015) comparison of the textual organization of research articles in civil engineering, software engineering and bio-medical engineering.

Further variation may also be anticipated in other linguistic and cultural communities, especially considering that these models have been developed in relation to the monolingual anglophone context. Hirano's (2009) comparison of CARS moves in the introductions to Brazilian Portuguese and English research articles, for example, shows how the English-language articles are much closer to the CARS model than the Brazilian ones. Likewise, Fakhri (2004) highlights significant divergences from CARS in the introductions to Arabic articles.

The translator of a research article generally needs to recognize the ST's discursive moves and be able to identify the linguistic resources employed to fulfil the various communicative purposes that are central to the research article. Depending on the intended use of the TT, translators may then need to decide whether and how to fulfil those communicative functions in the TL, allowing for cross-cultural and epistemological variation where appropriate. The next section discusses in more detail how scientists use linguistic resources to interact with their material and their readers in the texts they produce.

Metadiscourse

As noted above, key functions of research articles are to put forward knowledge claims and to seek to have those claims accepted as credible or significant by the discourse community, of which the author is also a part. This requires writers to use the text and its linguistic resources to support their position and to build relationships with readers. The term 'metadiscourse' is used to designate 'the self-reflective expressions used to negotiate interactional meanings in a text, assisting the writer (or speaker) to express a viewpoint and engage with readers as members of a particular community' (Hyland 2005: 37). Thus, metadiscourse is an umbrella term encompassing a range of devices used by writers to organize their text, engage their readers and signal their attitudes to their text and their audience (Hyland and Tse 2004: 156). Hyland's contributions (e.g. 2005) form the basis of much of the research on metadiscourse in academic contexts.

Metadiscourse may be seen as **interactive resources** that help to organize the discourse and the reader's interaction with the information flow, for example, by signalling that the topic is shifting, or that there is a sequence of ideas or connections between ideas (Hyland and Tse 2004: 157). Transitions can be realized through the use of conjunctions (e.g. *because*, *and*) and adverbials (e.g. *therefore*, *in addition*) showing the author's understanding of the logical relations between ideas (ibid.: 162). Frame markers refer to text or discourse sequences or acts (e.g. *to conclude*, *my aim here is to*). Endophoric markers refer to information in other parts of the text (e.g. *as noted above*, *see Fig.* 2). Evidentials refer to sources of material outside of the text, that is, citations and references in academic texts. Code glosses provide a reformulation (e.g. as an expansion or reduction) or an exemplification to help the reader to understand, introduced by expressions like *namely*, *in other words* and *for example*.

Metadiscourse may be seen also as **interactional resources** signalling the writer's attitude to specific aspects of the text and to the reader (Hyland and Tse 2004), showing the writer's stance and engagement. Devices that do this include hedges, boosters, attitude markers, engagement markers and self-mentions. Hedges and boosters are particularly important in this respect in academic texts, because they either downplay or heighten the author's commitment to a proposition. Hedges convey the author's reluctance to accept or present a knowledge claim or proposition as absolute or categorical. In Swales' space-creating terms, hedges project 'honesty, modesty and proper caution' and 'diplomatically' create space among other researchers (Swales 1990: 175). Hedges have also been described as politeness strategies in the social interaction of academic publishing (Myers 1989). Frequent hedging devices in English include modal auxiliaries expressing possibility (e.g. *may*, *might*, *could*, *would*), epistemic verbs (e.g. *suggest*, *indicate*, *seem*), and epistemic adverbs and adjectives (e.g. *probably*, *likely*, *perhaps*, *mainly*).

Boosters, on the other hand, emphasize the force of a proposition (Hyland and Tse 2004: 168) and the author's level of confidence in it. This can be done through modal auxiliaries (e.g. *must*, *will*), epistemic verbs (e.g. *show*, *demonstrate*, *find*), epistemic adjectives and adverbs (e.g. *clearly*, *actually*) and epistemic *that* constructions, for example, *it is clear that*. Attitude markers convey the author's attitude to the propositional information (e.g. *surprisingly*, *unfortunately*), while engagement markers explicitly address readers through questions or directives (e.g. *note that*, *consider*) and by using second-person pronouns. Self-mentions (e.g. through first-person pronouns) make explicit reference to authors, highlighting their presence.

Research articles perform specific rhetorical functions in specific social contexts, as outlined above. Reader–writer interaction of this kind, through metadiscourse, is key to the successful fulfilment of those functions. As Hyland and Tse (ibid.: 175) note, metadiscourse is not just about stylistic choices, but rather about how authors serve their needs by supplying certain cues to readers to ensure that their propositional content is understood and accepted. What discourse communities regard as professional, understandable, acceptable or convincing can vary across communities. Thus, translators need to understand cross-cultural and cross-disciplinary facets of metadiscourse if they wish to produce texts that that match the expectations and norms of the target discourse community. McGrath and Kuteeva (2012), for example, show that articles in pure mathematics have a comparatively low number of hedges, since authors in this field have to have very strong conviction in a proposition in order for results to be published. This contrasts markedly with writing in many humanities or social science disciplines, where findings and conclusions are often more tentative. There, hedging frequently signals the scope for alternative interpretations by others.

While a lot of the research on metadiscourse has centred on English academic discourse, there are also some cross-cultural, contrastive studies. For example, Dahl's (2004b) study shows that French research articles in economics and linguistics use different metadiscursive patterns from those of Norwegian and English articles from the same fields. However, she notes that there is little metadiscursive variation across the three languages in a comparison of research articles from another field, medicine. Mur Dueñas (2007, 2011) highlights significant differences in the overall frequency in metadiscourse features, and in the particular choices of linguistic resources in comparisons of Spanish and English research articles from the field of business management. Further examples of cross-cultural studies include Abdi's (2009) comparison of metadiscourse in English and Persian research articles, Vold's (2006) examination of epistemic modality in French, Norwegian and English articles, and Pisanski Peterlin's (2008) study of Slovene research articles and their translations into English.

Grammatical metaphor

We noted above that the English-language research article has undergone some changes over the past few centuries, and that one such development was towards a greater level of abstraction and information density, with a focus on processes rather than researchers. In linguistic terms, this is achieved by the process of grammatical metaphor, that is, the replacement of one grammatical category by another, as defined and discussed by Halliday (2004). One of Halliday's non-scientific examples to illustrate grammatical metaphor (2004: 57) comprises the following pair of utterances: (1) *The driver drove the bus too rapidly down the hill, so the brakes failed;*

and (2) *the driver's overrapid downhill driving of the bus caused brake failure*. The various shifts in rank and structure between (1) and (2) reflect a reconstrual of the event. The structure of (2) is typical of scientific and technical discourse in English, as another of Halliday's examples shows: *increased responsiveness may be reflected in feeding behaviour*. We noted similar structures in the Hardiebacker TDS in Chapter 4 and in the patent specification in Chapter 5. We can see that nominal groups (noun phrases) are used here, not for concrete objects or things, but for experiences, processes and qualities, like *failure* or *responsiveness*. Thus a quality or a process is conveyed by means of a noun (rather than a verb or adjective), so it becomes a virtual entity. As such, it can then be modified, for example, *increased responsiveness*, and it can then participate in other processes (e.g. *may be reflected in*). These metaphors reconstrue experience; they create virtual phenomena that can be theorized and that can lead to new understandings and new organizations of knowledge. These abstractions can become established as terms and distilled into taxonomies of abstract, virtual entities. They make scientific and technical discourse more compact. The syntax may be simple, for example, a nominal group followed by a verbal group followed by a second nominal group or a prepositional phrase, as in the examples above, but the lexical density can be high, with a lot of lexical items packed inside the simple structure, as another of Halliday's (2004) examples shows: *the theoretical program of devising models of atomic nuclei has been complemented by experimental investigations*.

Further exemplification of how experiences are transformed into abstractions can be seen in Hyland and Tse's analyses (2009: 117). Studying discourse from several different disciplines, they show that the word *process* is frequent in all of the domains but it is far more likely to be encountered as a noun in science and engineering disciplines than in social science. Examples of how *process* is embedded into abstract and complex nominal groups in their data include: *a constant volume combustion process, processing dependent saturation junction factors* and *the graphical process configuration editor* (ibid.).

Other consequences of grammatical metaphor can be the removal of the actor, thus creating an impression of objectivity and diminishing personal accountability. Processes, procedures and events lose their transparency. The lexically dense, abstract discourse sets itself apart as the discourse of the expert; it may be perceived as authoritative and it gives processes and events a perceived technicality and rationality (Halliday 2004: 128).

Grammatical metaphor, like other features discussed in this section, is intrinsic to English scientific discourse, but may be less a part of scientific discourse in other cultures and languages, since the way it reconstrues experience is a reflection of the approach to the scientific method which developed predominantly in the anglophone world. Thus, as translators, it is crucial that you identify and understand these features of language when dealing with English texts. The question of how to translate them must then be taken in the context of your translation situation, the translation commission, as well as your own professional ethical position.

Scientific abstracts

As we saw in the first section of this chapter, the abstract of a research article is sometimes translated to be published alongside the SL abstract and article. Abstracts, whether produced monolingually or multilingually, are widely used in indexing and cataloguing research articles, providing something akin to a summary or synopsis which gives readers an insight into the key aspects and findings of the research. On the basis of the abstract, readers will often decide whether they need to read the full article. Therefore, the abstract is a research and retrieval tool (Salager-Meyer 2009: 366) and an advertisement for the article (Van Bonn and Swales 2007), and it has to function both as an accompaniment to the full article and as a stand-alone genre (Bhatia 1993). The promotional function of the abstract is not to be underestimated; as Hyland (2000: 64) argues, it has to persuade readers, who are busy and overburdened with the quantity of research publications being produced, that an article is worth reading. The abstract 'selectively sets out the stall' and tries to draw the reader in (ibid.).

One way of describing the abstract is that it presents, in condensed form, the macropropositions of the article (Salager-Meyer 2009: 367). This means it may be expected to present the moves which are typical of scientific enquiry. Salager-Meyer proposes four (purpose, methods, results and conclusions), but Hyland's (2000: 67) model of five moves is widely applied, and includes the Introduction move.

- Introduction: establishes the context of the paper and motivates the research or discussion;
- Purpose: indicates purpose, thesis or hypothesis, outlines the intention behind the paper;
- Method: provides information on design, procedures, assumption, approach, data, etc.;
- Product: states main findings or results, the argument, or what was accomplished;
- Conclusion: interprets or extends results beyond scope of paper, draws inferences, points to applications or wider implications.

Hyland notes that only 5 per cent of the papers in his multidisciplinary corpus included all five steps (ibid.: 68). However, almost all included a Product statement, underlining the promotional nature of the genre. A study by Samraj (2005) of abstracts from two disciplines, conservation biology and wildlife behaviour, noted that only about half of the abstracts contained a Methods move, although methods were an important part of the research article itself, thus demonstrating that the abstract is not merely a synopsis of the article.

As with research articles, Hyland's corpus of abstracts also shows extensive disciplinary variation, underlining again that discourse communities have their own specific ways of persuading and communicating credibility and significance (2000: 70). Introductions often make a claim about the centrality or significance of the topic (ibid.: 76), for example, by highlighting benefits, novelty or importance of the research. As in research article introductions, gaps in knowledge are sometimes identified, demonstrating insider knowledge and showing that the author belongs to the discourse community, which may also be signalled by reference to familiar, traditional or well-known approaches or assumptions (ibid.: 80).

Thus, these short texts are not mere summaries of the research article but are themselves performing a series of important rhetorical moves. As was the case with research articles, the metadiscourse of abstracts can also reveal how authors interact and engage with their material and their readers (see Gillaerts and Van de Velde (2010) for a study of how the metadiscursive elements of abstracts have evolved over time). Being able to understand how abstracts fulfil those communicative purposes will help you to take decisions when translating them. It is also useful to have an understanding of variations across scientific disciplines and languages, and to be able to consider possible explanations for moves and variations, discussed in the next section.

Variation across languages and in translation

Variation is disciplinary but may also be anticipated in other linguistic and cultural communities. Some research focuses on that variation and compares language pairs, for example: Alharbi and Swales (2011) for Arabic and English; Melander et al. (1997) for Swedish and English; Busch-Lauer (1995) for German and English; Johns (1992) for Portuguese and English; Dahl (2004a) for Norwegian, French and English; Montesi and Urdiciain (2005) and Martín-Martín and Burgess (2004) for Spanish and English; Yakhontova (2006) for English, Ukrainian and Russian; Xiao and Cao (2013) for English and Chinese. Examples of studies are outlined below, for French, Spanish and Chinese, as illustrations of the kind of research being undertaken. These show how even abstracts, as very short texts, nonetheless reflect epistemological and rhetorical cross-cultural differences.

French and English

Van Bonn and Swales (2007) compare French and English abstracts in the field of linguistics. In terms of structure the two sets of abstracts were found to be similar, but they differed in how they situated the research, that is, how they justified it and how they related it to other research. Generally the English abstracts did more to situate the research in both of these respects, while the French abstracts frequently did not try to justify the research and did not cite other work so frequently. Van Bonn and Swales offer the possible explanation that the French authors are operating within a smaller academic community, so they do not need to justify or defend their research as much as tends to be the case in international contexts. Moreover, the competition to publish internationally has led Hyland (2000) and Hyland and Tse (2005) to highlight an increasing use of promotional elements in abstracts; in other words, authors (particularly targeting anglophone publications) have to work at 'selling' the research.

Van Bonn and Swales (2007) note that the French abstracts were more likely than the English to use what they call 'purposive' language, overtly signalling the goal of the research, that is, statements like *this paper attempts* or *the goal of the research is*. This reinforces their observation that French abstracts focus more on the 'what' of the research and the presentation of data, while the English abstracts, with statements justifying the research, focus on the 'why' of the research.

The English abstracts used more first-person pronouns than the French, and where the French used them, it was always in the plural, that is, *nous, notre*, even if there was a single author. The English, by contrast, used singular *I, my* when there was a sole author and *we, our* when there were multiple authors. This difference in how authors refer to themselves is explained in terms of different cultural expectations regarding what is appropriate formal academic style (Van Bonn and Swales 2007).

Another significant linguistic differences was observed in the use of connectors or 'transition words' (Van Bonn and Swales 2007), categorized as addition/enumeration (e.g. *also, as well as, first, second, third, d'abord, de plus*), contrast/concession (e.g. *however, whereas, despite, although, pourtant, tandis que, bien que*) and cause/effect (e.g. *therefore, thus, because, since, donc, alors, parce que, car*). The researchers noticed that the French abstracts used connectors to indicate addition much more frequently than in English and much more frequently than the other connector types. The most common type in

English was the contrast/concession. Van Bonn and Swales (ibid.) see this as evidence that French academic discourse tends to reveal a series of facts, one on top of the other; while English academic discourse is more contrastive, as it does more to relate this research or research gaps to previous research. Thus, French and English academic discourse seem to reflect different qualities of academic prose in the two languages: French as 'deductive, data- and fact-based' and English as 'inductive, argument-based' (ibid.: 95).

They conclude that the main differences, highlighted here, between the English and French abstracts, can be explained sociologically in terms of the differences between the academic communities, in size and maturity. They highlight the need for English abstracts to situate the research within a wider context where they will reach a larger and wider readership than the French ones.

Spanish and English

Martín-Martín (2003) investigates differences and similarities between abstracts in English published in international journals and Spanish abstracts in Spanish journals, both in the domain of experimental social sciences. This study aims to investigate the potential impact of sociocultural factors on preferences for certain rhetorical strategies, when the two different scientific communities were compared.

Focusing attention on the introductions to the abstracts, Martín-Martín (2003) observes that Swales' CARS model was also valid for introduction in abstracts; that is, most abstracts executed specific rhetorical moves to (i) establish a territory, (ii) establish a niche, and (iii) occupy the niche. Both in English and Spanish, the abstracts introduced the purpose of the study (*These experiments deal with*, *Este trabajo analizó*), usually in present tense and active voice, and established the relevance of the work for the scientific community. A significant difference between the English and Spanish abstracts is that the English abstracts more often justified the work in the research field, for example by indicating a gap. This could be introduced by an adversative sentence introduced by the connector *however* or by a question. Martín-Martín (ibid.) speculates that the Spanish authors may consider it unconventional to criticize the work of their colleagues in establishing a niche, since it is a small field, while the international community is a more competitive one. This may therefore account for lower rhetorical complexity in the Spanish abstracts.

The methods section in both languages was usually present but short, sometimes only one sentence describing data sources and methods, and sometimes embedded into the introduction unit, perhaps to save space. Some Spanish methods sections tended to be slightly longer. The methods section often used the past tense and passive voice in English, also common in Spanish.

The results unit was introduced by inanimate nouns such as *the findings, the results, the analyses* in subject position, with verbs such as *show, reveal, indicate* in the past tense. Some hedging was present also in the English abstracts, but generally not in the Spanish abstracts, which often did not have a results unit at all.

The conclusion unit was present in most Spanish and English abstracts, written usually in the present tense, with the function signalled explicitly through lexical choices, for example *these findings suggest*, the *conclusion drawn is that*. Often the passive voice was used and frequent verbs were *suggest, indicate, reveal, conclude*. A significant difference between English and Spanish here was that most of the English abstracts used hedging devices (e.g. epistemic verbs *tend, suggest, seem*, and modals *can, may, could*), while the Spanish abstracts seldom hedged.

One tentative explanation offered by Martín-Martín (2003) is that hedging, as a move to avoid threatening face, may be less needed when Spanish writers address Spanish readers in their relatively small and not highly competitive field, compared with the international field where there is need for considerably more face-saving. He speculates that the lower rhetorical complexity in the Spanish abstracts and the rhetorical variation results from the nature of that relationship between writers and their discourse communities (ibid.: 40). However, he also notes that the non-hedged discourse may be 'institutionalised by most Spanish academics as part of a long-established writing style' (ibid.: 41).

Perales-Escudero and Swales (2011) also compare translations of abstracts, as published in the journal *Ibérica*. The researchers analyse English abstracts and their Spanish translations, and Spanish abstracts and their translation into English. For features such as text-referring expressions (i.e. expressions referring to the whole of the article, like *paper, study, article, articulo, estudio, trabajo*), there was a high degree of convergence across the languages. However, there were also some notable differences. As in Martín-Martín's study, the Spanish abstracts showed stronger epistemic commitment to propositions (i.e. more boosting and less hedging), the authorial attitude was more amplified, and the authors showed greater authorial presence and sometimes used more periphrastic expressions than the corresponding English. Both boosting ('most significant') and periphrasis in the Spanish version can be seen in the following example (Perales-Escudero and Swales 2011: 58):

There was a statistically significant difference in . . .

Uno de los resultados más destacados fue que existe una relación estadísticamente significativa . . .

[Back translation: One of the most significant results was that there is a statistically significant difference . . .]

A second example shows how a hedged proposition in English is not hedged in Spanish (Perales-Escudero and Swales 2011: 59):

To our knowledge, little research has been carried out on . . .

Hay aún escasas publicaciones sobre cómo los científicos españoles . . .

[Back translation: There are few publications on how Spanish scientists . . .]

Attitudinal markers are amplified by authors adding markers in Spanish to replace a weaker marker or hedging in English. For example:

. . . the term 'engineering' is rarely used.

. . . parece sorprendente la ausencia del término 'ingeniería'.

[Back translation: . . . the absence of the term 'engineering' seems surprising]

The authors note the trend towards a plural personal pronoun, *we*, and the Spanish *-mos* form, even when there is a single author; it is concluded that the English abstracts may be influenced by the Spanish in this regard.

Finally, some of the periphrasis in Spanish seems to be accounted for by the use of lexical bundles instead of possible one-word equivalents (Perales-Escudero and Swales 2011: 59). Some of these expressions were used when presenting results, like *poner de manifiesto* (for *demonstrate* in the English text) and *ser testigos de* (for *stress* in the English text). Others were common in purposive statements, for example: *The aim of this paper is* rendered as *El objetivo primordial de este artículo es*. Explanations elicited from the authors in interviews indicated that they often saw these Spanish expressions as preferred 'chunks'. As Perales-Escudero and Swales conclude, if these periphrastic expressions are rhetorically salient and more frequent in Spanish prose than their one-word equivalents, translators should know about this divergence. They go further to argue that translators should 'preserve whatever uniqueness there is to the rhetorical patterns of other languages by using those that are most distinct from English whenever appropriate' (ibid.: 67).

Chinese and English

Hu and Cao (2011) compare the use of boosters and hedges in English abstracts in English-language journals with the usage in English and

Chinese abstracts in Chinese-language journals (all from the field of applied linguistics). One of their main findings is that abstracts written in Chinese for Chinese journals use fewer hedges and more boosters than the English abstracts in English-language journals. Thus, the Chinese abstracts convey more authorial certainty, commitment and assertiveness (ibid.: 2802). The authors of the English abstracts, using epistemic verbs like *suggest*, *argue* and modal auxiliaries like *could*, *may* and *might*, and fewer boosters, are more tentative and cautious. Hu and Cao explain these differences in historical, sociocultural and rhetorical terms; different traditions of knowledge construction and communication require Chinese writers to adopt positions of authority and credibility in their writing, announcing knowledge, rather than hedging or qualifying their claims and anticipating counterarguments, as is typical in anglophone academic discourse. In addition, they argue that post-positivism in anglophone linguistics discourse acknowledges subjectivity and multiple interpretations and rejects scientism, while the trend in China in recent decades has been in the other direction, with linguistics scholarship becoming increasingly positivistic (ibid: 2805).

Since Hu and Cao could also compare the English translations of the Chinese abstracts with both the source texts and the abstracts written in English, they could also make observations on the translation process. The high level of boosters in the Chinese abstracts was diminished in their English translations; this may indicate an awareness of those internationally preferred rhetorical norms on the part of the Chinese authors translating the abstracts. However, it was striking that the use of hedges in the translation did not differ from those in the Chinese abstracts. They were therefore less frequent than in the English-language abstracts. Hu and Cao suggest that the author–translators might have been expected to introduce some hedging if they wished to conform to anglophone norms of tentative authorial stances. They conclude that the English proficiency of the authors may not have been sufficiently sophisticated to be able to make full use of a wide range of metadiscoursal strategies.

Exercise 6.1: Using the AVL for English

The AVL for English can be accessed at www.academicvocabulary. info. This website offers you the AVL in two forms (lemma-based and word families), also for download. Use the online search interface to search for or browse specific items. In particular, carry out some searches to compare frequency across some of the nine different academic domains available. Examine the other data available to you, including synonyms, collocates, sample concordances and definitions, and assess the usefulness of this resource for your own translating and writing work.

Exercise 6.2: Compiling an academic vocabulary list for another language

Find out if you can access an academic vocabulary list for your other language(s). If you cannot, you could carry out your own corpus research to compile one for a specific academic discipline. The following instructions are based on procedures followed by Hyland and Tse for ESP study (2007), adapted here to the needs of translators and simplified to make it feasible as a practical task.

1. For the language of your choice, collect research articles from a specific discipline of science, engineering, social science or the humanities. Consider whether it may make sense for you to expand your corpus to include texts from other academic genres, for example: textbooks, abstracts, postgraduate dissertations. If you have more resources and time, you could also expand this exercise to more than one academic discipline.
2. Compile your corpus using a suitable corpus-processing tool. See Chapter 2 for details of corpus tools and how to use them.
3. If you have access to a reference corpus for your language, compare your academic corpus with the reference corpus (e.g. using KeyWords within Wordsmith Tools or Sketch Engine). The keyword list that is produced should contain mostly terms and core academic vocabulary. Remember that you are trying to identify the core vocabulary that is typical of academic discourse, not the specialist vocabulary of the domain.
4. If you do not have access to a reference corpus, use your corpus software to generate a frequency list (e.g. Wordlist within Wordsmith Tools or Sketch Engine) for the corpus (and also for subcorpora if you have included more than one discipline). This list will include generally common words as well as academic and technical vocabulary so you will have to separate manually the generally common words from the academic and technical vocabulary. You may find it helpful to use an English academic vocabulary list as reference (e.g. the AVL, available at www.academicvocabulary.info) and go through your list in the other language to try to identify equivalents.
5. Once you have your list in the second language you can compare it with an English list, if you have not already done so. Make a note of differences in frequencies or positions on the two lists. These may indicate differences in usage that need to be examined further and that may be indicative of different rhetorical strategies and communicative purposes of the two discourse communities.
6. For a set of the most common academic words in both languages, examine the collocates and concordance lines and note particular collocates and recurrent phrases, in both languages.
7. Record your findings from this exercise in a spreadsheet, database or termbase, so that you can use it as a reference tool when preparing your translations.

Exercise 6.3: Understanding grammatical metaphor

Taking a paragraph of a research article in English, identify some of the abstractions or reconstruals produced by the process of grammatical metaphor. A useful starting point is nominalizations, although grammatical metaphor also includes other shifts. For some instances, try to reverse this process, for example, to reconstruct the sentence by denominalizing. Can it be done? If not, why not? What were the effects (benefits and shortcomings) of using grammatical metaphor in these instances?

Exercise 6.4: Identifying the moves of research article abstracts

Following the example of the contrastive studies (for French/Spanish/Chinese and English) outlined in this chapter, carry out a small-scale investigation of abstracts in your TL and SL for a specific academic discipline, either by comparing a set of abstracts and their translations or by collecting two sets of abstracts, one in the SL and one in the TL. Identify the moves of the abstract and note similarities and differences between languages. Identify the academic vocabulary or phrases that help to signal the moves, noting any correspondences between SL and TL.

Exercise 6.5: Examining the metadiscourse of research article abstracts

For the set of abstracts compiled for the previous task, identify the interactive resources that help to organize the discourse and the reader's interaction with the information flow, for example: signals of topic shift, transitions, frame markers, reference to other parts of the text, references to material outside the text, code glosses. Then identify the interactional resources that signal the writer's attitude to aspects of the text and to the reader, that is: hedges, boosters, attitude markers, engagement markers and self-mentions. Try to relate your findings to sociocultural factors of doing, reporting and publishing research in the countries and languages concerned, for example: patterns and strategies of national and international publishing and scholarship, language policies, epistemologies of science, English as lingua franca.

Exercise 6.6: Translating a research article

For a topic of your choice, select a research article and design a hypothetical translation brief. Consider the discussion in this chapter on epistemicide and outline your options and likely approach for this task.

Draw up a plan for the research you need to do to prepare to translate. Carry out your research, using corpus, terminology or TM tools and documentation as appropriate to assist you in your analysis and in recording relevant data (e.g. terms, academic vocabulary) for future use. Translate your text or a section of it. Discuss the translation process and your translation decisions.

Further reading: Learning more about the translation of science

For a selection of historical case studies of scientific translation, read Montgomery (2000). For a range of methodological and theoretical approaches to the study of scientific translation, consult the special issue of *The Translator* devoted to the translation of science (Olohan and Salama-Carr 2011).

Key points from this chapter

- Research articles and abstracts perform a range of communicative purposes in scientific and academic discourse communities and authors use linguistic resources in a variety of complex ways to fulfil those functions.
- Studies drawing on genre-analysis techniques have focused on English in particular, but variation across disciplines and cultures also represents a fruitful area of analysis. Differences can often be ascribed to the natures of the discourse communities, smaller or larger, more or less familiar, more or less competitive, and to differences in epistemologies.
- Research in these genres is motivated by the need for scholars in many scientific disciplines worldwide to publish in English and the desire to provide guidance and training in EAP circles.
- The need to publish in English also motivates translations, both of articles and of abstracts, usually pre-publication.
- When commissioned to translate research articles for publication, translators are mindful of their role in the scientific publishing process. They need to understand the science but also the genre-related conventions, and they are generally expected to apply their specialist knowledge to help authors to get their research published.
- Where genre conventions and metadiscourse, but perhaps also epistemologies are very different, cross-cultural awareness may help the translator to explain those kinds of differences to their clients, who may not be so aware of them but who may wish to understand them. This level of analytical ability and awareness should also enable translators to justify some of their own translational choices, whether they are aiming to propagate or subvert genre conventions.

References

Abdi, Reza (2009) 'Projecting Cultural Identity through Metadiscourse Marking: A Comparison of Persian and English Research Articles', *Journal of English Language Teaching and Learning* 1(212): 1–15.

Academic Vocabulary List (n.d.) online at: www.academicvocabulary.info (accessed 30 January 2015).

Alharbi, Lafi M. and John M. Swales (2011) 'Arabic and English Abstracts in Bilingual Language Science Journals: Same or Different?', *Languages in Contrast* 11(1): 69–85.

Bazerman, Charles (1988) *Shaping Written Knowledge: The Genre and Activity of the Experimental Article in Science*, Madison, WI: University of Wisconsin Press.

Bennett, Karen (2007) 'Epistemicide! The Tale of a Predatory Discourse', *The Translator* 13(2): 151–69.

—— (2013) 'English as a Lingua Franca in Academia', *The Interpreter and Translator Trainer* 7(2): 169–93.

Bhatia, Vijay K. (1993) *Analysing Genre: Language Use in Professional Settings*, London: Pearson Education.

Brett, Paul (1994) 'A Genre Analysis of the Results Section of Sociology Articles', *English for Specific Purposes* 13(1): 47–59.

Busch-Lauer, Ines A. (1995) 'Abstracts in German Medical Journals: A Linguistic Analysis', *Information Processing and Management* 31(5): 769–76.

Coxhead, Averil (2000) 'A New Academic Word List', *TESOL Quarterly* 34(2): 213–38.

Dahl, Trine (2004a) 'Some Characteristics of Argumentative Abstracts', *Akademisk Prosa* 2: 49–67.

—— (2004b) 'Textual Metadiscourse in Research Articles: A Marker of National Culture or of Academic Discipline?', *Journal of Pragmatics* 36(10): 1807–25.

Eriksen, Marcus, Laurent C. M. Lebreton, Henry S. Carson, Martin Thiel, Charles J. Moore, Jose C. Borerro, Francois Galgani, Peter G. Ryan, Julia Reisser (2014) 'Plastic Pollution in the World's Oceans: More than 5 Trillion Plastic Pieces Weighing over 250,000 Tons Afloat at Sea', *PLoS ONE* 9(12): e111913, online at: http://dx.doi.org/10.1371/journal.pone.0111913 (accessed 9 February 2015).

Fakhri, Ahmed (2004) 'Rhetorical Properties of Arabic Research Article Introductions', *Journal of Pragmatics* 36(6): 1119–38.

Gardner, Dee and Mark Davies (2014) 'A New Academic Vocabulary List', *Applied Linguistics* 35(3): 305–27.

Gillaerts, Paul and Freek Van de Velde (2010) 'Interactional Metadiscourse in Research Article Abstracts', *Journal of English for Academic Purposes* 9(2): 128–39.

Goldstein, Miriam C., Andrew J. Titmus and Michael Ford (2013) 'Scales of Spatial Heterogeneity of Plastic Marine Debris in the Northeast Pacific Ocean', *PLOS ONE* 8(11): e80020, online at: http://dx.doi.org/10.1371/journal.pone.0080020 (accessed 30 January 2015).

Halliday, M.A.K. (2004) *The Language of Science*, Jonathan J. Webster (ed) London and New York: Continuum.

Hirano, Eliana (2009) 'Research Article Introductions in English for Specific Purposes: A Comparison between Brazilian Portuguese and English', *English for Specific Purposes* 28(4): 240–50.

Hu, Guangwei and Feng Cao (2011) 'Hedging and Boosting in Abstracts of Applied Linguistics Articles: A Comparative Study of English- and Chinese-Medium Journals', *Journal of Pragmatics* 43(11): 2795–809.

Hyland, Ken (2000) *Disciplinary Discourses: Social Interactions in Academic Writing*, London: Longman.

—— (2005) *Metadiscourse: Exploring Interaction in Writing*, London: Bloomsbury Publishing.

—— (2010) 'Constructing Proximity: Relating to Readers in Popular and Professional Science', *Journal of English for Academic Purposes* 9(2): 116–27.

Hyland, Ken and Polly Tse (2004) 'Metadiscourse in Academic Writing: A Reappraisal', *Applied Linguistics* 25(2): 156–77.

—— (2005) 'Hooking the Reader: A Corpus Study of Evaluative That in Abstracts', *English for Specific Purposes* 24(2): 123–39.

—— (2007) 'Is There an 'Academic Vocabulary'?', *TESOL Quarterly* 41(2): 235–53.

—— (2009) 'Academic Lexis and Disciplinary Practice: Corpus Evidence for Specificity', *International Journal of English Studies* 9(2): 111–29.

Johns, Tim (1992) 'It Is Presented Initially: Linear Dislocation and Inter-language Strategies in Brazilian Academic Abstracts in English and Portuguese', *Ilha Do Desterro* 27: 9–32, online at: https://periodicos. ufsc.br/index.php/desterro/article/view/10426 (accessed 15 January 2015).

Kanoksilapatham, Budsaba (2015) 'Distinguishing Textual Features Characterizing Structural Variation in Research Articles across Three Engineering Sub-discipline Corpora', *English for Specific Purposes* 37: 74–86.

Knorr Cetina, Karin (1999) *Epistemic Cultures: How the Sciences Make Knowledge*, Cambridge, MA: Harvard University Press.

McGrath, Lisa and Maria Kuteeva (2012) 'Stance and Engagement in Pure Mathematics Research Articles: Linking Discourse Features to Disciplinary Practices', *English for Specific Purposes* 31(3): 161–73.

Martínez, Iliana A., Silvia C. Beck and Carolina B. Panza (2009) 'Academic Vocabulary in Agriculture Research Articles: A Corpus-Based Study', *English for Specific Purposes* 28(3): 183–98.

Martín-Martín, Pedro (2003) 'A Genre Analysis of English and Spanish Research Paper Abstracts in Experimental Social Sciences', *English for Specific Purposes* 22(1): 25–43.

Martín-Martín, Pedro and Sally Burgess (2004) 'The Rhetorical Management of Academic Criticism in Research Article Abstracts', *Text* 24: 171–95.

Melander, Björn, John M. Swales and Kirstin M. Fredrickson (1997) 'Journal Abstracts from Three Academic Fields in the United States and Sweden: National or Disciplinary Proclivities?', in Anna Duszak (ed) *Culture and Styles of Academic Discourse*, Berlin: Walter de Gruyter, pp. 251–72.

Montesi, Michela and Blanca Gil Urdiciain (2005) 'Recent Linguistics Research into Author Abstracts: Its Value for Information Science', *Knowledge Organization* 32(2): 64–78.

Montgomery, Scott L. (2000) *Science in Translation: Movements of Knowledge Through Cultures and Time*, Chicago: University of Chicago Press.

—— (2009) 'English and Science: Realities and Issues for Translation in the Age of an Expanding Lingua Franca', *Journal of Specialised Translation* 11: 5–16, online at: www.jostrans.org/issue11/art_montgomery.php (accessed 15 January 2015).

Mur Dueñas, Pilar (2007) "I/we Focus On . . . ': A Cross-Cultural Analysis of Self-Mentions in Business Management Research Articles', *Journal of English for Academic Purposes* 6(2): 143–62.

—— (2011) 'An Intercultural Analysis of Metadiscourse Features in Research Articles Written in English and in Spanish', *Journal of Pragmatics* 43(12): 3068–79.

—— (2012) 'Getting Research Published Internationally in English: An Ethnographic Account of a Team of Finance Spanish Scholars' Struggles', *Ibérica* 24: 139–55.

Myers, Greg (1989) 'The Pragmatics of Politeness in Scientific Articles', *Applied Linguistics* 10(1): 1–35.

Olohan, Maeve and Myriam Salama-Carr (eds) (2011) *The Translator*, special issue on science in translation, 17(2).

Perales-Escudero, Moisés and John M. Swales (2011) 'Tracing Convergence and Divergence in Pairs of Spanish and English Research Article Abstracts: The Case of *Ibérica*', *Ibérica* 21: 49–70.

Pisanski Peterlin, Agnes (2008) 'Translating Metadiscourse in Research Articles', *Across Languages and Cultures* 9(2): 205–18.

—— (2013) 'Attitudes towards English as an Academic Lingua Franca in Translation', *The Interpreter and Translator Trainer* 7(2): 195–216.

Root-Bernstein, Meredith and Richard J. Ladle (2014) 'Speaking unto Nations', *Times Higher Education*, 26 June 2014: 30.

Salager-Meyer, Françoise (2009) 'Discoursal Flaws in Medical English Abstracts: A Genre Analysis per Research- and Text-Type', *Text – Interdisciplinary Journal for the Study of Discourse* 10(4): 365–84.

Samraj, Betty (2005) 'An Exploration of a Genre Set: Research Article Abstracts and Introductions in Two Disciplines', *English for Specific Purposes* 24(2): 141–56.

Stoller, Fredricka L. and Marin S. Robinson (2013) 'Chemistry Journal Articles: An Interdisciplinary Approach to Move Analysis with Pedagogical Aims', *English for Specific Purposes* 32(1): 45–57.

Swales, John M. (1990) *Genre Analysis: English in Academic and Research Settings*, Cambridge: Cambridge University Press.

—— (1997) 'English as Tyrannosaurus Rex', *World Englishes* 16(3): 373–82.

—— (2004) *Research Genres: Explorations and Applications*, Cambridge: Cambridge University Press.

Taviano, Stefania (2013) 'English as a Lingua Franca and Translation', *The Interpreter and Translator Trainer* 7(2): 155–67.

Van Bonn, Sarah and John M. Swales (2007) 'English and French Journal Abstracts in the Language Sciences: Three Exploratory Studies', *Journal of English for Academic Purposes* 6(2): 93–108.

Vold, Eva Thue (2006) 'Epistemic Modality Markers in Research Articles: A Cross-Linguistic and Cross-Disciplinary Study', *International Journal of Applied Linguistics* 16(1): 61–87.

Xiao, Richard and Yan Cao (2013) 'Native and Non-native English Abstracts in Contrast: A Multidimensional Move Analysis', *Belgian Journal of Linguistics* 27(1): 111–34.

Yakhontova, Tatyana (2006) 'Cultural and Disciplinary Variation in Academic Discourse: The Issue of Influencing Factors', *Journal of English for Academic Purposes* 5(2): 153–67.

7 Popular science

This chapter focuses on popular science news articles, as a genre that is frequently published and translated. We start by considering what it means to popularize science and how science discourse interacts with other public discourses. We continue by tracing a popular science story from professional journal article to press release to news item, and we identify some typical features of popular science news reporting and some cross-cultural differences. Finally the cultural specificity of popular science reporting is highlighted with reference to examples of translated news stories from *National Geographic* magazine.

Introducing popular science discourse

The Royal Society, founded in 1662, is the national academy of science in the UK. In January 2015 it appointed Professor Brian Cox to a new role as Professor for Public Engagement in Science. In creating this position, the Royal Society acknowledged the importance of engaging with the public to publicize the Royal Society's activities and to stimulate public interest and enthusiasm for science. However, the appointee's remit goes further than that; the Royal Society was looking for someone, an excellent communicator with media experience, who could also 'contribute to a greater public understanding of science and the importance of experiment, evidence and understanding uncertainty', who could 'increase public understanding of scientific issues which inform policy debates on important issues' and whose public engagement would 'strengthen the case for increased support for science' (Royal Society n.d.). This appointment is just one illustration of the current significance of science as public discourse. However, it is also illustrative of science's dependence on public funding and relationships between science and government policy. With much scientific research being publicly funded, there is increasing awareness of the need for the fruits of that activity to be made more accessible, not just to the funding bodies, but also to the general public whose taxes contribute to government coffers. It also highlights a need, as perceived by scientific institutions, for scientific communication not only to focus on breakthroughs and significant findings, but also to impart to the public an understanding of scientific methods, to underline the importance of evidence in drawing conclusions and to draw attention to the uncertainty inherent in much scientific endeavour.

Before examining some examples it is useful to reflect briefly on what it means to popularize science. Popularization is often understood as the simplification, distortion or dumbing down of science, a view that is reflected also in the term 'vulgarization'. Professional science and popular science are commonly conceived of and analysed as two separate discourses. As Myers (2003: 266) explains, in critiquing this view, it rests on the assumptions that scientists are the experts on what constitutes science, informing an ignorant public, and that scientific knowledge moves in one direction only, from scientists to society, through written statements. According to this perspective, professional scientific discourse is translated and simplified to produce popular science discourse. However, those assumptions are questioned in a special issue of *Discourse Studies* introduced by Myers' contribution. Here he suggests that we instead view popularization as a continuum and that we think about how scientists are involved in a range of genres, from informal conversations with colleagues to writing grant proposals, from giving lectures to writing journal articles. Thus, it is helpful to think in terms of degrees of popularization, rather than a stark distinction between two discourses.

Below are some scenarios, among many, which exemplify various degrees of popularization.

- Articles in popular science magazines like *Scientific American* are aimed as an educated readership with an interest in science. This readership includes professional scientists who are not specialists in the field about which they are reading. The high degree of specialization of branches and sub-branches of science means that professional scientists in one domain may have little specialist understanding of science from other domains, thus requiring accounts that are accessible to them.
- Most scientific funding proposals require applicants to produce accessible versions or summaries of their research proposal. This is because the proposals are evaluated by subject specialists, but also by people who are experienced in other fields but who may not be specialists in that particular field of knowledge. Once the funding has been awarded, accessible summaries may also be used by funding organizations to publicize the kinds of research being funded, perhaps also to show transparency of the evaluation system or to justify the use of public funds.

- Television documentaries on scientific themes are widely consumed by audiences who may expect to be informed but for whom being entertained may also be an important motivating factor in watching. The audiovisual dimension of the communication is key in achieving those aims.
- Popular science news websites, for example, Science News (www.sciencenews.org) and Science Daily (www.sciencedaily.com), also use multiple communication modes to engage readers.
- Science museums explain exhibitions for those who may not have much specialist knowledge. Many also organize interactive exhibits for children, often targeting them by age group or education stage.
- Citizen science initiatives bring non-professionals into the sphere of scientific practice. Non-scientists are motivated not only to become informed about science, but also to participate in scientific activity themselves and thus contribute to scientific research. This kind of initiative helps to counter the prevalent perception of professional science and its discourse as being elitist and exclusionary.

In the previous chapter we examined the communicative purposes of research articles within the academic community. We can take a similar approach here to think about who is involved in producing and consuming popularized accounts of science, what is communicated and how this discourse interacts with other discourses. On this final point, as Myers (2003) also argues, the view of popular science as predominantly functioning to inform an ignorant public is not tenable; the public holds knowledge and opinions, and makes connections between scientific news and what they already know, feel or believe. Scientific discourse interacts with other public discourses, whether economic, cultural or political. Below are two examples of how popular science discourses themselves influence and in turn are influenced by other discourses.

- The UK government's Advisory Council on the Misuse of Drugs (ACMD) is tasked with making recommendations to government on the control of dangerous and otherwise harmful drugs. In October 2008 Professor David Nutt was appointed Chairman of the ACMD, but, following a series of disagreements, he was sacked by the Home Secretary in October 2009. The disagreements concerned the classification of drugs and the estimation of drug harms. An ACMD report in February 2009 had recommended the reclassification of ecstasy from Class A to Class B, based on the low numbers of deaths per year attributable to ecstasy and its 'relatively few adverse health effects' (Advisory Council on the Misuse of Drugs 2009). Nutt, prior to taking office, had also published an editorial in the *Journal of Psychopharmacology* in which he compared the harms of horse riding with the harms of taking ecstasy (Nutt 2009). In July 2009 Nutt gave a lecture in London in which he was critical of the government's recent reclassification of cannabis from Class C to Class B. The ACMD had recommended that it stay as Class C, and, in Nutt's view, the government's cautious approach had the potential to mislead the public and to devalue scientific evidence. Much media coverage after the lecture focused on the claim that alcohol and tobacco were more dangerous than ecstasy or cannabis. Nutt's sacking was justified by the Home Secretary on the basis that Nutt could not be simultaneously a government advisory and a campaigner against government policy (Johnson 2009). The then Prime Minister, Gordon Brown, said 'we cannot send mixed messages' (BBC News 2009), the government's desirable message being that drug use was not politically, socially or morally acceptable. This led to a group of leading scientists publishing a set of principles for the treatment of independent scientific advice which was agreed by government and accepted into the Ministerial Code in June 2010 (Sense About Science n.d.).

• A World Health Organization report (2015) assessing the factors that contributed to difficulties containing the Ebola virus in West Africa discusses the clashes between the Western medical understanding of the virus, reflected in the advice health workers communicated to local communities, and traditional cultural understandings and practices of healing and compassionate care in the community and ceremonial burial rites. As noted in the report, one problem which impeded containment of the virus, especially in the early stages, was that health messages to the public 'repeatedly emphasized that the disease was extremely serious and deadly, and had no vaccine, treatment, or cure' (ibid.). This message, designed to counteract persistent beliefs that Ebola was not real, had the opposite effect to that intended; families decided that, if medicine could not help anyhow, they preferred to care for their dying loved ones at home, where they would be more comfortable in familiar surroundings.

In this book we are focusing on genres that are widely translated, so we will not discuss funding proposals or museum exhibitions (although the latter are occasionally translated). Of the genres mentioned so far, scientific news articles are clearly important for translation, so we will look more closely at them in the next section.

Science in the news

The science writing that we will focus on first is produced by scientific research organizations and institutions who seek to disseminate their research findings beyond the scientific research community, for some or all of the reasons mentioned above. In some cases, the institutions write directly for the public who access their websites or for websites which aggregate science news, like www.futurity.org. In other cases they issue press releases and other material designed for science journalists to read and communicate to the general public through their own publications. In most of these situations we can identify layers of mediation between scientists and the public, performed, for example, by press officers or journalists, as well as translators. To get an insight into the transformation from scientific journal article to news item, we take the example of a press release triggered by publication of a scientific study and some news reports generated in turn by the press release. For reasons of space we will confine this exploration to headlines and standfirsts (i.e. the highlighted text between the headline and the body of the article) and the use of sources in quotations (see Dahl 2015 for analysis of a different scientific story with similar areas of focus). Our aim is to identify some of the specific ways in which the discourses are constituted and framed, relating linguistic choices to the communicative purposes of the news stories and their contexts of production. We will then link our observations to some previous research identifying a set of typical features of popular science news reporting.

From research publication to press release

The publication of a professional scientific article can trigger a press release from the research organization, which, in turn, can trigger coverage in other outlets, for example, print and broadcast media, science news websites and blogs. Our example relates to a large European research project being led by investigators at the University of Cambridge; results of one study from this project were published as an article in the *American Journal of Clinical Nutrition* (*AJCN*) on 15 January 2015. The University of Cambridge issued a press release to publicize the research, and the story was picked up by broadcast and print media in the UK on the same day (for example featuring on BBC Radio 4's *Today* programme). The full text of the press release can be found in Appendix 4 (reproduced courtesy of the University of Cambridge).

Headline and standfirst

Excerpt 7.1 presents the headline and abstract outline of the *AJCN* article, and the headline and standfirst of the University of Cambridge press release. In the title of the *AJCN* article, we can identify many of the features typical of professional science, notably the use of medical terminology which may not be immediately understood by non-specialists, namely *all-cause mortality* and *overall adiposity* and *abdominal adiposity*. It also gives the full name for the large-scale European study of which this was a part, the *European Prospective Investigation into Cancer and Nutrition Study* and the corresponding acronym, *EPIC*. We might also recognize the two-part structure of *AJCN*'s title, with separation via a colon, as a common structure for academic paper titles, particularly where the first part is formulated to grab attention and the second to provide more information, although that is not the case here. With its 27 words and footnote reference, this title can hardly be described as snappy or particularly attention-grabbing. A final observation about the title is that it tells us that the study focuses on the relationship between physical activity and adiposity, but it gives no indication of the outcome or findings. These are, however, summarized in the abstract; the proportion of premature deaths among people categorized as moderately inactive was smaller than the proportion of premature deaths among people in the inactive classification. This reduced mortality was observed across different levels of body fat and waist circumference. It was therefore estimated theoretically that even small increases in physical activity among inactive people could reduce mortality to a greater degree than reductions in obesity levels.

EXCERPT 7. 1

AJCN article

Title: Physical activity and all-cause mortality across levels of overall and abdominal adiposity in European men and women: the European Prospective Investigation into Cancer and Nutrition Study (EPIC)[1–6]
[Abstract divided into headed sections: background, objective, design, results, conclusion. Followed by keywords.]

University of Cambridge press release

Headline: Lack of exercise responsible for twice as many deaths as obesity
Standfirst: A brisk 20 minute walk each day could be enough to reduce an individual's risk of early death, according to new research published today. The study of over 334,000 European men and women found that twice as many deaths may be attributable to lack of physical activity compared with the number of deaths attributable to obesity, but that just a modest increase in physical activity could have significant health benefits.

Unlike the professional science article, the lexis of the press release headline (*obesity*, *lack of exercise*) is widely used and meaningful to most people. The headline focuses on the main outcome, that is, the putative relations of causation between lack of exercise and death, and between obesity and death, and the comparison between them (one *responsible for twice as many deaths* as the other). The main verb and articles are omitted to produce the elliptical, epigrammatic format typical of headlines in English. There is no hedging of the causal relation in the headline, and the negative relation is the one highlighted, that is, death from lack of exercise. The standfirst then introduces the study and emphasizes the newness of this research (*new research published today*) but also frames the finding more positively in terms of the payoffs for the reader: a 20-minute walk may reduce your risk of early death. This is reiterated at the end of the standfirst in the form of *significant health benefits*, as is the relative ease with which the benefits can be experienced: *just a modest increase in physical activity*. Details of the study are included (number and type of participants). The 46-word sentence summarizing the study is longer than we might expect for a standfirst, and, unlike the headline, all claims in the standfirst are hedged: *could be enough to, may be attributable to, could have . . . benefits*. In addition, reference is to an *individual's risk*, rather than the reader's or everyone's, which generalizes but also potentially limits the scope of the promised payoff.

(Pseudo)quotation

The first four paragraphs of the press release follow a structure bearing some similarity to the kinds of moves we observed in professional science reporting in Chapter 6. They and the final two paragraphs could be summarized as follows:

- Paragraph 1: gives the context and rationale for the study.
- Paragraph 2: outlines the methods of the study with some precise details, a link to the website for the EPIC study and to the *AJCN* article itself.
- Paragraph 3: summarizes findings, including some quantitative information.
- Paragraph 4: extrapolates those findings to causes of European deaths more generally.
- Paragraph 5: quotes the lead researcher who emphasizes the simplicity of the key message and encourages us to increase levels of physical activity.
- Paragraph 6: quotes the director of the unit at Cambridge that is leading the research. He reiterates the key message on the desirability of increasing physical activity, but also relates the study's findings to the continued pursuit of reducing obesity in the population.

The final two paragraphs are of particular interest in that they comprise the kind of quotations typically used in press releases, namely quotations from people with some standing or reputation whose quotations are seen to lend impressions of credibility and objectivity to the message of the press release. These and other devices have been described by some scholars (Strobbe and Jacobs 2005; Sleurs et al. 2003) as **preformulating devices,** that is, devices used in press releases that are designed to facilitate reuse of the press release by journalists. Other preformulating devices include headlines, stand-firsts, comprehensive lead paragraphs and third-person (rather than first-person) references to the company or organization which is the subject of (and often producer of) the press release. The aim or ideal scenario for corporate press officers is that journalists simply copy those elements unchanged into their own piece. Sleurs et al. (ibid.) provide a more detailed analysis of quotation in particular, showing that the kind of quotation used in press releases tends to be constructed by the press officer and approved by the person quoted rather than occur naturally in interview or conversation. For this reason it may be called pseudo-quotation. Their studies also show how the quotes may be constructed with the specific aim of enabling journalists to reuse them.

In our example we have two quotations, presented as Excerpt 7.2. The first is from the lead investigator, Professor Ulf Ekelund, and the second is from the head of his research unit, Professor Nick Wareham. Both scientists are introduced with their academic title, and the full institutional affiliation (unit and university) is given for Ekelund and then referred to in abbreviated form for Wareham. The quotations are typical of those used in press releases in that the people quoted are put forward as authorities on the subject and their authority or standing is demonstrated in those ways. Although Wareham is also a co-author (with 46 others), he is quoted in his capacity as head of the unit, to lend further credibility to the report from a hierarchically superior position.

EXCERPT 7.2

Ekelund: *This is a simple message: just a small amount of physical activity each day could have substantial health benefits for people who are physically inactive. Although we found that just 20 minutes would make a difference, we should really be looking to do more than this – physical activity has many proven health benefits and should be an important part of our daily life.*

Wareham: *Helping people to lose weight can be a real challenge, and whilst we should continue to aim at reducing population levels of obesity, public health interventions that encourage people to make small but achievable changes in physical activity can have significant health benefits and may be easier to achieve and maintain.*

We will see below how the quotations were picked up and reused by journalists, but we can note here how the University of Cambridge press release on the University website reuses part of Ekelund's quotation by repeating part of it as a pull quote towards the top of the screen: *This is a simple message: just a small amount of physical activity each day could have substantial health benefits for people who are physically inactive – Ulf Ekelund.*

Both quotes are interesting in that they focus on the outcome and payoff of the research but also work to frame the main message against prevailing public health discourse in the UK. Wareham advocates continued pursuit of the aim of reducing the population's obesity levels, even if it is easier to achieve a small increase in physical activity than to lose weight. This is an explicit reference to much public health discourse of recent years, where obesity has been portrayed as the serious problem. Ekelund also contextualizes the payoff against prevailing public health messages about exercise; thus even if 20 minutes has been shown to make a difference, more exercise is even better. The latter is not a finding attributable to the study, but chimes with government guidelines such as those issued by the UK's National Health Service (see NHS 2013). Finally, Ekelund's use of both exclusive and inclusive *we* in the same utterance is worth noting; he both speaks with the authoritative voice of the scientist conducting the study but also places himself alongside the reader as part of the general public who should exercise.

From press release to news story

As noted above, press officers who construct press releases are generally hoping that their text will be picked up and reused by journalists, and they have certain textual resources at their disposal, labelled preformulating devices, when writing the releases to ease the transition from press release to news items. Reflecting a more critical stance to this practice, the word 'churnalism' has been coined to reflect the reuse of press releases as news articles with very little editing or addition. Whether viewed from press officer or journalism standards perspectives, the phenomenon is clearly acknowledged and can be traced by comparing press releases to news items, including in our own example. For illustration here, we can examine coverage of this story on news websites of two broadcasting bodies (BBC and ITV), two press organizations (the *Guardian* and the *Daily Mail*) and two organizations with a special interest in medical news (the British Heart Foundation and BootsWebMD). All are accessible online. The *Guardian*'s report can also be found in Appendix 4, reproduced courtesy of the *Guardian* Newspapers.

As examination of the headlines and standfirsts in Excerpt 7.3 indicates, emphasis is on the payoff rather than the methods or details of the research, which are reported to varying degrees later in the articles. The payoff or positive news (e.g. health benefits of exercise) does not, at first glance, seem particularly novel. However, the coverage received by the study shows that it was clearly deemed newsworthy; firstly, this seems to be not entirely because of what it says about physical activity, but because of what it says about obesity. Obesity has been at the forefront of the public health agenda for some time in the UK, as in many other countries, so in a somewhat twisted sense it is seen as good news if inactivity is revealed as more harmful than obesity. Thus it is the comparison of risk/harm associated with physical inactivity compared with obesity that is the main focus of the news coverage. Secondly, the study proposes a relatively simple remedy for inactivity which promises noticeable results, a daily 20-minute walk, so this is also highlighted.

EXCERPT 7.3

University of Cambridge press release

Headline: Lack of exercise responsible for twice as many deaths as obesity
Standfirst: A brisk 20 minute walk each day could be enough to reduce an individual's risk of early death, according to new research published today. The study of over 334,000 European men and women found that twice as many deaths may be attributable to lack of physical activity compared with the number of deaths attributable to obesity, but that just a modest increase in physical activity could have significant health benefits.

Daily Mail

Headline: Walk 20 minutes to live longer: Huge study reveals benefit of daily exercise (and how a lack of it kills twice as many people as obesity)
Standfirst: [as bulleted list of three items] A lack of exercise kills twice as many people as obesity, researchers warn

The Cambridge University study found even modest activity prolongs life

Twenty minutes of walking a day cuts premature risk of death by a third.

Guardian

Headline: Scientists recommend 20-minute daily walk to avoid premature death

Standfirst: Research into obesity establishes benefits of engaging in moderate levels of daily exercise.

BBC News

Headline: Inactivity 'kills more than obesity'

Standfirst: A lack of exercise could be killing twice as many people as obesity in Europe, a 12-year study of more than 300,000 people-suggests.

ITV News

Headline: Brisk 20-minute walk each day could help avoid an early death

Standfirst: none.

BootsWebMD

Headline: Inactivity causes more deaths than obesity: Study

Standfirst: none.

British Heart Foundation

Headline: Lack of exercise may lead to twice as many deaths as obesity, study claims

Standfirst: Physical inactivity may be associated with twice as many deaths as obesity, according to research.

Headlines and standfirsts

The *Daily Mail* headline, perhaps more unusually, comprises three parts, and here the second and third parts certainly elaborate on the first by summarizing a study finding and supplying more detail in parentheses. The use of parentheses in headlines in this way may be more typical of the *Daily Mail* than of other publications. At 26 words, the *Daily Mail* headline is long, but the way in which it is chunked into three parts maintains a snappiness, which is reinforced by the use of an active verb in each chunk and in particular by the reader being directly addressed by the imperative *walk* as the first word of the first part.

Most of the news headlines focus on the main finding, though to varying degrees and in different ways. The British Heart Foundation's headline is very similar to the press release, though the introduction of a modal verb has a hedging effect: *responsible for* vs *may lead to*. BootsWebMD and the BBC are less explicit about the comparison: *more* vs *twice as many*. The *Daily Mail* also makes reference to the relationship and comparison, but in the parenthetical part of the headline. It dramatizes by opting for the vivid *kills*, as does the BBC. In the BBC's case, *kills more than obesity* is enclosed within quotation marks, but it is striking that there is no such quote in the article, nor does this wording appear in any other written coverage. The quotation marks seem to be used to give the impression of a quotation and likewise the impression of credibility and objectivity that can come with quotation from an authoritative source.

The press release and the news items published by the British Heart Foundation, the BBC and BootsWebMD all place the prime cause in subject position, whether *lack of exercise* or *inactivity*. The *Guardian* diverges from other coverage in putting *scientists* in subject position. As noted, the *Daily Mail* headline starts by exhorting their readers to perform an action.

The news items make no reference to the name of the study in their headlines, though the *Daily Mail* mentions *huge study*, the British Heart Foundation and BootsWebMD also signal that it is a *study*, and the *Guardian* makes *scientists* the subject of its headline, thus also implying that there has been a study. The other sources do not make reference to the study in the headline. The BBC introduces the study and some details about it (duration and approximate number of participants) in the standfirst. The British Heart Foundation and the *Guardian* both mention *research* in their standfirsts, backing up previous mentions of *study* or *scientists* in their headlines. Of the news sites, the *Daily Mail* has the longest standfirst as well as the longest headline. Its standfirst mentions *researchers* and repeats *study* with a modifier to indicate the research institution. The University of Cambridge's standfirst is longer than those of the news articles and gives more detail on the study itself.

The *Daily Mail* headline is the only one which addresses the reader explicitly, exhorting them to *walk 20 minutes to live longer*. This is a focus on a positive outcome of the study for readers and the action they need to take to benefit from it. The benefits are reinforced in the standfirst. The *Guardian* and ITV headlines do something similar, also focusing on the benefit of the 20-minute daily walk, that is, *to avoid premature death* or *avoid an early death*, and the *Guardian* standfirst reinforces this attention to the payoff.

Quotation

The British Heart Foundation news item does not use quotations from the University press release, but instead lends its own voice of authority through a quotation from one of its senior cardiac nurses, June Davison, seen in Excerpt 7.4. As with the quotations discussed above, the nurse's 'senior' status lends credibility. In addition, like the quotations in the University of Cambridge press release, Davison's quotation is used as an opportunity to link the research to other public health discourse and to the British Hearth Foundation's mission. Therefore the finding that *just a modest increase in physical activity can have health benefits* is immediately followed by a statement which quotes UK Government guidelines on amount and nature of recommended exercise. The quote concludes with examples of physical activity but links *keeping active daily* to a reduction in the *risk of developing coronary heart disease*, which was neither a subject nor a finding of the study.

EXCERPT 7.4

Davison: *The results of this study are a clear reminder that being regularly physically active can reduce the risk of dying from coronary heart disease. The research suggests that just a modest increase in physical activity can have health benefits. Adults should aim to do at least 150 minutes of moderate intensity activity a week, carrying it out in sessions of 10 minutes or more. Whether it's going for a walk, taking a bike ride or using the stairs instead of the lift, keeping active every day will help reduce the risk of developing coronary heart disease.*

Both the *Guardian* and the *Daily Mail* news items reproduce Ekelund's, Wareham's and Davison's quotes, in that order. These quotations, together with the text introducing the quoted people, account for around 40 per cent of the articles. BootsWebMD's report also reproduces all three quotes, using an excerpt from Ekelund's as a sub-heading, '*A simple message*'. It concludes with a fourth quotation from a health information officer from Cancer Research UK confirming the benefits of moderate exercise. Thus, we can see that many of the news reports situate the study's findings even more explicitly against the backdrop of prevailing UK public health discourse than was done by the press release and the scientists' quotations.

The shorter ITV item uses Ekelund's quotation in full, but only snippets from Wareham's and attributes them to the researchers. The BBC news item uses quotations in a slightly different way, because it draws on a BBC News interview with Ekelund. However, here too the quotations serve to emphasize that obesity should be tackled also, despite the study's findings: *But I don't think it's a case of one or the other. We should also strive to reduce obesity, but I do think physical activity needs to be recognized as a very important public health strategy.* The item employs section subheadings *Obese vs inactive* and *Tackle both* to reinforce that message, and it includes two additional quotations. One is from a spokesperson from Heart Research UK, commenting on the benefits of lifestyle changes for heart health. The final quotation is from the president of the Faculty of Public Health, who demands changes *to make exercise easier – We need substantial investment in cycling infrastructure to make our streets safer.* Here, he seems to be using the results of the study as support for a campaign for better infrastructure. This rhetorical move is in keeping with his role and the goals of his organization, one of which is to advocate in matters of public health (Faculty of Public Health 2010).

Finally, we can note that the *Daily Mail* also summarizes two other sources of information, with the effect of casting doubt on the simplicity of the message and its likely implementation, while also invoking some of its common themes relating to societal ills and socio-economic problems; it refers to findings of a recent survey and a report that *a third of people can barely manage to walk for 30 minutes over seven days* and, secondly, that *physical inactivity cost the economy up to £10 billion a year through sick days, healthcare costs and early deaths.*

Visuals

It is useful to comment briefly on the images chosen by news outlets to attract the readers' attention to this story. The composition of the images could be studied in greater detail, but this may not be necessary for our purposes, because images accompanying scientific news stories are often reused with translations or replaced by sub-editors. However, as translators, it is useful for us to consider the role of the images accompanying texts, since they are chosen by sub-editors to fulfil certain purposes. A main function may be to attract the readers' eye and attention to the story. In addition, they often provide further explanation or exemplification of points made in the text. They also act as framing devices for the story, influencing the way in which readers then read and interpret the text of the story.

The images used in our examples tend to fall into two categories, focusing either on the characteristics portrayed in the story as negative or undesirable, that is, obesity and inactivity, or on the state aspired to, namely healthiness, fitness and slimness. The BBC story mixes both messages in its images, reflecting and reinforcing the main argument in the text (*tackle both*); two images are used, one of an obese man lying on a sofa with a remote control in his hand and one of an obese woman jogging in a green field.

The ITV image is a photo of a slim woman jogging in a park, the *Guardian*'s of a slim, female hill-walker in sunny countryside, and the British Heart Foundation uses a photo of two middle-aged men on and beside a running machine in a gym, one apparently showing the other how to use the settings, thus emphasizing physical activity. The BootsWebMD story is accompanied by a thumbnail image of a family watching television. The University of Cambridge press release features a silhouette of a male, slim hill-walker striding across countryside.

The *Daily Mail* images fall out of line of the pattern we see elsewhere. Two photos are used, one of a young, slim woman, wearing a short dress and with bare shoulders and legs, curled up on a sofa reading. Unlike the BBC photo, this is not a typical couch-potato image or pose. The second photo is of two young, slim men, in business suits, walking across an urban green space, talking and smiling at one another, again not a typical 'brisk walk' image. Thus, it appears that the *Daily Mail* images have been selected more for their potential to please the eye than for their relevance to the story.

Typical features of popular science reporting

Although this is just one example and we have not examined the full text of all the articles, some features of popular science reports emerge here which have been observed in other studies and may be regarded as typical for anglophone contexts. Hyland (2010) groups several of these features together under categories of organization, argument, credibility, stance and engagement. He proposes that writers use rhetorical features to negotiate with readers what he calls 'proximity of membership' and 'proximity of commitment' (ibid.: 117). Proximity of membership refers to the way writers position themselves as disciplinary experts; it is about their relationship with their community. Proximity of commitment refers to how writers position themselves in relation to the material they present; it is about their relationship with their text. Hyland (ibid.) explores the different ways in which proximity is negotiated in professional science and in popular science. His findings in relation to English-language popular science reporting include the following observations, for which our examples above have also provided some evidence:

- The main claim is foregrounded in the headline or towards the beginning of the article, often with a background move that contextualizes the issue before the main outcome is presented.
- The novelty and importance of the topic is given more emphasis than the methodology.
- Claims for novelty rest on newsworthiness, presented in terms of breakthroughs or something of immediate or potential benefit to readers.
- Novelty is linked to assumptions about readers' interest and knowledge, rather than the research itself.

- Little attention is paid to the methods of the study; instead reporting focuses on the objects of the study.
- Writers frame information by tailoring it to readers, making connections and explicit links to what readers are assumed to know or believe already.
- Specialist terminology is avoided, and necessary terms are explained.
- Credibility and authority are conveyed through use of scientists' voices in direct quotations.
- Claims are made relatively emphatically, that is, with less hedging and tentativeness than is typical in professional science reporting.
- Attitude markers are used to indicate the writer's affective response to the material of the text or the response that the reader is expected to have.
- Writers engage readers by using pronouns to address them directly.
- Visuals are used to attract readers' attention.

Other features identified by Hyland (ibid.) as typical of popular science discourse that were not particularly relevant in this example but that we will encounter in later examples include the following:

- Similes or explicit links are used to make the unfamiliar more familiar (not a salient feature of this text, since it did not refer to unfamiliar concepts);
- Cohesive devices, including repetition, are used more than in professional science, to help clarify unfamiliar concepts;
- Questions are used by writers to create a connection with readers.

The notion of proximity is a useful one for considering the negotiation of the relationship between writers and their readers and material. However, it is important to note that these particular manifestations of proximity are based on anglophone genre conventions, rhetorical moves and linguistic features. Thus, while it might be expected that many scientific authors would wish to convey credibility and authority, this may be achieved in a variety of different ways within different discourse communities, but also within different linguistic and cultural communities.

International dissemination and translation of scientific news

Numerous services exist with the purpose of disseminating research news globally, using translation to do so multilingually; one example is AlphaGalileo (www.alphagalileo.org). International news agencies like

Reuters publish science news and, as with their other categories of news stories, these stories are often taken up by other media organizations and translated and adapted into other languages (see Bielsa and Bassnett 2008 for discussion of the mechanisms of news translation in general).

We will consider one example of a press release translated for international audiences, to illustrate some of the ways in which the genre can vary across languages and cultures. Our text comes from the University of Granada's (UoG) website, where the University's research news is published in the form of short reports or press releases in Spanish, English and French. In December 2014, a press release announced the publication of an article in the *Journal of Dental Research* (Marfil-Álvarez et al. 2014), with translations of the Spanish press release into English and French. These press releases were also published on the AlphaGalileo website in the three languages in January 2015. The Spanish ST and English translation are reproduced in Appendix 5, courtesy of the UoG.

We will focus our attention on the translation into English. It follows the structure, information content and organization of the Spanish text quite closely, and it diverges in various ways from some of the genre conventions and typical features noted in our previous examples of English-language press releases. These differences also come to light when we compare the UoG's translated press release with some anglophone news coverage of the same story. Only two aspects are discussed below, for the purpose of exemplification, although it would certainly be possible to extend the analysis further. Here we focus on the level of technicality and ways in which credibility is established.

EXCERPT 7.5

University of Granada Spanish headline: La periodontitis crónica, enfermedad inflamatoria de las encías, influye en la gravedad y en el pronóstico del infarto.
University of Granada English headline: Chronic periodontitis, an inflammatory gum disease, influences prognosis and the severity of heart attacks.

Technicality

As can be seen in Excerpt 7.5, the English headline follows the syntax of the Spanish closely and it contains a technical term which may not be understood by non-specialists, namely *chronic periodontitis*. For this reason, it is then explained in a parenthetical clause in the headline itself. This makes a rather unwieldy headline in English; it could be more effective to remove the specialist term but introduce it and explain it later (which is done, in any case, in the lead paragraph of the article). In addition, the definite article *the* before *severity* is redundant in the English headline and could be removed. Its deletion would mirror the deletion, already done, of the article *the* before *prognosis*.

By comparing the UoG press release to the available English-language news items triggered by this press release, shown as Excerpt 7.6, we can see how others have chosen to represent this research in headlines. *Pharmacy Times* is a US-based monthly journal that aims to provide practical information for pharmacists. Cosmetic Dentistry Guide is a website providing reference resources for those interested in cosmetic dentistry. The omission of articles is evident in all four headlines. It is worth noting that, despite the specialized readership expected at *Pharmacy Times*, its editor opts for *inflammatory gum disease* and *heart attack* in the headline, rather than the technical alternatives. The technical terms *periodontitis* and *myocardial infarction* are used in the *Pharmacy Times* article, along with other terms, but not in the headline. In addition, the somewhat long-winded UoG formulation of *prognosis and the severity of heart attacks* becomes a shorter *heart attack severity* in *Pharmacy Times*, or *severe heart attacks* or *risk of massive heart attacks* in the other sources. The quotation marks in the *International Business Times* headline are similar to those we saw from the BBC headline in our previous example, in that it is unclear what or who is being quoted. There is no such quotation in the news article nor in the press release. Quotation marks may simply be used to lend the text an impression of objectivity and credibility, in the same way that quotations from scientists are often used in the body of news items.

EXCERPT 7.6

University of Granada headline: Chronic periodontitis, an inflammatory gum disease, influences prognosis and the severity of heart attacks

Pharmacy Times headline: Inflammatory Gum Disease Influences Heart Attack Severity.

Cosmetic Dentistry Guide headline: New Study Links Severe Periodontal Disease to Severe Heart Attacks.

International Business Times headline: Severe gum disease 'increases risk of massive heart attacks'.

Moving on to consider the remainder of the text, we note that the UoG's press release is written with a relatively high degree of technicality. Take, for example, a section of the first paragraph which explains that the research has demonstrated that *the extent and severity of chronic periodontitis is related to the size of acute myocardial infarction through seric levels of troponin I and myoglobin (biomarkers of myocardial necrosis)*. Catering for its readership of pharmacists, the *Pharmacy Times* reuses most of this information. However, the information is slightly reordered and some repetition is introduced, thus reducing the level of specificity and technicality and increasing textual cohesion: *chronic periodontitis [. . .] was related to serum levels of 2 biomarkers indicating heart tissue death*. Thus the two biomarkers are not named at this point, and myocardial necrosis is substituted by *heart tissue death*. The two biomarkers are then named in the next sentence, and their relation with *MI necrosis* is reiterated. The staged introduction of the technical information with some repetition is likely to be helpful to readers, even those possessing specialist knowledge. This provides an example of another of the features highlighted above by Hyland (2010), namely the use of cohesive devices, including repetition, for enhanced explanation of unfamiliar concepts.

The other sources do not elaborate on this part of the research, referring only to the relation between acute myocardial infarction and periodontitis, in line with an expectation that their readers are not familiar with these scientific concepts and do not require this level of specificity. Of these sources, the publication aimed at the medically least specialized readership, the *International Business Times*, avoids the technical terms in the headline and also introduces them sparingly in the article.

Credibility

The UoG's press release is very focused on the academic context of the research. It foregrounds the publication of the article in the *Journal of Dental Research*, which it describes as *prestigious*, and it gives the full title of the academic article in the first paragraph of the press release. It devotes almost a paragraph to naming some of the authors, their departments and to describing the relationship between them (doctoral student and supervisors). All of this information figures in the English press release, which follows the Spanish closely in structure and content. As we might expect, none of this detail is reproduced in the news reports, however. Those news outlets mention only the source, that is, researchers from the UoG, with *Pharmacy Times* adding 'in Spain', presumably to avoid confusion for its US readers with the Caribbean Grenada. *Pharmacy Times* names the scientific journal but without the positive evaluation. The foregrounding of the work as an academic achievement in the press releases, rather than for its benefits or payoff, is strengthened by the inclusion of a single visual image with the press release, a group photo of some of the researchers, taken in a library or reading room. We might judge it unlikely that a news outlet would reuse this photo, since it does not relate directly to their emphasis, namely the payoff of the research. This provides us with a good example of cross-cultural variation in how the credibility of the research is established and variation in how academic reputation is valued or prioritized.

Finally we may note that two quotations from one of the researchers, Aguado, are presented in the press release. This inclusion of the scientist's voice, through direct quotation, lends credibility to the story. As such, both quotations are reproduced in the *Pharmacy Times* article, and the first one is also used in the *International Business Times*.

This partial analysis provides further examples of the features highlighted by Hyland (2010) above as typical of popular science discourse and shows how a close translation of the Spanish press release deviates considerably from what is typical for the genre in anglophone contexts. This deviation from anglophone conventions may be the reason why the news outlets chose not to reproduce several prominent features of the translated press release. As with other genres discussed, translators who are familiar with those conventions can decide on the extent to which they conform to or flout them, in the context of their commission and the communicative event in which the translation will figure.

International editions of popular science magazines

In the previous section we considered press releases and their adaptation into news reports in the same language and in other languages, often in outlets which mix science news with other news. In this section we focus on publishing outlets that are dedicated to popular science reporting and that set out to deliver multilingual editions. Popular science magazines have the scope to publish feature articles, themed dossiers and other long-form writing, as well as short news reports. Two well-known examples are *Scientific American* and *National Geographic*, both US-based and both published in multiple languages. *Scientific American* has been the subject of some analysis by translation researchers; see Shuttleworth's (2011) analysis of metaphor and Liao's (2011) study of reader–writer interaction. The translation of *National Geographic* headlines have also been analysed by Manfredi (2014).

The extent of the translation activity involved in the production of multilingual science magazines is first illustrated using the example of *National Geographic* magazine. We then trace some of the translation decisions made in relation to two *National Geographic* articles, primarily with the aim of showing how a science story, originally written for American readers, has been reframed for target readers of other languages.

National Geographic magazine and translation

The *National Geographic* magazine was first published in English in 1888 by the National Geographic Society. Local-language editions have since been added to the portfolio, with Azerbaijani becoming the 40th language edition to launch in 2014 (National Geographic Society 2014a). According to its website, the magazine, in those various editions, reaches more than 60 million readers per month. The magazine covers themes and topics related to science, nature and technology, and is particularly known for its high-quality photojournalism.

National Geographic international publishing follows a licensing model whereby a local publisher signs a partnership agreement to gain the rights to translate editorial content into a local language. *National Geographic* provides the partner publisher with editorial and marketing support and rights to use the *National Geographic* name and trademarks (National Geographic Society n.d.). As noted by the executive vice president Terry Adamson, on the launch of the Ukrainian language edition, the Society is keen to offer readers 'a magazine that speaks to them in their own language', whose 'smart localized content and photography [. . .] is relevant and engaging' to those readers (National Geographic Society 2013).

The addition of local-language editions began in the 1990s with Japanese, Spanish (two editions, for Spain and Latin America respectively), Italian, Hebrew, Greek, French, German and Polish. In the 2000s, Korean, Portuguese (two editions, for Portugal and Brazil), Danish, Swedish, Norwegian, Dutch, Chinese (traditional for Taiwan and simplified for China), Finnish, Turkish, Thai, Czech, Hungarian, Romanian, Russian, Croatian, Bahasa Indonesia, Bulgarian, Slovene, Serbian and Lithuanian were added. Since 2010, there has been further expansion, with editions also produced in Arabic, Estonian, Latvian, Georgian, Mongolian, Farsi, Ukrainian and Azerbaijani.

This licensing model has been extended to other publications in the National Geographic Society stable. For example, *National Geographic Traveler* magazine was launched in the USA in 1984, with a first local-language edition established in 2002 in China. Further editions followed for the Czech Republic, India, Indonesia, Israel, Italy, Latin America, the Netherlands, Mongolia, Poland, Romania, Russia, Spain and the UK. The 15th local-language edition launched in 2014 as *National Geographic Traveller Australia & New Zealand* (National Geographic Society 2014b). *National Geographic Kids* has 17 local-language editions (available in the USA and in Bulgaria, Egypt, Germany, Indonesia, Israel, Italy,

Lithuania, Mongolia, the Netherlands, Slovenia, South Africa (Afrikaans and English), Spain, Turkey and the UK).

Reframing of popular science discourse in translation

In this section, we illustrate how science news stories are localized and reframed in translation, to take account of the knowledge, interests and opinions of the target audience in another geographic location, and to situate the scientific discourse in the context of other public discourses. Two *National Geographic* texts and some of their translations are used for exemplification:

- Text 1, about 3-D printing technology
  - 'Just Press Print', December 2014
  - '3-D-Druck: Einfach "Drucken" drücken', December 2014
  - 'Basta Carregar na Tecla', December 2014
  - 'Alles uit de printer', December 2014
  - 'Butona Bas ve Yarat', December 2014
  - 'Drukarki 3-D: po prostu wciśnij "drukuj"', December 2014
  - '3D-skriveren revolusjonerer verden', December 2014.
- Text 2, about growing bioartificial organs for transplant
  - 'The Big Idea: Organ Regeneration. Miracle Grow', March 2011
  - 'Des organes "bioartificiels" pour les patients en attente d'une greffe', June 2013
  - 'Nachwachsende Organe: Ein Ohr, bitte!', March 2011.

Cultural specificity: place names, institutions and other proper nouns

Some research organizations, institutes, universities and multinational companies are well known internationally and are reproduced without change in other languages or are transcribed but not translated or explained. Examples in this category from Text 1 include *Harvard*, *NASA* and *Airbus*.

Proper nouns may be translated into the TL, for example, the *International Space Station* in the ST is referred to as *die Internationale Raumstation (ISS)* in German, *Estação Espacial Internacional* in Portuguese, *internationale ruimtestation (ISS)* in Dutch, *Uluslararası Uzay İstasyonu* in Turkish and *Międzynarodowej Stacji Kosmicznej* in Polish. Although this is the only reference to the International Space Station in the text, the ISS abbreviation, derived from English, is also given in German and Dutch, because readers may be familiar with it.

Organization names may be reproduced in the TT but accompanied by expansion, additional information or explanation. Taking examples from Text 1, *GE*, *Cornell University* and *the Victoria and Albert Museum* are expanded as follows in the German translation: *der Konzern General Electric (GE)*, *die Cornell-Universität in den USA*, *[das] Victoria and Albert Museum für Kunst und Design*. Likewise the Norwegian text specifies *Cornell University i USA*.

The abbreviated *GE* is not initially used but is expanded into *General Electric* in several language versions. Expansion may lead to an increase in specificity of information, for example when Amsterdam's *Buiksloter Canal* is translated as *Buiksloter Canal in Amsterdam-Nord* in German and similarly *Buiksloterkanaal in Amsterdam-Noord* in Dutch. This increase in specificity may be justified on the basis that the German and Dutch readerships may be more familiar with Amsterdam's waterways than, for example, US, Portuguese or Turkish audiences.

Institutional information may be condensed or omitted in the translation, for example, *Wake Forest Institute for Regenerative Medicine in Winston-Salem, North Carolina* in Text 2 is rendered in French as *Wake Forest Institute de médecine régénératrice (Caroline du Nord)*, thus relegating the state to appear inside brackets and omitting the name of the town in which the institute is located. Similarly, in German the name of the institute is translated and written in accordance with German compounding or hyphenation conventions and the town name is also omitted: *Wake-Forest-Institut für Regenerative Medizin in North Carolina*. In Text 1 a California firm, Solid Concepts, is rendered in German as *[e]in Unternehmen in Kalifornien*, while the Portuguese version includes the company name but omits its location. These details are given as examples of 3-D printing initiatives, and the reduction in level of specificity may be justified on the basis that it is the example of what is printed that is more relevant than who printed it or where in the USA they were located.

Text 1 makes reference to the US television science-fiction series *Star Trek*, because the author draws a comparison between the fictional capabilities of the *Starship Enterprise*'s on-board replicator to synthesize objects and the now realistic potential offered by 3-D printers. This reference is kept in the German translation, where the series is referred to by its German title, *Raumschiff 'Enterprise'*. Similarly, the Dutch translation also refers to the *Star Trek* series explicitly. However, perhaps this is less familiar to Portuguese readers, since a more general reference to the realm of science fiction is made in that translation, omitting explicit mention of *Star Trek*, the starship or the synthesizer device: *Aquilo que antes parecia saído do mundo da ficção científica*. The Turkish text also does not name the TV series, but it reminds readers of the spaceship replicator which could synthesize everything: *izleyenler hatırlayacaktır, uzay aracının replikatörü her şeyi sentezleyebiliyordu.*

Cultural specificity: measurements and currency

When texts are adapted for different readerships, it may be necessary to convert measurements of various kinds, particularly when translating between US, imperial or metric systems. Text 1 supplies us with a typical example. The printer producing construction components for the house to be built on the banks of the Buiksloter Canal in Amsterdam is described in the ST as being *a 20-foot-tall printer.* This is converted into a 3-metre tall printer in most of the translations. However, it is always possible for translators to trip up with conversions, as the Portuguese translator seems to have done, describing the printer as *uma impressora com 1,80 metros de altura.*

Currency is another area that may be converted to a more familiar system for target readers. For Text 1 the German translator has chosen not to convert dollars into another currency, but this leads to a slight mismatch between ST and TT. In the ST the printer and facilities to provide the Browning pistols cost *the better part of a million dollars*, and it is emphasized earlier in the paragraph that the manufacturing was neither simple *nor cheap.* The German text removes the reference to cost at that point and only mentions that production of this kind is not easy. The cost is then given as more than half a million dollars (*mehr als eine halbe Million Dollar*); thus the cost is played down to some extent. In the Dutch translation the cost is also given as more than half a million dollars (*ruim een half miljoen dollar*). The cost in Portuguese is *cerca de quatrocentos mil euros*, that is, around 400,000 euro, which is well short of half a million dollars at the prevailing exchange rate. We can argue that this miscalculation does not matter too much here, since the point is that it cost a lot of money. However, it does then seem incongruous to opt for a specific sum, which may be inaccurate at the time of reading, rather than a more general indication of cost, as the ST and the other translations have done.

Similes and comparison with familiar concepts

As noted by Hyland (2010) above, a typical strategy in popular science discourse to explain unfamiliar concepts is to draw comparisons with familiar concepts, using similes. In Text 1 the new 3-D printing technology, which may be unfamiliar to readers, is made more understandable and more concrete through the use of comparison and simile. Comparisons are made, for example, with buying something on iTunes and with printing using a conventional desktop printer. These comparisons work just as well in the translations as in the ST.

By contrast, a more culture-specific comparison requires a different strategy. The growing of bioartificial cells into organs is explained via simile in Text 2: *It's like baking a layer cake [. . .] You're layering the cells one layer at a time, spreading these toppings.* A similar cultural reference works well in French where the comparison is with a *mille-feuille* and its *couches.* However the German translator may not have found a cake simile helpful; in that text the new cells are simply described as being applied to or spread on the balloon scaffold.

The headline of Text 2, *Miracle Grow,* attracts the US readers' attention as a word play, because Miracle Gro is a well-known brand of plant food, thus also appealing playfully to something familiar. This headline appears with an overline, *The big idea: organ regeneration.* The US plant food reference is not used in the French or German translations. The headline and overline are combined in the German translation: *Nachwachsende Organe: Ein Ohr, bitte!* [Regenerated organs: An ear please!] with the second part performing the attention-attracting function by implying you would order an ear just as you might ask for something in a shop or café. The French headline explicates further by referring to the use of the bioartificial organs, that is, for transplant patients: *Des organes 'bioartificiels' pour les patients en attente d'une greffe.* This is an informative headline, with no attempt made at word play, humour or other attention-attracting techniques.

Relevance of information for target readers

Text 2 begins with reference to the number of people waiting for organ transplants in the USA (more than 100,000) and the number who die each day (18). This information is repeated in the French translation (although 100,000 is mistakenly reproduced as 10,000). However, this is followed by some information about the French situation, namely that 250 French people die every year due to lack of suitable organs for transplant, clearly information which will be of great interest to the French readership. The German translation goes even further in its localizing efforts. The numbers relating to the USA are omitted completely and are replaced by separate figures for the number of people waiting for kidney transplants in Germany and in Austria in 2009, the total number of transplants performed in those countries in the same year and the number remaining who did not receive a transplant.

Later, Text 2 describes how various research labs are working on growing bioartificial organs. Examples are given of a jawbone at Columbia University, a lung at Yale University, a rat heart at the University of Minnesota and a kidney at the University of Michigan. The German text replaces the examples of Columbia and Yale with an example of an Austrian scientist working in Boston on a lung. The French text includes all the US examples but also adds a reference to collaboration between Minnesota and Madrid. Both of the references to work being done in Europe or by European scientists serve to bring the issue closer to Europe-based readers.

Interaction with other public discourses

As noted in the introduction to this chapter, popular science discourse is not produced or consumed in a vacuum, and it is a misconception to think of popular science as merely serving to inform an otherwise ignorant public. Rather, readers relate this discourse to their own knowledge, opinions and beliefs, and popular scientific discourse interacts with other public discourses, whether economic, political or cultural. Some examples of this are provided by these two texts and their translations.

Text 2 refers to the potential usefulness of a stem cell bank, noting that Atala's team have shown that stem cells *can be collected without harming human embryos (and thus without political controversy) from amniotic fluid in the womb*. This is followed by a paragraph in which Atala expands on the benefits of a bank of 100,000 stem cell samples, *so that surgeons would order organs grown as needed*. The controversial nature of this idea is likely to be the reason why the French translation mentions the collection of stem cells from amniotic fluid but omits this final paragraph about growing organs to order. The German translation describes the collection of stem cells from embryos as 'ethically questionable', *ethisch bedenklich*, which is rather different from *politically controversial*, but omits all reference to a stem cell bank and Atala's wishful scenario of how it might be used. These adjustments serve to situate this discourse within the different legal and ethical frameworks of the target cultures; stem cell research regulations are less restrictive in the USA than in EU contexts.

Text 2 is accompanied by a photograph depicting the synthetic scaffold of an ear, described in the caption as *part of an effort to grow new ears for wounded soldiers*. The French translation makes similar reference to wounded soldiers (*oreilles pour les soldats blessés*). Like US soldiers, French soldiers are deployed to conflicts around the world at present, and returning injured soldiers are prominent in public discourse and consciousness. However, the German translation reads: *So sollen neue Ohren für Unfallopfer wachsen*, referring to growing new ears for 'victims of accidents', without reference to soldiers, reflecting perhaps a very different policy of military engagement in Germany and the reduced relevance of references to injured soldiers for the German readership.

Text 1 also provides us with an interesting example of the interrelationships between scientific discourse and other public discourse in their specific cultural context, and of how translators might deal with this when producing a text for another cultural context. The issue revolves around the gun culture of the USA. 3-D printing hit the international headlines in 2013, as described in Text 1, when an American, Cody Wilson, printed a handgun and test-fired it. The ST tells us it was *a single-shot, 38-caliber pistol*, called the Liberator, made out of $60 worth of plastic. The German translation also makes reference to this newsworthy event but with less technical detail about the gun, simply described as a single-shot gun (*eine einschüssige Pistole*).

The ST continues by voicing the initial but very real concerns of law-enforcement officials of the consequences of such disposable, untraceable guns being made available so easily. Since gun possession is much more strictly controlled in Germany than in the USA, the issue of traceability and law enforcement is less relevant, and the German translation instead poses a very general question about whether everyone will now be able to manufacture disposable guns. A similar generalization is made in the Dutch translation.

A later reference to the ability to print disposable guns uses US slang to refer to the gun as *a Saturday night special*. The Portuguese translator, who otherwise reproduces the same level of specificity regarding the guns which have been printed and publicized, replaces the reference to people printing a Saturday night special with a more generic reference to printing for their own projects (*imprimir os seus projectos*). This point is completely omitted by the German translator, since it seems quite specific to the US context.

These examples are useful to illustrate the cultural specificity of popular science reporting and the cultural and social embeddedness of popular scientific discourse (see Anderson 2009 for further illustration in relation to climate change debates). As we can see from this small selection of examples, these are factors that some of the *National Geographic* translators and editors are clearly aware of and take into account in their translations.

Other popular science genres and translation

Myers (2003) noted that most research on scientific popularization was done on texts, typically newspapers, and moreover that the focus of analysis was usually the words of the text, not other visual elements. He advocated more research on other genres, for example, lecture demonstrations or TV documentaries and museum exhibits.

From the perspective of translation, the scientific documentary film is one that should interest us, since many science documentaries are broadcast internationally in languages other than the SL.

Documentaries often rely predominantly on voice-over to accompany the visual and other auditory content, and this lends itself well to translation and revoicing. Thus, for example, many of the BBC nature documentaries narrated in their UK versions by David Attenborough (e.g. *Blue Planet* (2001), *The Life of Mammals* (2002), *Planet Earth* (2006), *Frozen Planet* (2011)) are sold in many countries worldwide and are broadcast with a translated script delivered by a dubbing artist or actor. In intralingual versions, these documentaries are often re-voiced in the USA by a more recognizable actor (e.g. Pierce Brosnan in *The Blue Planet*, Sigourney Weaver in *Planet Earth* and Alec Baldwin in *Frozen Planet*). Considering scientific discourse in its wider context of production, it is interesting to note the controversy surrounding the seventh and final episode of *Frozen Planet*, which the BBC sold to international broadcasters separately from the package of the first six episodes. The separate syndication of the seventh episode was reportedly because that episode, unlike the others, was presented by Attenborough in front of camera and thus did not lend itself so easily to translation via voice-over (Torrance 2011). In addition, Attenborough would not be familiar to those international audiences. However, other commentary suggested that some channels may have opted out of showing the seventh episode, called 'On Thin Ice', because it focused attention on human influence on global warming and would not be popular among climate-change sceptics (ibid.). Some US networks showed only the first six episodes, but Discovery Channel later reversed its initial decision not to broadcast the politically sensitive episode (ibid.).

Research centre websites constitute another site of translation. Most research centres now disseminate information about their own activities to the public via their websites, thus engaging in popularization of science and employing many of the techniques we have seen so far in selecting newsworthy items for dissemination and attracting readers' attention, through headlines and use of visual imagery. They make specialist knowledge accessible to non-specialists through terminological, lexical and phraseological choices, and organize scientific news in ways which stimulate the reader's interest and perform rhetorical functions for the centre, often bound up with making a case for the usefulness or applicability of the research. Some examples of research centres with bilingual or multilingual websites and a significant focus on popular science discourse (among many that could be cited) are the Centre National de la Recherche Scientifique (CNRS, ww.cnrs.fr) and the Max Planck Gesellschaft (www.mpg.de).

Another genre that is frequently translated is the popular-science book, particularly when written by well-known scientists. Many of the metadiscoursal features discussed above are also key to the success of the popular-science book, which generally aims to show the author's authority and command of the subject while also engaging the reader and communicating scientific ideas in a non-exclusionist and entertaining way.

To conclude, it is worth mentioning a range of translation activities involving popular science which are generally not undertaken as professional, paid activities, but rather by translation volunteers, who may or may not be trained translators. These kinds of activities may provide you with useful opportunities for practice during your studies. One example where scientific popularization and volunteer translation meet is the TED initiative (www.ted.com) and its TED Talks, disseminated online. These talks are described by Caliendo (2012) as a hybrid genre, like news articles in that they prioritize results over methods, and like lectures in that they are pre-planned and use multimedia resources. However, TED Talks tend towards more informality than would be typical in either of those genres, and the talks are delivered by the scientists themselves, so there is a sense of the audience having more immediate access to the scientific knowledge. Scotto di Carlo's (2014) analysis of a corpus of TED Talks draws on Hyland's (2010) notion of proximity, introduced above, to identify techniques used by the speakers to establish a relationship of proximity with the audience. An extensive volunteer translation effort goes into providing access to TED Talks for speakers of languages other than English (see Olohan 2014). However, there is little research examining how the metadiscoursal elements outlined above are dealt with in translation, that is, how translators' choices maintain, create or diminish audience engagement and relations of proximity in that multimodal context.

A final example of contexts in which popular science genres are translated by volunteer translators is citizen science. Increasingly nonscientists are becoming engaged in scientific endeavours through citizen-science initiatives, defined in various ways, and involving varying degrees of participation in the research process, from providing help with data processing or transcription to shaping research projects. See Franzoni and Sauermann (2014) for definitions and discussion of various forms of citizen science. One such initiative is Zooniverse (www.zooniverse.org). Zooniverse is 'a collection of web-based citizen science projects that use the efforts of volunteers to help researchers deal with the flood of data that confronts them'. The first Zooniverse project was Galaxy Zoo, launched in 2007, and it provides an example of how translation is used to enable people to participate in Galaxy Zoo in English, Spanish, Arabic, Italian, Polish, Russian, Portuguese, Hebrew, Hungarian, Ukrainian and Chinese (simplified and traditional). Some other projects, particularly those that require participants to interpret visual data, for example from astronomy projects, are made accessible in some other languages. Zooniverse translation is done by a small number of volunteers.

Like TED Talks or Wikipedia pages on scientific or technical topics, these kinds of citizen-science initiatives can provide you with the opportunity to become more directly involved in science communication, to gain valuable translation practice in scientific and technical domains, and to apply and extend your genre-related expertise.

Exercise 7.1: Exploring misrepresentations of science in the media

Read a selection of entries from Ben Goldacre's *Bad Science* blog (www.badscience.net) or on the US's Health News Review website (www.healthnewsreview.org) on the misrepresentation of science in the media. Based on your readings, discuss some of the perceived recurrent shortcomings of media coverage of science news.

Exercise 7.2: Producing popular science news

Select a professional science research article from a recent issue of a specialist journal, on a topic of your choice. Now imagine you want to write a short news item on this research for a selected science news website or blog, in English or another language. What are the specific challenges you would face in producing a news item for a non-specialist reader? Having discussed the difficulties, carry out the necessary research and produce the news item. If it is feasible, check whether the research generated any news coverage around the time of its publication, and compare your news story to those published by other outlets.

Exercise 7.3: Analysing reader–writer interaction

For a popular science news report and its translation, in languages of your choice, carry out a detailed analysis of the two texts, focusing on strategies of reader–writer interaction, referring back to the section on metadiscourse in Chapter 6 as well as the content of this chapter. Discuss your findings. Are the expectations of the source and target audiences likely to be different in this respect? Do the SL and TL offer different rhetorical and discursive means to negotiate the relationship between the writer, their readers and their material? Do the author's and translator's decisions reflect those differences?

Exercise 7.4: Reflecting on the socio-cultural significance of popular scientific discourse

For a scientific topic considered controversial in your country or region (e.g. hydraulic fracturing (fracking), nuclear energy, renewable energy, embryonic stem cell research, man-made climate change, evolutionary theory, specific dam or deforestation projects), find two popular science texts representing two opposing points of view. Consider how the writers construct and frame their arguments, how they link their ideas to prevailing public discourses and how they make assumptions about readers' beliefs and prior knowledge. Hypothesizing a realistic translation commission for both texts, consider how your own ideological stance could influence your translational decisions in both cases.

Exercise 7.5: Translating other popular science genres

For a popular science genre which is not a news report, design a hypothetical but realistic translation brief, carry out the necessary preparatory research and translate the text. Discuss your translation process and decisions.

Exercise 7.6: Engaging in volunteer scientific translation

If your language combinations make it feasible, find a volunteer translation initiative in scientific or technical domains to which you could contribute. As well as contributing your own translations, reflect analytically on the volunteer initiative. How is the translation activity set up and coordinated? How do translators and other collaborate? What role does technology play in the activities? What appears to motivate the translators? In what ways do you benefit from the activity?

Key points from this chapter

- Popular science genres can be regarded as scientific genres in their own right, rather than simplified versions of professional science.
- Popular science news reporting shares features with other forms of news reporting. It can also be characterized by the specific ways in which the discourse is organized, the arguments constructed and credibility conveyed, and the ways in which writers engage and interact with their readers.

- Popular science is intertwined with other public discourses. There is significant scope for science news stories to be framed and reframed for different social and cultural contexts and agendas, and translators participate in this reframing.
- Most studies of popular science discourse and translation have focused on the textual components of news and magazine articles; increasingly popular science discourse takes other forms and modes, and there is much potential for further study of how other popular science genres are translated.

References

Advisory Council on the Misuse of Drugs (2009) *MDMA ('Ecstasy'): A Review of Its Harms and Classification under the Misuse of Drugs Act 1971*, London: Advisory Council on the Misuse of Drugs.

Anderson, Alison (2009) 'Media, Politics and Climate Change: Towards a New Research Agenda', *Sociology Compass* 3(2): 166–82.

BBC News (2009) 'Minister "Appalled" by Nutt Exit', 3 November 2009, online at: http://news.bbc.co.uk/1/hi/uk_politics/8340686.stm (accessed 30 January 2015).

Bielsa, Esperança and Susan Bassnett (2008) *Translation in Global News*, London and New York: Routledge.

Caliendo, Giuditta (2012) 'The Popularisation of Science in Web-Based Genres', in Giuditta Caliendo and Giancarmine Bongo (eds) *The Language of Popularisation: Theoretical and Descriptive Models*, Bern: Peter Lang, pp. 101–32.

Dahl, Trine (2015) 'Contested Science in the Media Linguistic Traces of News Writers' Framing Activity', *Written Communication* 32(1): 39–65.

Faculty of Public Health (2010) 'Our Mission', *About Us*, online at: www.fph.org.uk/our_mission (accessed 15 January 2015).

Franzoni, Chiara and Henry Sauermann (2014) 'Crowd Science: The Organization of Scientific Research in Open Collaborative Projects', *Research Policy* 43(1): 1–20.

Hyland, Ken (2010) 'Constructing Proximity: Relating to Readers in Popular and Professional Science', *Journal of English for Academic Purposes* 9(2): 116–27.

Johnson, Alan (2009) Letter to the *Guardian*, 2 November 2009.

Liao, Min-Hsiu (2011) 'Interaction in the Genre of Popular Science', *The Translator* 17(2): 349–68.

Manfredi, Marina (2014) 'Translating Lexical and Grammatical Metaphor in Popular Science Magazines: The Case of *National Geographic (Italia)*', in Donna R. Miller and Enrico Monti (eds) *Tradurre Figure – Translating Figurative Language*, Bologna: Università di Bologna, online at: http://amsacta.unibo.it/4030/1/TradurreFigure_Volume_MillerMonti2014.pdf (accessed 15 January 2015).

Marfil-Álvarez, Rafael et al. (2014) 'Acute Myocardial Infarct Size Is Related to Periodontitis Extent and Severity', *Journal of Dental Research* 93(10): 993–8.

Myers, Greg (2003) 'Discourse Studies of Scientific Popularization: Questioning the Boundaries', *Discourse Studies* 5(2): 265–79.

National Geographic Society (2013) 'Sanoma Media Ukraine to Launch Local-Language Edition of National Geographic Magazine in April', *National Geographic Society Press Room* online at: http://press.nationalgeographic.com/2013/03/25/sanoma-media-ukraine-to-launch-ngm-in-april/ (accessed 20 January 2015).

—— (2014a) 'Garant Holding Signs On to Launch *National Geographic Magazine* in Azerbaijan in 2014', *National Geographic Society Press Room*, online at: http://press.nationalgeographic.com/2014/02/27/garant-holding-national-geographic-azerbaijan/ (accessed 20 January 2015).

—— (2014b) 'Australasian Edition of National Geographic Traveler Magazine To Launch in July in Partnership with Adventure World', National Geographic Society Press Room, online at: http://press.nationalgeographic.com/2014/05/08/australasian-edition-of-national-geographic-traveler-magazine-to-launch-in-partnership-with-adventure-world/ (accessed 20 January 2015).

—— (n.d.) 'International Publishing: Benefits of Partnership', online at: www.nationalgeographic.com/international-publishing/partnership/ (accessed 15 January 2015).

NHS (2013) 'Physical Activity Guidelines for Adults', NHS Choices, online at: www.nhs.uk/Livewell/fitness/Pages/physical-activity-guidelines-for-adults.aspx (accessed 30 January 2015).

Nutt, David J. (2009) 'Equasy–An Overlooked Addiction with Implications for the Current Debate on Drug Harms', *Journal of Psychopharmacology* 23(1): 3–5.

Olohan, Maeve (2014) 'Why Do You Translate? Motivation to Volunteer and TED Translation', *Translation Studies* 7(1): 17–33.

Royal Society (n.d.) 'Professorship for Public Engagement of Science', online at: https://royalsociety.org/grants/schemes/professorship-public-engagement/ (accessed 15 January 2015).

Scotto di Carlo, Giuseppina (2014) 'The Role of Proximity in Online Popularizations: The Case of TED Talks', *Discourse Studies* 16(4): 591–606.

Sense About Science (n.d.) 'Independent Scientific Advice: Principles for the Treatment of Independent Scientific Advice', online at: www.senseaboutscience.org/pages/independent-scientific-advice.html (accessed 30 January 2015).

Shuttleworth, Mark (2011) 'Translational Behaviour at the Frontiers of Scientific Knowledge: A Multilingual Investigation into Popular Science Metaphor in Translation', *The Translator* 17(2): 301–23.

Sleurs, Kim, Geert Jacobs and Luuk Van Waes (2003) 'Constructing Press Releases, Constructing Quotations: A Case Study', *Journal of Sociolinguistics* 7(2): 192–212.

Strobbe, Ilse and Geert Jacobs (2005) 'E-Releases: A View from Linguistic Pragmatics', *Public Relations Review* 31(2): 289–91.

Torrance, Caroline (2011) 'Majority of International Broadcasters Will Show All Frozen Planet Episodes', *BBC Worldwide Blog*, online at: http://blogs.bbcworldwide.com/2011/11/15/majority-of-international-broadcasters-will-show-all-frozen-planet-episodes/ (accessed 24 January 2015).

World Health Organization (2015) 'Factors That Contributed to Undetected Spread of the Ebola Virus and Impeded Rapid Containment', *WHO*, online at: www.who.int/csr/disease/ebola/one-year-report/factors/en/ (accessed 17 January 2015).

Appendix 1

The English instructions are reproduced here, courtesy of Lakeland (www.lakeland.co.uk) and can also be found online.

Lakeland Instruction BOOKLET
Hand Mixer Set MODEL 13653

INTRODUCTION

Thank you for choosing this stainless steel stick blender, complete with a range of accessories for blending, chopping and whisking. This powerful kitchen helper takes the time and effort out of many culinary tasks, and comes with a handy storage bag. Please take a few moments to read these instructions before using your blender for the first time, and keep them in a safe place for future reference.

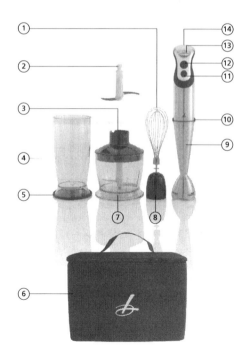

FEATURES

1. Balloon whisk
2. Chopping blade
3. Chopping bowl lid
4. 800ml blending beaker
5. Beaker base/cover
6. Storage bag
7. 500ml chopping bowl
8. Whisk collar
9. Blender stick
10. Release buttons
11. TURBO button
12. ON button
13. Speed selector
14. Power handle

Power: 800W
Operating voltage: 220-240V~50/60Hz

IMPORTANT SAFEGUARDS

When using this stick blender set, please follow these basic safety precautions.

1. Please read all instructions before using.
2. Make sure your electricity supply matches the voltage shown on the appliance.
3. This blender is for household use only. It is not suitable for commercial use, or for use outdoors. It must only be used for its intended purpose.
4. Do not let the power cord hang over the edge of the worktop or table, or touch hot surfaces, such as stovetops.
5. To avoid electric shock, do not immerse the power handle, cord or plug in water or any liquid. Please do not operate with wet hands, and never allow the cord or plug to get wet.
6. Handle the blender stick and chopping blade with care when assembling, emptying the bowl, and cleaning. Their blades are very sharp; never touch them when the blender is plugged in.
7. Make sure all parts are locked into place before switching on.
8. To prevent injury, keep fingers, hair, clothing and utensils well away from the blender stick during use. Never place your hands or any utensils inside the chopping bowl during use. If you need to scrape out the bowl, switch off and unplug the blender.
9. Let hot foods such as soup etc. cool to room temperature before blending.
10. To avoid overheating, run the blender for up to 1 minute at a time when preparing soft ingredients, or 10 seconds for hard foods.
11. Always switch off and unplug the blender before adding or removing parts, after use and before cleaning.

12. Using attachments not supplied by the manufacturer may lead to electric shock, fire or injury, and should be avoided.

13. The blender is not intended for use by children or infirm people unless they have been adequately supervised by a responsible person to ensure they can use it safely. Children should be supervised to ensure they do not play with the blender. It must not be left unattended during use.

14. Do not use the blender if the power cord or plug show any signs of damage, or if the appliance is dropped, damaged or working incorrectly. Call the helpline on 015394 88100 to arrange a repair by an authorised repairer, or a replacement. Never try to repair the blender yourself as this may cause electric shock.

BEFORE USING FOR THE FIRST TIME

Carefully unpack the blender and accessories, and remove any packaging. Take great care when handling the blender stick and chopping blade; always hold the chopping blade by its plastic spindle. Wipe the power handle and chopping bowl lid with a damp cloth, then dry. Do not immerse in water. All other parts can be cleaned in warm, soapy water, or in the dishwasher.

BLENDING

Soups, sauces, dips, mayonnaise, milkshakes and baby food can be blended in moments. Use the blending beaker, your own mixing bowl, or blend directly in a saucepan (take the pan off the heat and allow to cool first).

To prevent splashing, do not fill the blending beaker above 800ml. The beaker is supplied with an antislip base to help keep it steady on your worktop. Always keep a firm hold of the beaker, bowl or saucepan as you blend. We recommend that you begin blending at low speed, and gradually increase the speed as required.

CAUTION: before preparing baby food, always ensure the blender stick is thoroughly sterilised.

1. Making sure the blender is unplugged, push the blender stick onto the power handle; it will click into place. Plug into the mains socket.

2. Lower the blender into the food before you begin blending, to prevent splashing. Press and hold the ON button to start blending and use the speed selector dial to turn the speed up (+) or down (-). Keep a firm hold of the beaker, bowl or saucepan handle as you blend.

3. For maximum blending power, release the ON button, then press and hold the TURBO button.

4. Keep the blender upright and do not let any liquid reach the power handle. Release the ON or TURBO button at any time to stop blending. PLEASE NOTE: the blender should be used for no longer than 1 minute at a time, or 10 seconds for hard ingredients. Never blend dry ingredients without adding some liquid.

5.   Unplug the blender. To detach the blender stick for cleaning, press the two release buttons and remove the blender stick, keeping your hands well away from the blades. See CARE AND CLEANING.

WHISKING

The balloon whisk is suitable for whipping cream, egg whites, light sponge mixes and instant desserts. We recommend that you begin whisking at low speed, and gradually increase the speed as required.

1.   Firstly, assemble the whisk attachment by pushing the balloon whisk onto the whisk collar.
2.   Making sure the blender is unplugged, push the assembled whisk onto the power handle; it will click into place. Plug into the mains socket.
3.   To prevent splashing, lower the whisk into the food before you begin whisking. Press and hold the ON button to start whisking and use the speed selector dial to turn the speed up (+) or down (-). Keep a firm hold of the beaker or bowl as you whisk.
4.   For maximum whisking power, release the ON button, then press and hold the TURBO button.
5.   Keep the whisk upright and do not let liquid reach the whisk collar. Release the ON or TURBO button at any time to stop whisking. PLEASE NOTE: the whisk should be used for no longer than 2 minutes at a time.
6.   Unplug the blender. To detach the whisk for cleaning, press the two release buttons and remove the whisk. See CARE AND CLEANING.

CHOPPING

Meat, cheese, onion, fresh herbs, garlic and nuts can all be successfully chopped using the chopping bowl and blade. However, hard foods such as coffee beans, ice cubes, nutmeg and spices will damage the blade and should be avoided.

1.   Holding the chopping blade by its plastic spindle, slot the blade onto the pin in the chopping bowl. Keep fingers well away from the sharp blades.
2.   Cut your ingredients into small pieces (up to 1"/2.5cm) and add to the chopping bowl.
3.   Push the lid onto the chopping bowl, turning it clockwise to click into place. Sit the bowl on its antislip base to help keep it steady on your worktop.
4.   Fit the power handle into the lid.
5.   Plug the blender into a mains socket. Take a firm hold of the chopping bowl, then press and hold the ON button to start chopping. Use the speed selector to turn the chopping speed up (+) or down (-).
6.   For maximum chopping power, press and hold the TURBO button.
7.   Release the ON or TURBO button at any time to stop chopping. PLEASE NOTE: the chopping blade should be used for no longer than 10 seconds at a time when chopping hard ingredients.

8. When you have finished chopping, unplug the blender. Press the release buttons to detach the power handle from the lid. Be sure the blade has completely stopped before removing the lid; turn the lid anticlockwise to unlock. Carefully lift out the blade, then empty the bowl. See CARE AND CLEANING.

CHOPPING GUIDE

FOOD	MAXIMUM QUANTITY	APPROX. TIME
Meat	250g	8 secs
Fresh herbs	50g	8 secs
Walnuts	100g	8 secs
Cheese	100g	5 secs
Bread	80g (1 or 2 slices)	5 secs
Onion	150g	8 secs
Biscuits	150g	6 secs
Soft fruit	200g	6 secs

CARE AND CLEANING

Always unplug the blender before cleaning. Wipe the power handle and chopping bowl lid with a damp cloth, then dry. Do not immerse in water or any liquid.

All other parts can be washed in warm, soapy water, or in the dishwasher. Take care not to touch the sharp blades. If carrots etc. have discoloured the chopping bowl or blending beaker, rub with a cloth dipped in vegetable oil, then wash as normal.

Do not use abrasive cleaners or metal scourers as they will damage the product.

PLEASE NOTE: it is best to rinse the blades straight away after processing very salty food.

CAUTION: the blending beaker and chopping bowl are not microwave-safe.

RECYCLING YOUR ELECTRICALS

Along with many other high street retailers, Lakeland has joined a scheme whereby customers can take their unwanted electricals to recycling points set up around the country. Visit **www.recycle-more.co.uk** to find your nearest recycling point.

ELECTRICAL CONNECTIONS

THIS APPLIANCE MUST BE EARTHED

This appliance is fitted with a fused three-pin plug to BS1363 which is suitable for use in all homes fitted with sockets to current specifications. If the fitted plug is not suitable for your socket outlets, it should be cut off and carefully disposed of. To avoid an electric shock, do not insert the discarded plug into a socket.

Fitting a new plug

If for any reason you need to fit a new plug, the flexible mains lead must be connected as shown here. The wires in the mains lead fitted to this appliance are coloured in accordance with the following code:

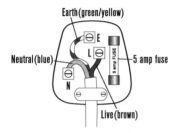

Connect BLUE to Neutral (N)
Connect GREEN & YELLOW to Earth (E)
Connect BROWN to Live (L)
5 amp fuse to be used

If the colours of the wires in the mains lead of this appliance do not correspond with the coloured markings identifying the terminals in your plug, proceed as follows. The wire which is coloured green and yellow MUST be connected to the terminal which is marked with the letter E (Earth) or coloured green. The wire which is coloured blue MUST be connected to the terminal which is marked with the letter N (Neutral) or coloured black. The wire which is coloured brown MUST be connected to the terminal which is marked with the letter L (Live) or coloured red.

Before refitting the plug cover, check that there are no cut or stray strands of wire inside the plug. Use a 5 amp BS1362 fuse. Only BSI or ASTA approved fuses should be used. If you are at all unsure which plug or fuse to use, always refer to a qualified electrician.

Note: after replacing or changing a fuse on a moulded plug which has a fuse cover, the cover must be refitted to the plug; the appliance must not be used without a fuse cover. If lost, replacement fuse covers can be obtained from an electrical shop. This appliance complies with the following EC Directives: 2006/95/EC (Low Voltage Directive) and 2004/108/EC (EMC Directive).

Appendix 2

This Technical Data Sheet is reproduced here, courtesy of James Hardie Building Products Ltd.

HardieBacker® CEMENT BACKERBOARD FOR TILE AND STONE — **TECHNICAL DATA SHEET**

WATER RESISTANT

MOULD RESISTANT

STRONGEST ON MARKET

EASY TO INSTALL

Description

HardieBacker® Cement Backerboard for tile and stone is a unique, cement based water resistant tile backerboard that can be used on walls, floors and countertops. HardieBacker® has high flexural and compressive strength, resulting in a superior tile bonding surface whilst adding value with its Mouldblock™ Technology.

Physical Properties

SPECIFICATIONS	HardieBacker® EZ Grid® 6mm		HardieBacker® 12mm
Dimensions	1500 x 900 x 6 mm	1200 x 800 x 6 mm	1200 x 800 x 12 mm
Weight	12.5 kg	9 kg	13.8 kg
Reaction to Fire	A1, S1-d0		A1, S1-d0

Basic Composition

Portland cement, sand, cellulose and selected additives. HardieBacker® Cement Backerboard for tile and stone doesn't contain asbestos, gypsum, glass fibre or formaldehyde.

Approved Products

- HardieBacker® Cement Backerboard for tile and stone has been evaluated by the BBA and approved with certificate no. 04/4100.
- The products meet the European standard for fibre cement - EN 12467 and its reaction to fire, in accordance with EN 13501-1, is A1,S1-d0. The product is therefore classified as fully non-combustible.
- HardieBacker® Cement Backerboard for tile and stone is covered by a **10-year limited product warranty**.

Health and safety

James Hardie® products contain respirable crystalline silica. During installation, use score and snap technique. During clean up use HEPA vacuums or wet cleanup methods. For further information, refer to our installations instructions and Material Safety Data Sheet (MSDS) available at: www.jameshardie.co.uk

HardieBacker® EZ Grid® 6mm Cement Backerboard for Tile and Stone

	General Property	Test Method	Unit or Characteristic	Requirement	Result
Physical Attributes	Dimensional Tolerances	EN 12467	Length	± 0.5%	Pass
		EN 12467	Width	± 5 mm	Pass
		EN 12467	Thickness	± 6%	Pass
	Weight		kg/m²	As reported	9.25
	Apparent density	EN 12467	Saturated, kg/m²	As reported	1300
	Water Impermeability	EN 12467	Physical Observations	No drop formation	Pass
	Compressive Strength	ASTM D2394			48 Mpa
	Flexural Strength	EN 12467	Equilibrium conditioned, MPa	> 10 MPa	Pass
	Category, class	EN 12467		As reported	NT Category C Class 2, level 3
Durability	Warm Water Resistance	EN 12467			Pass
	Heat/Rain Resistance	EN 12467			Pass
	Freeze/Thaw Resistance	EN 12467			Pass
	Soak/dry Resistance	EN 12467			Pass
Fire	Surface Burning Characteristics	EN13501-1	Fuel Contributed	As reported	A1
		EN13501-1	Smoke Development Index (SDI)	As reported	s1
		EN13501-1	Flames Droplets Index	As reported	d0
		EN13501-1	Euroclass	As reported	A1
	Combustibility		Suitable where non-combustible materials are specified in accordance with local building regulations.		
Thermal	Coefficient of Thermal Conductivity	EN 12667	k-value	As reported	0.19 W/(mK)
	Coefficient of Thermal Resistance	EN 12667	r-value	As reported	0.029 m².K/W
Weight capacity	Tile weight carrying capacity		kg/m²	As reported	100kg/m² *

* Please contact JH technical department when considering application of heavy tiles

PREVENTS
MOISTURE DAMAGE
MOULD GROWTH &
TILE FAILURE

 **JamesHardie**   www.jameshardie.co.uk

HardieBacker® 12mm Cement Backerboard for Tile and Stone

	General Property	Test Method	Unit or Characteristic	Requirement	Result
Physical Attributes	Dimensional Tolerances	EN 12467	Length	± 0.5%	Pass
		EN 12467	Width	± 5 mm	Pass
		EN 12467	Thickness	± 6%	Pass
	Weight		kg/m²	As reported	13.7
	Apparent density	EN 12467	kg/m³	As reported	1140
	Water Impermeability	EN 12467	Physical Observations	No drop formation	Pass
	Compressive Strength	ASTM D2394			45 Mpa
	Flexural Strength	EN 12467	Equilibrium conditioned, MPa	> 10 MPa	Pass
	Category, class	EN 12467		As reported	NT Category C Class 2, level 3
Durability	Warm Water Resistance	EN 12467			Pass
	Heat/Rain Resistance	EN 12467			Pass
	Freeze/Thaw Resistance	EN 12467			Pass
	Soak/dry Resistance	EN 12467			Pass
Fire	Surface Burning Characteristics	EN13501-1	Fuel Contributed	As reported	A1
		EN13501-1	Smoke Development Index (SDI)	As reported	s1
		EN13501-1	Flames Droplets Index	As reported	d0
		EN13501-1	Euroclass	As reported	A1
	Combustibility	Suitable where non-combustible materials are specified in accordance with local building regulations.			
Thermal	Coefficient of Thermal Conductivity	EN 12667	k-value	As reported	0.19 W/(mxK)
	Coefficient of Thermal Resistance	EN 12667	r-value	As reported	0.068 m² K/W
Weight Capacity	Tile weight carrying capacity		kg/m²	As reported	100kg/m² *

* Please contact JH technical department when considering application of heavy tiles

Applications

- HardieBacker® Cement Backerboard for tile and stone is intended as an internal substrate for tiling in residential and commercial properties. It is a water resistant board and can be used in wet areas in both new build and renovation.
- HardieBacker® Cement Backerboard for tile and stone is suitable for use in domestic steam rooms, saunas, swimming pool surrounds and changing areas.
- HardieBacker® Cement Backerboard for tile and stone can be used as backing for new domestic boilers.
- HardieBacker® Cement Backerboard for tile and stone can be used with multi-fuel or log burning stove installations as a reference plate or a decorative non-combustible lining sheet. * This installation is for masonry applications only. It is not to be used as a fire protection board.

How to install **Hardie**Backer® Cement Backerboard for Tile and Stone

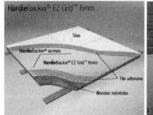
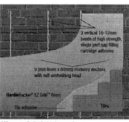

* Masonry application for interior use only.

Tel 0800 068 3103
Fax 0800 917 5424
info.europe@jameshardie.com

James Hardie Building Products Limited
7 Albermarle Street
LONDON W1S 4HQ
UNITED KINGDOM

JamesHardie   C E BBA   DO IT ONCE, DO IT RIGHT.™

Appendix 3

(19) Europäisches Patentamt
European Patent Office
Office européen des brevets

(11) **EP 0 916 952 B1**

(12) **EUROPEAN PATENT SPECIFICATION**

(45) Date of publication and mention
of the grant of the patent:
01.01.2014 Bulletin 2014/01

(51) Int Cl.:
G01N 35/04 (2006.01)   *G01N 35/02* (2006.01)

(21) Application number: **98121460.4**

(22) Date of filing: **11.11.1998**

(54) **Conveyor system for clinical test apparatus**

Fördersystem für Gerät für klinische Tests

Système de transport pour dispositif pour essais cliniques

(84) Designated Contracting States:
AT BE CH DE DK ES FI FR GB GR IE IT LI LU MC NL PT SE

(30) Priority: **14.11.1997 US 970549**

(43) Date of publication of application:
19.05.1999 Bulletin 1999/20

(73) Proprietor: **Siemens Healthcare Diagnostics Inc.**
Tarrytown, NY 10591 (US)

(72) Inventors:
• **Van Dyke Jr., Bingham Hood**
Gilbertsville, PA 19525 (US)
• **Barra, John Louis**
Glendora, New Jersey 08029 (US)

• **Hatcher, Thomas James**
Malver, PA 19355 (US)
• **Campanelli, Michael John**
Mahopac, New York 10541 (US)

(74) Representative: **Maier, Daniel Oliver et al**
Siemens AG
Postfach 22 16 34
80506 München (DE)

(56) References cited:
WO-A-95/03548   WO-A-96/25712
AT-B- 393 257   US-A- 4 798 095

Remarks:
The file contains technical information submitted after the application was filed and not included in this specification

EP 0 916 952 B1

Description

BACKGROUND OF THE INVENTION

[0001] This invention relates to conveyor devices for transporting biological material in containers to clinical test apparatus and more particularly to a conveyor system with a main transport lane for all containers to be tested and individual sidebar lanes associated with different clinical test apparatus, and traffic control gates at each sidebar lane for diverting separate groups of containers to their corresponding clinical test apparatus. The invention further relates to a system for supporting utility installations for the conveyor and its associated traffic control gates.

[0002] The term "clinical testing" is intended to refer to hematological tests, tests relating to immunoassay, toxicology, urinalysis and any other specific category of testing performed on biological or body material such as blood, serum, and urine for example. The clinical testing of blood, serum, urine or other body fluid provides invaluable information relative to the health status of an individual and clinical test results are commonly used for diagnostic evaluation, surgical decision making and the recognition of when a change or changes have occurred in a patient's health status.

[0003] Clinical testing often involves esoteric and costly procedures that must produce quality information with a high degree of accuracy. As new clinical tests are conceived and conventional clinical tests are improved, the expanding pool of information that is obtainable from various clinical tests must be weighed against the cost of obtaining such information. By reducing the cost of clinical tests, such tests can have the widest possible availability to those individuals who would benefit most from the tests.

[0004] One known way of reducing the costs for clinical testing is to perform such tests automatically and as quickly as possible. Thus diverse clinical test apparatus have been developed which operate independently of each other to perform different types of specialized tests with a minimal amount of personnel. The tests are usually performed on fluid samples that are contained in sample tubes, although other containment formats are also used, especially when the test material is not in fluid form.

[0005] However separate personnel and supervision teams are generally required to oversee each individual clinical test apparatus and separate work areas are often required for each specific category of clinical test apparatus. Thus, a laboratory which is engaged in diverse clinical testing procedures would require a relatively large facility space to accommodate the separate clinical test apparatus.

[0006] In a further attempt to reduce operating costs for clinical testing a common transport system has been developed to automatically deliver test material containers such as sample tubes to a variety of otherwise unrelated and independent clinical test apparatus. Such transport system includes a conveyor adapted to run along a predetermined travel path with different, unrelated clinical test apparatus located along the travel path of the conveyor. Each of the clinical test apparatus is adapted to operate on a common sample tube that is transported by the conveyor system.

[0007] The known conveyor systems for delivering sample tubes to different clinical apparatus are usually custom built for the particular needs of a test laboratory. In many instances the construction of conveyor systems for clinical test apparatus require dedicated installations of electrical power supply, plumbing service, vacuum and pressure service. Thus the known conveyor systems usually have the character of custom design, permanency and inflexibility once they are installed.

[0008] In WO 96/25712 a conveyor system with a main line and a spur line is disclosed. This conveyor system, however, does not offer the possibility to detachably fasten further auxiliary conveyors to the main line.

[0009] It is thus desirable to provide a conveyor system for clinical testing of biological materials in containers, which conveyor system can be constructed with modular stations for each clinical test apparatus, with simplified installations for plumbing, electricity, vacuum and pressure service that do not require ground, wall or ceiling installation.

OBJECTS AND SUMMARY OF THE INVENTION

[0010] Among the several objects of the invention may be noted the provision of a novel conveyor system for clinical test apparatus, a novel conveyor system that has a main transport lane and one or more auxiliary lanes corresponding to each clinical apparatus, a novel conveyor system for clinical test apparatus wherein auxiliary transport lanes are provided alongside main transport lanes for side by side movement of sample tubes on a main transport lane and on an auxiliary transport lane, a novel conveyor system for clinical test apparatus including a main transport conveyor and a plurality of separately run auxiliary conveyors, and wherein each auxiliary conveyor is associated with a separate clinical test apparatus, a novel conveyor system wherein each auxiliary conveyor is provided with traffic control gates including a diverter gate and an interface gate wherein the diverter gate selectively diverts sample tubes from the main transport conveyor to the auxiliary conveyor and the interface gate controls return of the diverted sample tubes to the main transport conveyor, a novel conveyor system for clinical test apparatus that also carries its own utility service lines such as electrical, plumbing, pressure and vacuum lines, a novel system for supporting the utility service lines, a novel conveyor system for clinical test apparatus wherein the main transport conveyor is separately driven by one motor while the auxiliary transport conveyors are each driven by separate motors, and novel gates for directing sample tubes to selected clinical apparatus for testing or other functional purpose.

[0011] Other objects and features of the invention will be in part apparent and in part pointed out hereinafter. These objects are met by the conveyor system according to claim 1.

[0012] In accordance with the present invention, the conveyor system for clinical test apparatus includes a main transport conveyor that defines a closed circuit travel path. The closed circuit travel path permits objects that remain on the conveyor to repeat the travel path when the conveyor moves in one direction. The main transport conveyor has straight line paths and curved paths. The conveyor system also includes a plurality of auxiliary conveyors that define a straight line travel path. The auxiliary conveyors, which are arranged in series with one another are located alongside the straight line travel paths of the main transport conveyor. Each auxiliary conveyor transports an object from one end of the auxiliary conveyor to the other end without retracing any point of travel when the auxiliary conveyor is moving in one direction, which is normally the same direction as the main transport conveyor.

[0013]   Each of the auxiliary conveyors is controlled by separate motors or drive means that are preferably independent of the motor or drive means for the main transport conveyor. In this manner the auxiliary conveyors can be arranged as modules alongside the main transport conveyor.

[0014]   Separation means are provided between the main transport conveyor and the auxiliary conveyor except at predetermined intersections between the main transport conveyor and the auxiliary conveyor. Such intersections are defined by gate controlled crossover openings that permit diversion of sample tubes from the main transport conveyor to the auxiliary conveyor and vice versa.

[0015]   One of the gate openings is controlled by a divert gate device which has actuatable diversion means for diverting movement of objects on the main transport conveyor to the auxiliary conveyor. The diversion means has one position that blocks off the flow of traffic on the main transport conveyor and at the same time directs such traffic to the auxiliary conveyor. The diversion means has another position

that does not interfere with traffic on the main transport conveyor and thus permits such traffic to bypass the auxiliary conveyor.

[0016]   Another crossover opening that provides a direct flow path from the auxiliary conveyor to the transport conveyor is controlled by an interface gate device that is located upstream of the crossover opening. The interface gate device as well as the divert gate device cooperate with label readers for the sample tubes. The sample tubes are thus rotated at each gate device to enable the label reader to obtain a reading of the sample tube label.

[0017]   A clinical test apparatus or other functional device which operates on the sample tubes is associated with each auxiliary conveyor. Thus one auxiliary conveyor can be associated with a load and unload station for the sample tubes. Other auxiliary conveyors are respectively associated with different clinical test apparatus that perform different categories of tests on sample tubes.

[0018]   If a sample tube is to be tested by a specific clinical test apparatus the system programming and the information on the individual sample tube label will cause activation of the gates in a manner which will direct the sample tube to the intended clinical test apparatus while enabling sample tubes that are not intended to be tested by a clinical test apparatus to bypass the auxiliary conveyor associated with that clinical test apparatus. Thus the sample tubes will go only to a clinical test apparatus that is to perform a required test on the sample tube.

[0019]   Sample tubes are unloaded from pucks when they are to be tested by a clinical test apparatus. The empty puck is reloaded with another sample tube that is exiting from the test apparatus. Thus the puck remains on the conveyor during unloading and reloading of sample tubes. The unloading and reloading of the pucks is accomplished by a robotic device that forms no part of the present invention.

[0020] Although the main transport conveyor and the auxiliary transport conveyors are separately driven and each clinical test apparatus operates independently of the other clinical test apparatus, the movement of all sample tubes and the operation of all the gates in the conveyor system is governed by a single process control means such as a computer.

[0021] Columns which support the conveyor system also support utility service for the conveyor system such as electrical lines, plumbing lines, air pressure lines and vacuum lines. The installation of such utility lines above ground and on the conveyor columns facilitates servicing and construction of the conveyor system.

[0022] The invention accordingly comprises the constructions hereinafter described, the scope of the invention being indicated in the claims.

DESCRIPTION OF THE DRAWINGS

[0023]   In the drawings,

Fig. 1 is a simplified schematic plan view of a conveyor system incorporating the present invention;

Fig. 2 is an enlarged simplified schematic plan view hereof with a reduced number of auxiliary conveyors;

Fig. 3 is a front elevational view thereof;

Fig. 4 is a sectional view thereof taken on the line 4-4 of Fig. 3;

Fig. 5 is an enlarged schematic plan view of a divert gate device employed in the conveyor system;

Fig. 6 is an enlarged schematic plan view of an interface gate device employed in the conveyor system;

Fig. 7 is a sectional view taken on the line 7-7 of Fig. 6;

Fig. 8 is a sectional view taken on the line 8-8 of Fig. 6;

Fig. 9 is a fragmentary elevational view of the support structure for the conveyor system;

Fig. 10 is a sectional view taken on the line 10-10 of Fig. 9;

Fig. 11 is a sectional view taken on the line 11-11 of Fig. 9;

Fig. 12 is a perspective view of the utility support system of the conveyor incorporating a further embodiment of the invention;

Fig. 13 is a fragmentary elevation view from the left side of Fig. 12;

Fig. 14 is an end view thereof, showing the utilities in a cabinet, with portions of the cabinet broken away;

Fig. 15 is an opposite end view thereof, on a reduced scale, showing the utilities below a drip pan of the conveyor;

Fig. 15A is an enlarged fragmentary detail partly shown in section of the structure shown in Fig. 15;

Fig. 16 is a top end view of a support column or stanchion of the utility support system;

Figs. 17 and 18 are fragmentary perspective views thereof showing adjustable securement members being joined to the support column to support the utility structure shown in Fig. 12;

Fig. 19 is a pictorial view of the utility structure supported on the support columns;

Fig. 20 is an enlarged schematic plan view of an interface gate incorporating another embodiment of the invention;

Fig. 21 is a sectional view thereof taken on the line 21-21 of Fig. 20;

Fig. 22 is a perspective view thereof;

Fig. 23 is an enlarged schematic plan view of a divert gate incorporating a further embodiment of the invention; and,

Fig. 24 is a side elevation thereof, partly shown in section.

[0024] Corresponding reference characters indicate corresponding parts throughout the several views of the drawings.

DETAILED DESCRIPTION OF THE INVENTION

[0025] A conveyor system for clinical test apparatus incorporating one embodiment of the invention is generally indicated by the reference number 10.

[0026] Referring to Fig. 1 the conveyor system 10 includes a main transport conveyor 12 defining a closed circuit travel path in a generally horizontal plane. The closed circuit travel path permits objects that remain on the conveyor 12 to repeat the path of travel when the conveyor 12 is moving in one direction. The closed circuit travel path includes two straight line paths 16 and 18 and two curved paths 22 and 24 at respective opposite ends of the straight line paths 16 and 18.

[0027] An auxiliary conveyor 30, which has a straight line travel path, is positioned alongside and parallel to the straight line travel path 16 of the main transport conveyor 12. The straight line travel path of the auxiliary conveyor permits objects

on the conveyor 30 to move from one point to another without retracing any point of travel when the conveyor 30 is moving in one direction.

[0028] The auxiliary conveyor 30 is associated with a load and unload station 40 that represents an initial and final transport point for sample tubes 106. Robots (not shown) at the station 40 remove tested sample tubes 106 from the conveyor 30 and replaces them with new sample tubes 106 to be tested. An auxiliary conveyor 32 is associated with a clinical test apparatus station 42 which performs a specific category of tests on a sample tube 106. Additional auxiliary conveyors 34, 36, 38 and 39, similar to the conveyors 30 and 32 are also provided alongside and parallel to the straight line paths 16 and 18 of the conveyor 12 in series with the auxiliary conveyors 30 and 32. Each auxiliary conveyor 34, 36, 38 and 39 is associated with a clinical test apparatus station such as 44, 46, 48 and 49 that perform separate and distinct categories of clinical tests. However the auxiliary conveyors 30-39 associated with the different stations 40-49 are generally similar in operation and construction.

[0029] The main transport conveyor 12 is arranged to run in a counterclockwise direction, although the direction of travel is a matter of choice. The auxiliary conveyor 30, and all other auxiliary conveyors 32-39 preferably run in the same direction as the main transport conveyor 12. The auxiliary conveyor 30, which has an upstream end 50 and a downstream end 52, travels in a generally horizontal plane that is preferably coplanar with the travel plane of the main transport conveyor 12. Pairs of gate devices 160 and 170 are provided on the conveyor system 10 between opposite ends 50 and 52 of any of the auxiliary conveyors 30-39. [0030] For purposes of clarity, reference will be made to a simplified conveyor system as shown in Fig. 2 which has the same operating structures as the conveyor system 10 of Fig. 1, but is more clearly illustrated on a larger scale than that of Fig. 1. [0031] The main transport conveyor 12 includes a known conveyor belt 60. The conveyor belt 60 defines a main transport lane also indicated by the reference number 60 since the main transport lane is the path traveled by objects on the conveyor belt 60. The conveyor belt 60 is bordered at opposite sides by edge walls 68 and 70 that are generally mirror images of each other. The edge walls 68 and 70 include ledge portions 76 and 78 (Fig. 4) located at a predetermined height above the conveyor belt 60 and projecting over the conveyor belt 60. The ledge portions 76 and 78 cooperate with the conveyor belt 60 to form a vertical confinement for generally cylindrical sample tube pucks 100 that travel on the conveyor belt 60 and hold a sample tube 106, which can be of different heights and diameter within a predetermined size range such as approximately 13 to 16 mm in diameter and 75 to 100 mm in height. [0032] The puck 100 includes resilient biasing means 104 (Fig. 6) which apply a slight retention force on the sample tube 106. The puck 100 maintains a stable positioning of the sample tube 106 as the conveyor belt 60 transports the puck 100 from one location to another along the conveyor belt travel path. The biasing mean 104 in the puck 100 permits removal and replacement of the sample tube 106 in the

puck 100 as often as is necessary. As used herein the term sample tube 106 is generally intended to include the puck 100 which holds the sample tube 106, unless otherwise indicated.

[0033] The auxiliary conveyor 30 includes a known conveyor belt 120. The conveyor belt 120 defines a sidebar lane also indicated by the reference number 120 since the sidebar lane is the path traveled by objects on the conveyor belt 120. The conveyor belt 120 is bordered on opposite sides by edge walls 128 and 130 (Fig. 4) similar to the edge walls 68 and 70. The edge walls 128 and 130 include ledge portions 136 and 138 which perform the same function as the ledge portions 76 and 78.

[0034] As most clearly sown in Fig. 4 the edge walls 70 and 130 are located adjacent each other between the edge walls 68 and 128. The adjacent edge walls 70 and 130 function as a separation or segregation means between the main transport lane 60 and the sidebar lane 120. The adjacent edge walls 70 and 130 include a sidebar entrance opening 146 (Fig. 2) proximate the upstream end 50 of the auxiliary conveyor 30 and a sidebar exit opening 148 proximate the downstream end 52 of the auxiliary conveyor 30. The entrance opening 146 and the exit opening 148 are also referred to as traffic intersections that are controlled by the gate devices 160 and 170.

[0035] The gate device 160, which is also referred to as a divert gate, is provided at the edge wall 68 of the transport conveyor 12 in substantial alignment with the sidebar entrance opening 146 at the upstream end 50 of the auxiliary conveyor 30. The gate device 170 which is also referred to as an interface gate is provided alongside the edge wall 128 of the auxiliary conveyor 30 a short distance upstream of the sidebar exit opening 148.

[0036] In order to efficiently control puck traffic at the intersections 146 and 148 between the main transport lane 60 and any of the sidebar lanes 120 the gate devices 160 and 170 must obtain a reading of information pertaining to each sample tube 106 passing through the gate device. Subsequent action on the sample tube 106 including a determination of the travel path, and the unloading and/or loading of the sample tubes 106 in the pucks 100 will be based on the information that is read from the sample tube 106 at the gates 160 and 170.

[0037] Each sample tube 106 is a reservoir of sample fluid that is later extracted or withdrawn from the sample tube at the clinical test apparatus in selected quantities for whatever tests are to be performed by one or more clinical test apparatus. Each sample tube 106 thus includes a label 108 (Fig. 7) with information relating to the identity of the individual supplying the test sample, the type of fluid in the sample tube and the type of test or tests that are to be performed on the material contained in the sample tube, hereinafter referred to as the label information. Under this arrangement each sample tube 106 is uniquely distinguishable from other sample tubes and can be individually identified. The label 108 applied to the sample tube 106 is preferably in a machine readable format such as a known bar code that can be automatically read or interpreted in a known manner by a known label reading device.

[0038] Thus a label reader device at the gates 160 and 170 will read the sample tube label and communicate the label information to a system control computer (not shown) that governs all processing operations performed by the conveyor system 10 and also governs the acceptance of the sample tubes 106 by the respective clinical test apparatus. The process control computer thus retains the label information and process activity information for each sample tube 106. This information is specifically used to control the gate devices 160 and 170 to direct the sample tube 106 to the appropriate clinical test apparatus in accordance with known programming techniques.

[0039] With regard to the control of puck traffic at the auxiliary conveyor 30, the divert gate 160 (Fig. 5) includes three pneumatically controlled plunger devices 180, 182 and 184 of known construction supported on a gate housing 186. The plunger devices 180 and 182 respectively include retractable fingers 192 and 194, and the plunger device 184 includes a retractable divert head 196 with an inclined surface 198. A puck rotating mechanism 190 is provided on the gate housing 186 between the plunger devices 180 and 182 to rotate the puck 100 and the sample tube 106 to allow the sample tube label 108 to be read by a known label scanner or reader device 200 (Fig. 7) shown at the gate 170 but also provided at the gate 160.

[0040] When the respective fingers 192 and 194 of the plunger devices 180 and 182 are in a protracted position as shown in Fig. 5 the combination of the plunger devices 180 and 182 with the puck rotating mechanism 190 constitute a singulator device that enables the label reader device 200 to read the label of one sample tube 106 at a time. The retractable fingers 192 and 194 are spaced apart a distance slightly larger than the puck diameter to permit the puck rotating mechanism 190 to rotate the puck 100 between the protracted fingers 192 and 194.

[0041] The puck rotating mechanism 190, which can be automatically controlled in a known manner for slight lateral movement toward and away from the main transport lane 60, includes a puck contacting belt 206 driven by wheels 208 and 210. Then a singulated sample tube 106 has been read by the reader device 200, the finger 194 retracts to permit the singulated sample tube 106 to move toward the plunger device 184. The finger 192 remains protracted to hold back the non-singulated sample tubes 106. The protracted or retracted position of the divert head 196 will determine whether the singulated sample tube 106 stays on the main transport lane 60 or is diverted to the sidebar lane 120. Retracted positions of the fingers 192, 194 and the divert head 196 are shown dotted in Fig. 5.

[0042] If all testing has been completed for the singulated sample tube 106 the divert head 196 (Fig. 5) will be protracted to block off the main transport lane 60. The singulated sample tube 106 will thus be diverted to the sidebar lane 120 of the auxiliary conveyor 30, which leads to the load/unload station 40. Completely tested singulated sample tube 106 will travel on the sidebar lane 120 to the interface gate 170. If further testing is required for the singulated sample tube 106 the divert head 196 will be retracted to enable the sample tube 106 to remain on the main transport lane

60 and thereby bypass the auxiliary conveyor 30 and the load/unload station 40.

[0043] When another sample tube 106 is to be singulated for label reading at the divert gate 160 the finger 194 is protracted and the finger 192 is retracted to permit the line of sample tubes 106 to proceed to the finger 194. The finger 192 is then protracted to singulate the next sample tube 106.

[0044] The interface gate 170 (Fig. 6) includes three pneumatically controlled plunger devices 220, 222 and 224 of known construction supported on a gate housing 226. The plunger devices 220, 222 and 224 respectively include retractable fingers 232, 234 and 236. Retracted positions of the fingers 232, 234 and 236 are shown dotted in Fig. 6.

[0045] One puck rotating mechanism 242, similar to the puck rotating mechanism 190 is supported on the gate housing 226 between the plunger devices 220 and 222 and another puck rotating mechanism 244, similar to the puck rotating mechanism 190 is supported on the gate housing 226 between the plunger devices 222 and 224. The combination of the plunger devices 220 and 222 with the puck rotating mechanism 242 constitute a singulator device that enables the label reader device 200 at the gate 170 (Fig. 7) to read the label 108 of one sample tube 106 at a time, in the same manner as described for the singulator device at the divert gate 160.

[0046] The completely tested sample tube 106 is thus lined up with other sample tubes 106 behind the protracted finger 234 of the plunger device 222 at the interface gate 170 while the finger 232 of the plunger device 220 is retracted. The retracted finger 232 of the plunger device 220 is then protracted to singulate sample tube 106, wherein the sample tube 106 is confined between the fingers 232 and 234 for rotation by the puck rotating mechanism 242. The label 108 (Fig. 7) on the rotating sample tube 106 is read by the reader device 200. The processor system control computer (not shown) that is linked to each of the label reader devices 200 maintains a history of the test activity for each and every sample tube 106 and a record of all testing not yet performed on any sample tube.

[0047]   If there is a confirmation at the interface gate 170 that all testing has been completed for a singulated sample tube 106 as determined during the label reading operation at the puck rotating mechanism 242, then the sample tube 106 is withdrawn from the puck 100 by a robot (not shown) while the puck 100 is singulated at the puck rotating mechanism 242. The unloaded puck 100 with exposed biasing spring 104 (Fig. 6) remains on the auxiliary conveyor 30 due to the vertical confinement provided by the ledges 136 and 138 (Fig. 4) at the conveyor edge portions 128 and 130.

[0048]   The unloaded puck 100 (Fig. 6) is then allowed to pass beyond the singulation point by retraction of the finger 234. The unloaded puck 100 is held from further movement by the protracted finger 236 at the plunger device 224. A robot (not shown) places a new sample tube 106 in the unloaded puck 100 while the puck is restrained by the finger 236. The new sample tube 106 in the reloaded puck 100 is rotated by the rotating mechanism 244 to permit an initial reading of test instructions and

sample identification from the label of the new sample tube 106. The rotating mechanisms 242 and 244 can have separate drive means or be commonly driven from a single drive means.

[0049] The finger 236 of the interface gate 170 is then retracted to permit the new sample tube 106 to proceed through the sidebar exit opening 148 (Fig. 2) to transfer from the sidebar lane 120 of the auxiliary conveyor 30 to the main transport lane 60. Other pucks 100 that are lined up for singulation at the interface gate 170 of the auxiliary conveyor 30 are similarly processed for reading of their respective sample tube labels. Thus, sample tubes 106 at the interface gate 170 of the auxiliary conveyor 30 will be unloaded if their testing is completed or allowed to pass beyond the gate 170 if further testing is indicated by the label reader 200.

[0050] The newly loaded sample tubes 106 and the older retained sample tubes 106 that still require further testing pass through the interface gate 170 (Fig. 2) at the load/unload station 40 and exit at the exit opening 148 from the auxiliary conveyor 30 to the main transport lane 60. The main transport lane 60 carries the sample tubes 106 to the divert gate 160 at the intersection of the auxiliary conveyor 32 and the main transport lane 60. The sample tubes 106 are initially held in line at the divert gate 160 by the protracted finger 194 (Fig. 5). The sample tubes 106 are then singulated for label reading in a manner similar to that previously described for the divert gate 160 at the auxiliary conveyor 30.

[0051]   When the label of a singulated sample tube 106 has been read the process computer receives the information and will cause the plunger device 184 to protract the divert head 196 if the sample tube 106 is to be tested by the clinical apparatus 42 that is associated with the auxiliary conveyor 32. Protraction of the divert head 196 will block off the main transport lane 60 and direct the sample tube 106 onto the sidebar lane 120 of the auxiliary conveyor 32.

[0052] If the label for the sample tube 106 at the divert gate 160 of the auxiliary conveyor 32 indicates that the sample tube 106 is not to be tested by the clinical apparatus associated with the auxiliary conveyor 32 the process control computer will cause the divert head 196 to be retracted. With the divert head 196 in a retracted position the sample tube 106 will continue to travel on the main transport lane 60 thereby bypassing the auxiliary conveyor 32 and the clinical apparatus 42.

[0053] Assuming the sample tube 106 is to be tested at the clinical apparatus 42 such sample tube 106 will be diverted onto the sidebar lane 120 which moves the sample tube 106 to the interface gate 170. The sample tube 106 is held in line at the interface gate 170 by the protracted finger 234 (Fig. 6) which holds sample tube 106 and other sample tubes 106 in line for singulation and label reading in a manner as previously described with respect to the interface gate 170 at the auxiliary conveyor 30. Label reading at the interface gate 170 is used to confirm that the sample tube 106 is to be tested by the clinical test apparatus 42.

[0054] Once the confirmatory reading has been taken at the interface gate 170 of the auxiliary conveyor 32, a robot (not shown) will remove the sample tube 106 from its

singulation position for transfer to the clinical test apparatus 42. The unloaded puck 102 remains on the auxiliary conveyor 132 due to the vertical confinement provided by the ledges 136 and 138 (Fig. 4) at the conveyor edge portions 128 and 130. The plunger device 222 (Fig. 6) is then activated to retract the finger 234 and permit the unloaded puck 102 to travel to the next protracted finger 236 where it is held back by the finger 236 at the next puck rotating mechanism 244. The unloaded puck 102 is then reloaded with a sample tube 106 that has already been tested at the clinical test apparatus 42.

[0055] It should be noted that the sample tube 106 that was robotically removed from the puck 100 at the singulator mechanism for transfer to the clinical test apparatus 42 is generally not the same sample tube 106 that is loaded in the empty puck 102 when the empty puck 102 is at the rotating mechanism 244 (Fig. 6). The unloading of the sample tube 106 from a puck 100 and the reloading of the puck 100 with a different sample tube 106 is due to the clinical test apparatus 42 being operated in continuous fashion.

[0056] Thus the clinical test apparatus 42 receives input sample tubes 106 to be tested simultaneously as it delivers output sample tubes 106 that have been tested. The label of the sample tube 106 that is at the puck rotating mechanism 244 is read by the label reader device at the puck rotating mechanism 244 and provides information to the process computer that the sample tube 106 has been tested at the clinical test apparatus 42. The plunger device 224 (Fig. 6) is then activated to retract the finger 236 and permit the sidebar lane 120 of the auxiliary conveyor 32 to move the sample tube 106 through the exit opening 148 of the interface gate 170 onto the main transport lane 60 in the direction of the clinical test apparatus.

[0057] The main transport lane 60 will carry the sample tube 106 to the next intersection that is governed by the next divert gate 160, namely the auxiliary conveyor 34 (Fig. 1) that is associated with the clinical test apparatus 44. Depending upon the information on the label 108 of the sample tube 106 and the information stored in the process control computer memory, the sample tube 106 will be either diverted onto the auxiliary conveyor 34 or allowed to stay on the main transport lane 60. If the sample tube 106 does not require any further testing it will not be diverted to any other auxiliary conveyors associated with clinical test apparatus and will usually be diverted to the auxiliary conveyor 30 for unloading at the unload station 40.

[0058] Each of the auxiliary conveyors 30-39 is powered by separate and independent motor devices. Thus the inclusion of additional auxiliary conveyors into the conveyor system 10 can be easily accomplished since the adjacent edge walls 70 and 130 of the main conveyor and the auxiliary conveyor can be detachably fastened together in any suitable known manner. Furthermore, the extrusions which form the edge walls 68, 70, 128 and 130 can be formed in standard sizes with and without the exit and entrance openings 146 and 148 to facilitate the addition of any other auxiliary conveyors.

[0059] If desired, auxiliary conveyors can be provided not only for transfer of tubes to clinical test apparatus but also for transfer of tubes to stations that perform other functions that may be considered beneficial for the processing of the sample tubes. For example, the next sequential station 42 from the load and unload station 40 rather than being associated with a clinical test apparatus can be used as a label check station for the purpose of checking whether a sample tube label 108 has a proper bar code, whether the label 108 has been properly affixed to the sample tube 106 and whether any other identification function is lacking in connection with the sample tube. The label check station will operate to remove any questionable sample tubes 106 from the conveyor system for remediation or disposal. The label check station will also operate to confirm that a sample tube has been properly labeled, and upon such confirmation the sample tube will be returned to the main transport lane 60.

[0060] Another embodiment of a divert gate is generally indicated by the reference number 330 in Fig. 23. The divert gate 330 is provided at the edge wall 68 of the transport conveyor 12 in substantial alignment with the sidebar entrance opening 146 at the upstream end 50 of the auxiliary conveyor 30. The divert gate 330 (Fig. 23) includes three pneumatically controlled plunger devices 332, 334 and 336 of known construction supported on a gate housing 338. The plunger devices 332 and 334 respectively include retractable fingers 340 and 342, and the plunger device 336 includes a retractable divert head 344 with an inclined surface 346.

[0061] Referring to Fig. 24 a strip of tape 350 is secured to an inside surface 352 of the edge wall 70 directly across from the plunger devices 332 and 334. The tape 350 constitutes a contact surface that makes slight contact with the periphery of the pucks 100 when the pucks are directly across from the plunger devices 332 and 334. The movement of the conveyor belt 60 along with the slight touching of the tape 350 against the periphery of the pucks 100 causes a slight rotation of the pucks 100 as they move on the conveyor belt 60 past the tape 350.

[0062] A known label scanner or reader device 356 (Fig. 23) reads the bar code label 108 of a puck 100 that is held in position between the protracted fingers 340 and 342. A mirror 358 (Figs. 23 and 24) is supported on a horizontal surface 360 of the edge wall 70 across from the plunger devices 332 and 334. The mirror 358 is positioned to reflect the bar code 108 of the sample tubes 106 when the bar code 108 is positioned in front of the mirror 358. Under this arrangement a bar code reading of the sample tube 106 can be obtained by the label scanner device 356 when the bar code label 108 faces the scanner device 356 or when the bar code label 108 faces the mirror 358. The slight rotation of the puck 100 by contact with the tape 350 facilitates reading of the bar code label 108 by the reader device 356. Thus the divert gate 330 does not require the puck rotating mechanism 190 of the divert gate 160.

[0063] If the bar code label 108 is oriented in a position that does not permit the scanner device 356 to obtain a reading of the bar code label 108, then the puck 100 will not be diverted to the side bar lane 120 and will remain on the main transport lane 60. However based on past performance there is a 95% chance that the sample tube 106 will have an orientation that permits the reader device 356 to obtain a reading of the bar code label 108.

[0064] When the respective fingers 340 and 342 of the plunger devices 332 and 334 are in a protracted position, the combination of the plunger devices 332 and 334 constitute a singulator device that enables the label reader device 356 to read the bar code label 108 of one sample tube at a time. The retractable fingers 340 and 342 are spaced apart a distance slightly larger than the puck diameter to permit the puck to rotate slightly between the protracted fingers 340 and 342 as previously described.

[0065] When the retractable finger 340 is in a protracted position as shown in Fig. 23 it retains the queue of pucks 100. Thus after a puck 100 has been singulated between the fingers 340 and 342 the puck label is read and the finger 342 can be retracted to release the singulated puck. If the bar code information indicates that the singulated puck should be diverted from the main transport lane 60 to the sidebar lane 120 the divert head 344 will remain in a protracted position to divert the singulated puck 100 in the manner shown in Fig. 23. If the bar code label information on the singulated puck 100 indicates that the puck 100 should remain on the main transport lane 60 the divert head 344 will be retracted to enable the singulated puck 100 to continue being moved on the main transport lane 60.

[0066] Regardless of whether the singulated puck 100 is or is not diverted from the main transport lane 60 to the sidebar lane 120 the puck 100 will pass across a beam

364 (Fig. 23) of a sensor 366. The sensor 366 upon sensing the puck 100 will signal the control means (not shown) of the conveyor system 10 to activate the plunger 334 to protract the finger 342 as shown in Fig. 23 for singulation of another puck 100 in the queue of pucks held back by the finger 340. The plunger device 332 will thus be activated to retract the finger 340 to enable the leading puck 100 in the queue of pucks that are held back by the finger 340 to move into engagement with the now protracted finger 342.

[0067] The sensor device 370 senses the presence of a puck 100 that has progressed to the finger 342 and signals the control means to activate the plunger device 332 to protract the finger 340 thereby singulating the progressive puck 100 between the protracted fingers 340 and 342. Another sensor device 372, in alignment with the plunger device 332 senses the presence of a puck 100 upstream of the protracted finger 340 to recognize that the sensed puck is being held back by the protracted finger 340.

[0068] Another embodiment of the interface gate is generally indicated by the reference number 380 in Figs. 20-22. The interface gate 380 includes a star wheel device 382 (Fig. 22) rotatable on a fixed support plate 384. The support plate 384 constitutes a portion of the gate housing for the interface gate 380 that is joined to the edge wall 128 (Fig. 21) of the sidebar conveyor belt 120.

[0069] The star wheel device 382 (Fig. 21) includes an upper rotatable plate 388 having four radially spaced sample tube recesses 392 shown in phantom outline in Fig. 20. The sample tube recesses 392 are wider than the sample tubes 106

and do not contact any portion of the sample tubes 106. The recesses 392 are also narrower than the outside diameter of the pucks 100, as most clearly shown in Fig. 20 to prevent the puck from elevating above the recesses 392 when a sample tube 106 is withdrawn from a puck 100.

[0070] Four generally triangular segments 398 are each secured to the upper rotatable plate 388 such that one of the segments 398 is provided between any two consecutive sample tube recesses 392. The segments 398 have a vertical thickness that is slightly less than the distance between the upper rotatable plate 388 and the fixed lower plate 384. The segments 398 are thus freely movable with the rotatable upper plate 388 relative to the fixed lower plate 384.

[0071] Referring to Figs. 21 and 22 a shaft 402 has an upper end keyed to the center of the upper rotatable plate 388. An opposite lower end of the shaft 402 is keyed to a pulley 404 driven by a motor 406 (Fig. 22) via a belt 408. Thus the motor 406 rotates the upper plate 388 and the segments 398 in a counterclockwise direction as shown in Fig. 22.

[0072] Referring again to Figs. 21 and 22 a puck rotating collar 414 with peripheral "O" rings 416 is spaced between the upper plate 388 and the fixed lower support plate 384. A sleeve 412 concentric to the shaft 402 and freely rotatable relative to the shaft 402 has an upper end keyed to the puck rotating collar 414. A pulley 418 is formed at an opposite end of the sleeve 412 and is rotatable in a clockwise direction by a motor 420 via a belt 422 that passes around a motor pulley 424. The collar 414 is thus rotatable by the motor 420 between the upper plate 388 and the lower plate 384 in a clockwise direction as shown in Fig. 22.

[0073] A pair of biasing units 430 are provided on the fixed lower support plate 384 to bias the pucks 100 against the puck rotating collar 414 when the pucks 100 are guided past the biasing units 430 by the star wheel device 382. Each biasing unit 430 includes a plate 432, slidable in a recess 434 of the lower support plate 384. A pair of biasing rollers 435 are rotatably mounted on the support plate 384 to engage a surface portion of the pucks 100 that is opposite the puck rotating collar 414, to urge the pucks against the collar 414. The slide plate 432 has a guide slot 436 that receives spaced guide pins 438 fixed to the lower support plate 384 that permit the slide plate 432 to move toward the pucks 100 with a limited range of movement. A pair of biasing springs 440 are secured at one end to a post 442 on the slide plate 432 and at an opposite end to a post 444 on the support plate 384 to urge the slide plate 432 and the rollers 435 toward the pucks 100.

[0074] Referring to Figs. 20 and 22 a deflector member 446 on the edge wall 130 of the side bar lane 120 deflects a puck 100 from the sidebar lane 120 into a tube recess 392 of the star wheel device 382.

[0075] A sensor 450 at the gate 380 (Fig. 20) senses that a sample tube 106 has entered the tube recess 392 at the 5 o'clock position of the star wheel device 382. The sensor signals the control means for the conveyor system 10 to actuate the motor 406 to rotate the star wheel device 382 and the entered puck 100 approximately 90 degrees to the 2 o'clock position of Fig. 20. The biasing unit 430 at the 2 o'clock position urges the entered puck 100

against the puck rotating collar 414 to rotate the sample tube 106 for bar code reading purposes.

[0076] A sensor 452 at the gate 380 senses the presence of the rotating sample tube 106 and signals the control means of the conveyor system 10 to cause the bar code reader device (not shown) to read the bar code of the rotating sample tube 106 in the 2 o'clock position. A robot (not shown) removes the sample tube from the puck in the 2 o'clock position and transfers such sample tube to an analysis system (not shown) for processing. Thus the puck at the 2 o'clock position of the star wheel device 382 in Fig. 20 is emptied of its sample tube. The sensor 452 senses the removal of the sample tube from the puck 106 in the 2 o'clock position and signals the control means for the conveyor system 10 to cause the motor 406 to rotate the star wheel device 382 another 90 degree increment to the 11 o'clock position of Fig. 20.

[0077] A sensor 454 at the gate 380 senses that there is no sample tube in the puck 100 at the 11 o'clock position of Fig. 20. A robot (not shown) transfers a processed sample tube from the sample analysis system at the gate 380 (not shown) to the empty puck at the 11 o'clock position of Fig. 20. The sensor 454 at the gate 380 senses when the sample tube 106 has been placed in the puck 100 at the 11 o'clock position and signals the control means to actuate the motor 406 to rotate the star wheel device 382 approximately 30 degrees to move the puck 100 from the 10 o'clock position into alignment with the biasing unit 430 at the 9 o'clock position of Fig. 20. The biasing unit 430 at the 9 o'clock position urges the puck 100 against the puck rotating collar 414 to rotate the sample tube 106 to permit a bar code label reading of the sample tube 106 by a scanner (not shown).

[0078] After the bar code label of the puck 100 in the 9 o'clock position has been read by the scanner device, the control means actuates the motor 406 to rotate the star wheel device 382 to the 7 o'clock exit position as shown in Fig. 20. The puck 100 can thus exit the interface gate 380 at the 7 o'clock position to move onto the sidebar lane 120. Further rotation of the star wheel device 382 will not begin until the 7 o'clock position is empty. Thus a sensor device 456 at the gate 380 senses when the puck 100 has left the 7 o'clock exit position of the star wheel device 382.

[0079] Under this arrangement, each time the star wheel device 382 indexes 90 degrees an additional puck 100 can be diverted by the deflector member 446 into the 5 o'clock position of the star wheel device 382 as shown in Fig. 20 for pick-up of a sample tube from the diverted puck and replacement of another sample tube in the empty puck as previously described. It should also be noted that a puck entering the gate 380 can exit the gate 380 without removal of its sample tube 106 if the information read on the bar code label 108 indicates that the tube 106 is not to be processed by the analysis system at the gate 380.

[0080] The main transport conveyor 12 and the auxiliary conveyors 30-39 are commonly supported on identical column members 360 (Figs. 9-12) that are spaced a predetermined distance from each other. The column members 360 are a known structure for supporting conveyors. As shown in Figs. 16-18, the column member 260 includes

vertical slots 262 that are open at a top end of the column. The slots 262 are engageable by a rectangular securement plate 264 having an opening 266 for a fastener 268.

[0081] The securement plate 264 can be installed in the vertical slot 262 at the top end of the column 260, or if desired, the plate 264 can be initially installed with the narrow side up in the slot 262. The securement plate 264 can then be rotated in a known manner to a locking orientation as shown in Fig. 18.

[0082] Bracket members 270 (Fig. 4) are provided near an upper end of each of the columns 260 to join the edge wall 68 of the conveyor 12 to the column 260. The adjacent edge walls 70 and 130 are integrally joined in any suitable known manner.

[0083] For example, although not shown, the fasteners 268 can be passed through the bracket members 270 (Fig. 4) to access one or more of the securement plates 264 in one or more of the vertical slots 262 of the column members 260.

[0084] In addition a joining member 274 (Figs. 7 & 8), which supports the conveyor 12, joins the edge wall 68 to the edge wall 70. Another joining member 276, which supports the auxiliary conveyors 30-39, and is similar to the joining member 274, joins the edge wall 128 to the edge wall 130. Thus the bracket members 270 extending from the column members 260 support the conveyors 12 and 30-39 as well as the respective edge walls 68, 70, 128 and 130 in cantilever arrangement with respect to the column members 260.

[0085] It will be noted that the edge walls 68, 70, 128 and 130 as well as the bracket members 270 and the joining members 274 and

276 can each be formed as extrusions of predetermined length. [0086] A drip pan 278 (Figs. 4 & 15) for collecting any drippage from the conveyor can also be secured to the columns 260 below the conveyor. Thus, referring to Fig. 15, the securement plate 264 and the fastener are used in the manner previously described to secure the drip pan 278 to the column 260.

[0087] Service support brackets 290 (Figs. 9, 15 & 15A) are joined to the column members 260 between the bracket members 270 (Fig. 4) and a base portion 300 (Figs. 9 & 15) of the column members 260, also using the securement plate 264 and the fasteners 268 to lock onto the column members 260. The service support brackets 290 (Figs. 9, 15 & 15A) hold boxes 306 for electrical service, conduits 308 for air pressure and vacuum service and conduits 312, including a waste line 312A, for plumbing service to the conveyor system 10 and to any of the clinical test apparatus associated with the conveyor system 10. Any suitable known valving, switches and solenoid devices 313 (Figs. 13 & 14) are provided on the conduits 306-312 to control the utility service to the conveyor system 10.

[0088] Under this arrangement all utilities which service the conveyor system 10 are carried by the support columns 260 of the conveyor system. No extraneous drops, cords or wires need be suspended over the conveyor or recessed in the ground below the conveyor. In addition much if not all of the cabinetry for the conveyor can be supported by the support system in the manner shown in Figs. 3, 9, 14, 15, 15A and 19.

[0089] Some advantages of the invention evident from the foregoing description include a conveyor system having a main transport lane and a sidebar lane that are substantially parallel to each other and operate side-by-side, a novel conveyor system which includes a main transport conveyor that runs in an endless circuit and auxiliary conveyors provided alongside the main conveyor at the straight line paths of the main conveyor to permit crossover between the main conveyor and the auxiliary conveyor and vice versa, a novel conveyor system wherein the main conveyor and auxiliary conveyors are each powered by separate motors, a novel conveyor system wherein the main conveyor and the auxiliary conveyor can be built as modules to permit inclusion of any selected number of auxiliary conveyors as well as the elimination of unwanted auxiliary conveyors should they no longer be needed at some future time, a novel conveyor system having traffic control gates that can be positioned directly alongside the main conveyor and the auxiliary conveyor, a novel conveyor system having traffic control gates wherein two puck rotating mechanisms can be incorporated in a single gate operating from a single motor, a novel conveyor system having utility service connected to column supports for the conveyor for convenient access to such utility service and convenient installation of such utility service, and a novel conveyor system that provides common transport of sample tubes to different clinical apparatus and provides for the bypassing of such clinical apparatus if tests are not required at a particular clinical test apparatus.

[0090] In view of the above, it will be seen that the several objects of the invention are achieved and other advantageous results obtained.

[0091] As various changes can be made in the above constructions without departing from the scope of the invention, it is intended that all matter contained in the above description or shown in the accompanying drawings shall be interpreted as illustrative and not in a limiting sense.

Claims

1. A conveyor system for clinical test apparatus comprising,

    a) a main transport conveyor defining a closed circuit path of travel in a generally horizontal plane, the closed circuit path of travel permitting objects on the conveyor to repeat the path of travel when the conveyor is moving in one direction, the closed circuit path of travel including a straight line path and a curved path,

    b) a plurality of auxiliary conveyor modules, each comprising an auxiliary conveyor defining a straight line path of travel in a generally horizontal plane, the straight line path of travel permitting objects on the conveyor to move from one point to another without retracing any point of travel when the conveyor is moving in said one direction, said auxiliary conveyor having an upstream end and a downstream end relative to said one direction of movement,

    c) said auxiliary conveyor being positioned alongside the straight line path of travel of said first transport conveyor to run in the same direction as said first conveyor,

    d) segregation means between the straight line path of said main transport conveyor and said auxiliary conveyor for normally preventing objects from said transport conveyor from moving onto said auxiliary conveyor and vice versa,

    e) said segregation means including first and second openings spaced a predetermined linear distance from each other along said straight line path,

    f) a divert gate device provided at one of said openings proximate an upstream end of said auxiliary conveyor, said divert gate device having diversion means for diverting movement of objects on said main transport conveyor through said one of said openings in said segregation means to said auxiliary conveyor,

    g) an interface gate provided downstream of said one opening and upstream of said other opening in said segregation means, and

    h) said other opening providing a flow path that leads directly from said auxiliary conveyor to said main transport conveyor,

    said conveyor system including first motor means for moving said main transport conveyor and second motor means independently operable of said first motor means for moving said auxiliary conveyor of said auxiliary conveyor modules said auxiliary conveyor modules being detachably fastened to said main transport conveyor.

2. The conveyor system as claimed in claim 1 wherein said divert gate has a first protractible and retractable hold back means having a protracted position for holding back the movement of objects on said main transport

conveyor as said objects approach said divert gate, said first hold back means being operable independently of said diversion means.

3. The conveyor system as claimed in claim 1 wherein said diversion means includes a protractible and retractable diversion member having a protracted position for diverting movement of objects on said main transport conveyor to said auxiliary conveyor and a retracted position wherein objects on said main transport conveyor can continue to move on said main transport conveyor past said divert gate device through said one of said openings in said segregation means.

4. The conveyor system as claimed in claim 1 said plurality of said auxiliary conveyor modules is positioned alongside the straight line path of travel of said main transport conveyor in series such that each of said auxiliary conveyors is at a different location along the closed circuit path of travel of said main transport conveyor and each of said auxiliary conveyors has one of said divert gates and one of said interface gates and a set of said first and second openings is provided between each of said auxiliary conveyors and said main transport conveyor.

5. The conveyor system as claimed in claim 1 including support means for supporting said main transport conveyor and said auxiliary conveyor in cantilever arrangement.

6. The conveyor system as claimed in claim 5 wherein said support means includes a base position

for ground contact, said support means including means for supporting utility service including plumbing, electrical and pneumatic pressure lines between said base portion and said main transport conveyor such that said utility service for said conveyor system is above ground.

Patentansprüche

1. Förderanlage für eine Vorrichtung für klinische Tests, welche aufweist:

a) einen Haupttransportförderer, der eine geschlossene Kreislauf-Fahrstrecke in einer im Allgemeinen waagrechten Ebene definiert, wobei die geschlossene Kreislauf-Fahrstrecke ermöglicht, dass Gegenstände auf dem Förderer die Fahrstrecke wiederholen können, wenn sich der Förderer in eine Richtung bewegt, wobei die geschlossene Kreislauf-Fahrstrecke eine geradlinige Strecke und eine gekrümmte Strecke aufweist,
b) mehrere Hilfsförderermodule, von denen jedes einen Hilfsförderer aufweist, der eine geradlinige Fahrstrecke in einer im Allgemeinen waagrechten Ebene definiert, wobei die geradlinige Fahrstrecke ermöglicht, dass sich Gegenstände auf dem Förderer von einem Punkt zu einem anderen bewegen, ohne sich noch einmal zu irgendeinem Punkt der Fahrstrecke zurückzubewegen, wenn sich der Förderer in die eine Richtung bewegt, wobei der Hilfsförderer relativ zu der einen Bewegungsrichtung ein stromaufwärtiges und ein stromabwärtiges Ende aufweist,

c) wobei der Hilfsförderer entlang der geradlinigen Fahrstrecke des ersten Transportförderers derart angeordnet ist, dass er in dieselbe Richtung wie der erste Förderer läuft,

d) Trennungsmittel zwischen der geradlinigen Strecke des Haupttransportförderers und des Hilfsförderers, um normalerweise zu verhindern, dass sich Gegenstände von dem Transportförderer auf den Hilfsförderer bewegen und umgekehrt,

e) wobei das Trennungsmittel erste und zweite Öffnungen aufweist, die in einer vorgegebenen geradlinigen Entfernung voneinander entlang der geradlinigen Strekke angeordnet sind,

f) eine Umleitgattervorrichtung, die an einer der Öffnungen nächst einem stromaufwärtigen Ende des Hilfsförderers bereitgestellt ist, wobei die Umleitgattervorrichtung Umleitmittel zum Umleiten der Bewegung von Gegenständen auf dem Haupttransportförderer durch die eine der Öffnungen in dem Trennungsmittel zu dem Hilfsförderer aufweist,

g) ein Übergangsstellengatter, das stromabwärts der einen Öffnung in dem Trennungsmittel und stromaufwärts der anderen Öffnung in dem Trennungsmittel bereitgestellt ist, und

h) wobei die andere Öffnung einen Durchlaufweg bereitstellt, der direkt von dem Hilfsförderer zu dem Haupttransportförderer führt,

wobei die Förderanlage erste Motormittel zum Bewegen des Haupttransportförderers und zweite Motormittel, die

unabhängig von dem ersten Motormittel betreibbar sind, zum Bewegen des Hilfsförderers der Hilfsförderermodule aufweist, wobei die Hilfsfördermodule lösbar an dem Haupttransportförderer befestigt sind.

2. Förderanlage nach Anspruch 1, wobei das Umleitgatter ein erstes aus- und einfahrbares Rückhaltemittel aufweist, das eine ausgefahrene Stellung zum Zurückhalten der Bewegung von Gegenständen auf dem Haupttransportförderer, wenn sich die Gegenstände dem Umleitgatter nähern, aufweist, wobei das erste Rückhaltemittel unabhängig von dem Umleitmittel betreibbar ist.

3. Förderanlage nach Anspruch 1, wobei das Umleitmittel ein aus- und einfahrbares Umleitglied aufweist, das eine ausgefahrene Stellung zum Umleiten der Bewegung von Gegenständen auf dem Haupttransportförderer zu dem Hilfsförderer und eine eingefahrene Stellung, wobei sich Gegenstände auf dem Haupttransportförderer weiterhin auf dem Haupt transportförderer an der Umleitgattervorrichtung vorbei durch eine der Öffnungen in dem Trennungsmittel bewegen können, aufweist.

4. Förderanlage nach Anspruch 1, wobei die mehreren Hilfsförderermodule in einer Reihe entlang der geradlinigen Fahrstrecke des Haupttransportförderers angeordnet sind, derart, dass jeder der Hilfsförderer an einem anderen Ort entlang der geschlossenen Kreislauf-Fahrstrecke des Haupttransportförderers angeordnet ist und jeder der

Hilfsförderer ein Umleitgatter oder ein Übergangsstellengatter aufweist und ein Satz aus den ersten und zweiten Öffnungen zwischen jedem der Hilfsförderer und dem Haupttransportförderer bereitgestellt ist.

5. Förderanlage nach Anspruch 1, die ein Tragmittel zum Tragen des Haupttransportförderers und des Hilfsförderers in einer Kragträgeranordnung aufweist.

6. Förderanlage nach Anspruch 5, wobei das Tragmittel einen Basisabschnitt für Bodenkontakt aufweist, wobei das Tragmittel Mittel zum Tragen von Versorgungsdiensten wie Rohrleitungen, Elektroleitungen und Pneumatikdruckleitungen zwischen dem Basisabschnitt und dem Haupttransportförderer aufweist, derart, dass die Versorgungsdienste für die Förderanlage oberirdisch sind.

Revendications

1. Système de convoyeur pour une installation d'essais cliniques, comprenant :

a) un convoyeur principal de transport définissant un trajet de circuit fermé de déplacement dans un plan d'une manière générale horizontal, le trajet de circuit fermé de déplacement permettant à des objets sur le convoyeur de refaire le trajet de déplacement, lorsque le convoyeur se déplace dans un sens, le trajet de circuit fermé de déplacement comprenant un trajet en ligne droite et un trajet en courbe,

b) un pluralité de modules de convoyeur auxiliaire, chacun comprenant un convoyeur auxiliaire définissant un trajet en ligne droite de déplacement dans un plan d'une manière générale horizontal, le trajet en ligne droite de déplacement permettant à des objets sur le convoyeur de se déplacer d'un point à un autre sans retrouver un point de déplacement, lorsque le convoyeur se déplace dans ledit un sens, le convoyeur auxiliaire ayant une extrémité en amont et une extrémité en aval par rapport audit un sens de déplacement,

c) le convoyeur auxiliaire étant placé le long du trajet en ligne droite de déplacement du premier convoyeur de transport pour aller dans le même sens que le premier convoyeur,

d) des moyens de ségrégation entre le trajet en ligne droite et le convoyeur principal de transport et le convoyeur auxiliaire pour empêcher normalement des objets du convoyeur de transport d'aller sur le convoyeur auxiliaire et vice versa,

e) les moyens de ségrégation comprenant des première et deuxième ouvertures à une distance linéaire déterminée à l'avance l'une de l'autre le long du trajet en ligne droite,

f) un dispositif de déviation à porte prévu à l'une des ouvertures à proximité d'une extrémité en amont du convoyeur auxiliaire, le dispositif de déviation à porte ayant des moyens de déviation pour dévier un déplacement des objets sur le convoyeur principal de transport vers le convoyeur auxiliaire en passant par ladite une des ouvertures des moyens de ségrégation,

g) une porte d'interface prévue en aval de ladite une ouverture et en amont de l'autre ouverture des moyens de ségrégation, et

h) l'autre ouverture procurant un trajet d'écoulement qui mène directement du convoyeur auxiliaire au convoyeur principal de transport,

le système de convoyeur comprenant des premiers moyens à moteur pour déplacer le convoyeur principal de transport et des deuxièmes moyens à moteur, pouvant fonctionner indépendamment des premiers moyens à moteur, pour déplacer le convoyeur auxiliaire des modules de convoyeur auxiliaire, les modules de convoyeur auxiliaire étant fixés de manière amovible au convoyeur principal de transport.

2. Système de convoyeur suivant la revendication 1, dans lequel la porte de déviation a un premier moyen de retenue déployable et rétractable ayant une position déployée pour retenir le mouvement des objets sur le convoyeur principal de transport, alors que ces objets se rapprochent de la porte de déviation, les premiers moyens de retenue pouvant fonctionner indépendamment des moyens de déviation.

3. Système de convoyeur suivant la revendication 1, dans lequel les moyens de déviation comprennent un élément de déviation déployable et rétractable ayant une position déployée pour un mouvement de déviation des objets sur le convoyeur principal de transport vers le convoyeur auxiliaire et une position rétractée, dans laquelle des objets sur le convoyeur principal de transport peuvent continuer à se déplacer sur le

convoyeur principal de transport au-delà du dispositif de déviation à porte en passant par ladite une des ouvertures des moyens de ségrégation.

4. Système de convoyeur suivant la revendication 1, la pluralité des modules de convoyeur auxiliaire étant placés le long du trajet en ligne droite de déplacement du convoyeur principal de transport en série, de manière à ce que chacun des convoyeurs auxiliaires soit en un emplacement différent le long du trajet de circuit fermé de déplacement du convoyeur principal de transport et de manière à ce que chacun des convoyeurs auxiliaires ait l'une des portes de déviation et l'une des portes d'interface et un jeu de première et deuxième ouvertures est prévu entre chacun des convoyeurs auxiliaires et le convoyeur principal de transport.

5. Système de convoyeur suivant la revendication 1, comprenant des moyens de support pour supporter le convoyeur principal de transport et le convoyeur auxiliaire en porte-à-faux.

6. Système de convoyeur suivant la revendication 5, dans lequel les moyens de support comprennent une partie de socle pour un contact avec le sol, les moyens de support comprenant des moyens pour supporter un service de commodité comprenant de la plomberie, des lignes électriques et pneumatiques sous pression entre la partie de socle et le convoyeur principal de transport, de manière à ce que le service de commodité pour le système de convoyeur soit au-dessus du sol.

Appendix 4

Lack of exercise responsible for twice as many deaths as obesity

A brisk 20 minute walk each day could be enough to reduce an individual's risk of early death, according to new research published today. The study of over 334,000 European men and women found that twice as many deaths may be attributable to lack of physical activity compared with the number of deaths attributable to obesity, but that just a modest increase in physical activity could have significant health benefits.

Physical inactivity has been consistently associated with an increased risk of early death, as well as being associated with a greater risk of diseases such as heart disease and cancer. Although it may also contribute to an increased body mass index (BMI) and obesity, the association with early death is independent of an individual's BMI.

To measure the link between physical inactivity and premature death, and its interaction with obesity, researchers analyzed data from 334,161 men and women across Europe participating in the European Prospective Investigation into Cancer and Nutrition (EPIC) Study. Between 1992 and 2000, the researchers measured height, weight and waist circumference, and used self-assessment to measure levels of physical activity. The participants were then followed up over 12 years, during which 21,438 participants died. The results are published today in the American Journal of Clinical Exercise.

The researchers found that the greatest reduction in risk of premature death occurred in the comparison between inactive and moderately inactive groups, judged by combining activity at work with recreational activity; just under a quarter (22.7%) of participants were categorized as inactive, reporting no recreational activity in combination with a sedentary occupation. The authors estimate that doing exercise equivalent to just a 20 minute brisk walk each day – burning between 90 and 110 kcal ('calories') – would take an individual from the inactive to moderately inactive group and reduce their risk of premature death by between 16-30%. The impact was greatest amongst normal weight individuals, but even those with higher BMI saw a benefit.

Using the most recent available data on deaths in Europe the researchers estimate that 337,000 of the 9.2 million deaths amongst European men and women were attributable to obesity (classed as a BMI greater than 30): however, double this number of deaths (676,000) could be attributed to physical inactivity.

Professor Ulf Ekelund from the Medical Research Council (MRC) Epidemiology Unit at the University of Cambridge, who led the study, says: 'This is a simple message: just a small amount of physical activity each day could have substantial health benefits for people who are physically inactive. Although we found that just 20 minutes would make a difference, we should really be looking to do more than this – physical activity has many proven health benefits and should be an important part of our daily life.'

Professor Nick Wareham, Director of the MRC Unit, adds: 'Helping people to lose weight can be a real challenge, and whilst we should continue to aim at reducing population levels of obesity, public health interventions that encourage people to make small but achievable changes in physical activity can have significant health benefits and may be easier to achieve and maintain.'

Reference

Ekelund, U et al. Activity and all-cause mortality across levels of overall and abdominal adiposity in European men and women: the European Prospective Investigation into Cancer and Nutrition Study (EPIC). American Journal of Clinical Nutrition; 14 Jan 2015

Reproduced courtesy of The Guardian Newspapers, from www. theguardian.com/lifeandstyle/2015/jan/14/scientists-recommend-20-minute-daily-walk-premature-death

Scientists recommend 20-minute daily walk to avoid premature death

Research into obesity establishes benefits of engaging in moderate levels of daily exercise

Lack of exercise is twice as likely to lead to an early grave than obesity, research has shown.

A brisk 20-minute walk each day could be all it takes to avoid dying prematurely, the findings suggest.

Scientists looked at the effects of obesity and exercise on 334,161 European men and women whose progress was followed for 12 years. They found that people who engaged in moderate levels of daily exercise – equivalent to taking an energetic 20-minute walk – were 16% to 30% less likely to die than those classified as inactive.

Although the impact of exercise was greatest among people of a normal weight, even those with a high body mass index (BMI) levels saw a benefit.

Overall, avoiding inactivity theoretically reduced the risk of death from any cause by 7.35%, said the scientists. Having a BMI lower than obesity levels, defined as a score of 30 or more, was estimated to lower mortality by 3.66%. Keeping waists trim, irrespective of BMI, had a similar impact on death rates as exercise.

BMI is calculated by dividing a person's weight in kilograms by their height in metres squared and is a standard tool used to assess whether someone is overweight or obese.

Lack of exercise was thought to have caused almost 700,000 deaths across Europe in 2008.

Study leader Prof Ulf Ekelund, from the Medical Research Council (MRC) epidemiology unit at Cambridge University, said: 'This is a simple message: just a small amount of physical activity each day could have substantial health benefits for people who are physically inactive.

'Although we found that just 20 minutes would make a difference, we should really be looking to do more than this – physical activity has many proven health benefits and should be an important part of our daily life.'

Participants in the research, who had an average age of about 50, were recruited to the European Prospective Investigation into Cancer (Epic) study conducted across 10 European countries, including the

UK. All had their height, weight and waist sizes measured and provided self-assessments of physical activity levels.

Just under a quarter (22.7%) were categorised as inactive, working in sedentary jobs without engaging in any recreational exercise.

The findings, which are published in the American Journal of Clinical Nutrition, say the greatest reductions in the risk of premature death were seen when comparing moderately active groups with those who were completely inactive.

Using the most recent available public data, the researchers calculated that 337,000 of the 9.2m deaths that occurred in Europe in 2008 could be attributed to obesity, but physical inactivity was thought to be responsible for almost double this number – 676,000 deaths.

Co-author Prof Nick Wareham, director of the MRC epidemiology unit, said: 'Helping people to lose weight can be a real challenge and, whilst we should continue to aim at reducing population levels of obesity, public health interventions that encourage people to make small but achievable changes in physical activity can have significant health benefits and may be easier to achieve and maintain.'

June Davison, senior cardiac nurse at the British Heart Foundation, said: 'The results of this study are a clear reminder that being regularly physically active can reduce the risk of dying from coronary heart disease.

'The research suggests that just a modest increase in physical activity can have health benefits. Adults should aim to do at least 150 minutes of moderate intensity activity a week, carrying it out in sessions of 10 minutes or more.

'Whether it's going for a walk, taking a bike ride or using the stairs instead of the lift, keeping active every day will help reduce the risk of developing coronary heart disease.'

Appendix 5

La periodontitis crónica, enfermedad inflamatoria de las encías, influye en la gravedad y en el pronóstico del infarto

Investigadores de la Universidad de Granada han demostrado por primera vez que la periodontitis crónica, una enfermedad inflamatoria de las encías que provoca la pérdida gradual de los dientes, guarda relación con la mayor extensión del infarto agudo de miocardio, comúnmente conocido como ataque al corazón.

En un trabajo pionero titulado Acute myocardial infarct size is related to periodontitis extent and severity y publicado en la prestigiosa revista Journal of Dental Research, los investigadores han demostrado que la extensión y la severidad de la periodontitis crónica se relaciona con el tamaño del infarto agudo de miocardio determinado por niveles séricos de troponina I y mioglobina (biomarcadores de necrosis miocárdica).

Esta investigación, es parte de los resultados de la tesis doctoral de Rafael Martín Marfil Álvarez, dirigida por los profesores de la UGR Francisco Mesa Aguado (departamento de Estomatología), José Antonio Ramírez Hernández (departamento de Medicina) y Andrés Catena Martínez (departamento de Psicología Experimental). En ella, analizaron 112 pacientes que habían sufrido un infarto agudo de miocardio, pertenecientes a la Unidad de Gestión Clínica de Cardiología del Hospital Universitario Virgen de las Nieves de Granada. A todos ellos se les realizó una valoración cardiológica, bioquímica y de salud periodontal.

Como explica el profesor Francisco Mesa Aguado, uno de los autores, según los resultados de este trabajo, que habrá que confirmar con otros estudios, 'la periodontitis crónica se configura como un factor de riesgo de mortalidad y juega un importante papel en el pronóstico del infarto agudo de miocardio'.

Los investigadores señalan que será necesario realizar un seguimiento de los pacientes periodontales que han sufrido un infarto de miocardio para determinar si tienen una peor evolución clínica (un nuevo evento coronario, un fallo cardíaco o incluso la muerte).

'Si es el caso, la periodontitis crónica, debería ser considerada como predictora en el desarrollo del infarto de miocardio y ser incluida en los scores de estratificación de riesgo', afirma Mesa Aguado.

Chronic periodontitis, an inflammatory gum disease, influences prognosis and the severity of heart attacks

Researchers from the University of Granada have demonstrated for the first time that chronic periodontitis, an inflammatory gum disease which provokes gradual teeth loss, is closely related to the severity of acute myocardial infarction, commonly known as heart attack.

In a pioneering research, published in the prestigious *Journal of Dental Research*, and titled '*Acute myocardial infarct size is related to periodontitis extent and severity*', this team have demonstrated that the extent and severity of chronic periodontitis is related to the size of acute myocardial infarction through seric levels of troponin I and myoglobin (biomarkers of myocardial necrosis).

This research results in part from the conclusions of Rafael Martín Marfil Álvarez's doctoral dissertation, which was directed by UGR professors Francisco Mesa Aguado (Stomatology Department), José Antonio Ramírez Hernández (Medicine Department), and Andrés Catena Martínez (Experimental Psychology Department). This research analyzed 112 patients who had suffered from acute myocardial infarction, at the Virgen de las Nieves University Hospital Cardiology Unit. They all underwent a series of cardiological, biochemical and periodontal health checks and tests.

According to professor Francisco Aguado, one of the authors of this research (which will have to be confirmed through further research), 'chronic periodontitis appears as a death risk factor and it plays an important role in the prognosis of acute myocardial infarction'

Researchers point out that it will be necessary to conduct follow-up checks with periodontal patients who have suffered myocardial infarction in order to determine the severity (or lack of it) of their clinical evolution (new coronary events, cardiac failure, or even death)

'If that happens to be the case, chronic periodontitis should be considered as a predictor in the development of myocardial infarction, and be therefore included in the risk stratification scores', according to Mesa Aguado.

Glossary

ad-hoc corpus
a collection of texts compiled quickly to form a corpus for a specific purpose or task. Also known as DIY (do it yourself) corpus or disposable corpus.

associative relation
a relation other than generic/partitive that links one **concept** to another.

audience design
the ways in which text producers vary their linguistic choices responsively to accommodate various roles of their text receivers.

booster
the linguistic expression of the writer's conviction towards the material of their text (see **metadiscourse**).

code gloss
additional information supplied by the writer through reformulation or exemplification (see **metadiscourse**).

colligation
the likely co-occurrence of grammatical patterns and lexical items.

collocation
the likely co-occurrence of lexical items.

concept
a unit of knowledge defined by means of its characteristics.

concordance
instances of the node word, phrase or pattern retrieved from a corpus and displayed with some surrounding co-text, usually in KWIC (key word in context) format.

discourse community
a group that has shared goals and uses communication and conventionalized **genres** to achieve those goals.

documentary translation
translation that documents the communication between the source-text (ST) author and the ST receiver.

endophoric marker
a reference to another part of the text (see **metadiscourse**).

epistemic verb
verb used to express the speaker's degree of certainty, doubt or commitment (i.e. epistemic stance) towards their utterance or a proposition.

epistemic adverb
adverb used to express the speaker's degree of certainty, doubt or commitment (i.e. epistemic stance) towards their utterance or a proposition.

evaluative epithet
attitudinally loaded adjective.

evidential
a reference to a source of textual information outside of the text (see **metadiscourse**).

frequency list
list of words in a corpus, ordered according to the frequency with which they occur in the corpus. Also referred to as word list.

genre
a conventionalized communicative event that occurs regularly in a **discourse community** and that is characterized by a set of mutually understood communicative purposes.

generic relation
hierarchical relation between **concepts** whereby one concept is a superordinate and the other is its subordinate.

grammatical metaphor
the replacement of one grammatical category by another.

hedge
the linguistic expression of a writer's lack of commitment to the material of the text (see **metadiscourse**)

illocutionary force
the speaker's intention when producing an utterance (see **speech act**).

keyword
a word form or phrase that is more frequent in a text than would be expected based on its frequency in a reference corpus, that is, it displays the property of keyness.

lemma
a set of word forms that are inflectional variants of a common headword or stem.

lexical bundle
a string of words that follow each other more frequently than expected by chance.

lexical density
a measure of the proportion of content words (lexical words) to function words (grammatical words) in a corpus.

metadiscourse
linguistic devices used by writers to organize their text, engage their readers and signal their attitudes to their text and their audience.

move
a rhetorical and discoursal unit that performs a coherent communicative function in written or spoken discourse.

multimodality
co-occurrence of two or more modes of communication (e.g. verbal, visual).

n-gram
sequence comprising *n* numbers of words (e.g. bigram is a two-word sequence, tri-gram a three-word sequence).

partitive relation
hierarchical relation between **concepts**, whereby one concept is part of the other.

phraseology
the set of phrases that occur in a text more often than would be expected by chance.

preformulating device
a device used in press releases designed to facilitate reuse of the press release by journalists.

proximity of membership
the way in which writers position themselves as disciplinary experts and members of their **discourse community.**

proximity of commitment
the way in which writers position themselves in relation to the material they present in their texts.

semantic prosody
affective meaning (positive, negative or neutral) of a word established through use with its typical collocates.

speech act
an action performed by an utterance, beyond the sense conveyed by its lexical items.

term
designation for a **concept**.

termbase
a database containing terminological and conceptual information, usually organized by **concept**.

terminology
the set of specialized **terms** for a subject domain.

terminology management
the researching, recording, storing, managing and maintaining of **terms** and accompanying terminological and conceptual information.

text type
classification of text based on the rhetorical purpose it fulfils in its context, realized by linguistic features.

translation memory
software designed for translators to store, search, retrieve and reuse previous translations during the translation process.

Index

3-gram *see* n-gram
abbreviation 27, 86–8, 90, 95, 194–5
Abdi, Reza 157
academic vocabulary 145–9, 166–8
Academic Vocabulary List (AVL)
    147, 165–6
Across 45
action statement 59–61, 64, 68–70,
    75
African Intellectual Property
    Organization 121
African Regional Intellectual
    Property Organization 121
Aixelá, Javier Franco 76
Alexander, Kara Poe 52, 55
Amare, Nicole 55
Amstad score 53
Anderson, Alison 199
AntConc 28, 48
Anthony, Laurence 28
Aparacio, Antonio 8
Arabic 47, 56, 6–8, 71, 122, 138,
    144, 155, 160, 193, 201
Arbeitskreis Deutsch als
    Wissenschaftssprache (ADAWiS)
    140
ASTM F2575 standard 23
attitude marker 156, 167, 188
audience design 19
Azerbaijani 193

Bad Science see Goldacre, Ben
Bahasa Indonesia 193
Bassnett, Susan 189
Bazerman, Charles 108, 149

Beeby, Allison 14
Benis, Michael 8
Bennett, Karen 139, 140
Bhatia, Vijay K. 16, 159
Biber, Douglas 18
Bielsa, Esperança 189
bi-gram *see* n-gram
Bloom's taxonomy (of educational
    objectives) 4
Bluff, Julia 74
booster 97–9, 156–7, 164–5, 167;
    see also hedge
BootCaT 37, 48
brand identity *see* corporate
    identity; product name
Brazilian Portuguese 90, 94
Brett, Paul 153
British National Corpus 28, 41, 48,
    98
British Standards Institution 13, 20,
    24, 52, 62–3, 66, 74
Bulgarian 193
Burgess, Sally 160
Busch-Lauer, Ines A. 160
Byrne, Jody 53

Caliendo, Giuditta 201
Cao, Feng 164–5
Cao, Yan 160
CARS *see* move
CAT *see* computer-assisted
    translation
Catrambone, Richard 52
Chartered Institute of Linguists
    (CIoL) 8

Chinese 54, 83, 90, 92, 94, 102, 120, 122–6, 142–4, 160, 164–5, 167, 193, 201
Christensen, Tina Paulsen 49
churnalism 181
citizen science 175, 201, 202
code gloss 156, 167
cognitive load 65
cohesive device 188, 191; *see also* repetition
colligation 28, 29
Collins Wordbanks Online 48
collocation 28–9, 35, 41, 98, 146, 165–6
colloquial language 97–8
Comité Européen de Normalisation 88
communicative event 16–18, 107, 192
communicative purpose 6, 15–21, 24, 51, 75, 80, 101, 107, 138, 145, 155, 160, 166, 168, 175, 177
comparative form 98, 154
completeness 72–3
computer-assisted translation 26, 42–5
concept 7, 16–17, 24, 27, 42–43, 54, 99, 124, 131; *see also* term
concordance 28–9, 35–6, 41, 48, 165–6
consistency 44, 49, 73–4, 83, 99, 104, 129–30
content word 30, 54
contracted form 97
corporate identity 82–4, 101
corpus 26–9, 31, 35–8, 41, 48, 138, 146–7, 160, 166, 168, 201; ad-hoc 37; reference 31–3, 38, 48, 132, 166
Corpus of Contemporary American English (COCA) 28, 41, 48, 147
Coxhead, Averil 145–6
Coxhead's Academic Word List 145–7

credibility: in scientific publishing 138, 184, 188, 190–2
Croatian 92, 193
Cross, Graham 8
Cross, Martin 134
Cross-Lingual Information Retrieval 124–6
cultural adaptation 67–8, 94, 97, 157, 160–5, 195–9
currency *see* unit of measurement
Cyr, Dianne 55
Czech 94, 102, 144, 193

Dahl, Trine 157, 160, 177
Danish 144, 193
Davies, Mark 145–7
decimal marker 86–7
declarative information: in instructions 64, 70
Déjà Vu 45
Dell'Orletta, Felice 54
desktop publishing (DTP) 13, 85
design patent *see* patent
direct address *see* interpersonal reference
Directorate-General for Translation 10–11, 14–15, 45
disclosure: of invention 44, 106, 108
discourse: community 16–18, 24, 26–7, 137, 139, 140, 146, 148–9, 154–5, 157, 160, 163, 166, 168, 188; legal 106–7, 130; marketing 80, 85, 93–5, 104
documentary film 175, 199
documentary translation 128–30, 135
Doherty, Stephen 46, 49
Dozuki 74, 77
Dunne, Elena S. 12
Dunne, Kieran J. 12
Durban, Chris 19
Dutch 47, 94, 102, 124, 193–6, 199

ECHA-term termbase 92–3, 102
Eiriksdottir, Elsa 52

EN15038 13; standard 23
endophoric marker 156
engagement marker 148, 156, 167
English 2, 3, 5, 11, 18, 29–31, 37–8,
      46–8, 52–3, 56–7, 60, 67–70,
      72–4, 80–3, 87– 90, 94–101,
      111, 115–6, 120, 122–4, 126–7,
      132–3, 147, 149–50, 155–8,
      160–8, 179, 187, 189–91, 193–4,
      201–2; as scientific lingua franca
      137–145; hegemony of 138–42
English for Academic Purposes
      (EAP) 139, 145
English for Specific Purposes
      (ESP) 145
enTenTen corpus 31
epistemic culture 154
epistemic verb 156, 163, 165
epistemicide 139–40, 167
epistemology 139–40, 145, 167, 168
Eriksen, Marcus 150
Espacenet 110, 120, 133–4
Estonian 193
ethics 104, 159, 198, 203
Eurasian Patent Office 121–2
Eurasian Patent Organization 121
EuroParl Corpus 38, 41
European Association for Technical
      Communication 23
European Chemicals Agency 92,
      101–2
European Masters in Translation
      (EMT) 14–15
European Patent Convention 107
European Patent Office (EPO) 46,
      106–7, 110–12, 119–22, 126–7
European patent with unitary
      effect 127
European Space Agency 11–12
evaluative lexis 98–9, 102
evidential 156; see also quotation

Fakhri, Ahmed 155
Farkas, David K. 56, 58–9, 61, 64
Farsi 193

Finnish 46, 193
Flesh Kincaid Reading Ease 53
Forman, Paul 7
frame marker 156, 167
Franzoni, Chiara 201
freelance translation
      see translation
French, 11, 47, 57, 70, 83, 86, 94,
      97, 101–2, 110–11, 115, 117,
      120, 122–7, 138, 142–4, 157,
      160–2, 167, 189, 193, 195,
      197–8
function word 30–1

Galaxy Zoo 201
Ganier, Franck 52–3
Gardner, Dee 145–7
Gellevij, Mark 56
genre: conventions 4, 13, 16–17, 69,
      77, 104, 137, 139–40, 145, 149,
      168, 188–9, 192, 195; hybridity
      18, 201
Georgian 193
German 1, 9, 11, 46, 53–4, 56,
      67–9, 71–3, 80, 83, 86, 88–91,
      94, 96–8, 100–2, 110–11, 115,
      117, 120, 122, 124–7, 138,
      140–1, 144, 160, 193–9
Gillaerts, Paul 160
gist translation 121, 126, 144
Globally Harmonized System of
      Classification and Labelling of
      Chemicals 91–2
glossary 42, 56, 72, 101–2;
      see also termbase
Gnecchi, Manusca 14
Goldacre, Ben 202
Goldstein, Miriam C. 153
Google Translate 46, 126
grammatical metaphor 90, 132,
      137, 157–8, 167
graphics 54–5, 66, 73–5, 81–5, 87,
      93, 95, 101, 186–7, 200
Greek 90, 138, 193
Gunning Fog Score 53

Halliday, MAK 90, 132, 157–8
Hancke, Julia 54
Hatim, Basil 18
HealthNewsReview 202
Hebrew 193, 201
hedge 101, 148, 156–7, 163–5, 167, 179, 184, 188
Helmers, Christian 109, 110
Hirano, Eliana 155
Holz-Mänttäri, Justa 19
Hu, Guangwei 164, 165
Hungarian 193, 201
Hyland, Ken 138, 146–8, 155–61, 166, 187–8, 191–2, 196, 201

IATE termbase 43, 47
iconicity 54–5
IEEE Transactions on Professional Communication 76
illocutionary force 108
image see graphics
IMRAD model 150–4
information density 89–90, 157
information-to-persuasion ratio 99
in-house translation see translation
INID code 110–11
innovation patent see patent
Institute of Scientific and Technical Communicators 23
Institute of Translation and Interpreting (ITI) 8, 19, 23
institutional titles: translation of 195
instrumental translation see documentary translation
Intellectual Property Office 107, 118
intellectual property right 106–8, 119–21, 128, 135
International Bureau 123
International Patent Classification 111, 122
International Preliminary Reports on Patentability 123
international search report 123
interpersonal reference 95–7, 188

ISO/TS 11669 standard 19, 23
Italian 36–8, 46–7, 53–4, 86, 94, 97, 100–2, 120, 122, 125, 193, 201
itTenTen corpus 38

Jacobs, Geert 180
Japanese 83, 120, 122–6, 143, 193
Johns, Tim 160
Journal of Specialised Translation (JoSTrans) 77
Journal of Business and Technical Communication 76
Journal of Technical Writing and Communication 76

Kane, Yukari Iwatani 110
Kanoksilapatham, Budsaba 150, 154–5
Karreman, Joyce 52, 65
Kelly, Dorothy 14
Kelly, Nataly 8
Kenny, Dorothy 46, 49
keyword list 29–41, 166
Kilgarriff, Adam 28, 30, 32, 37
Kiraly, Donald 14
Knorr Cetina, Karin 154
Knowles, James 112
Korean 83, 120, 122–5, 143, 193
Krathwohl, David R. 4
Kress, Gunther 55
Kum, Doreen 84
Kuteeva, Maria 157
KWIC see concordance

Ladle, Richard J. 141–2
language service provider (LSP) 8, 9, 13, 18, 85, 142
Latin 138
Latvian 193
learnability 52, 55
legal language see discourse; terminology
lexical bundle 147–9
lexical density 54, 158
lexical repetition see repetition

lexical variation 132
Liao, Min-Hsiu 192
lingua franca: of science 137–40,
    143, 167
Liptak, Adam 107
Lithuanian 193
localization 13, 23, 94
London Agreement 120, 126
Loorbach, Nicole 65

machine translation 13, 26, 45–6,
    49, 106, 119–21, 124, 126–8,
    134; statistical (SMT) 45, 46, 49,
    120, 126; see also Google
    Translate; PatentTranslate;
    post-editing; TAPTA
Manfredi, Marina 192
Manning, Alan 55
Marfil-Álvarez, Rafael 189
MarketWatch 8
Martínez, Iliana A. 145, 146
Martín-Martín, Pedro 160, 162–3
Mason, Ian 18–19
MateCat 45
material safety data sheet see safety
    data sheet
Maylath, Bruce 14
Mazenc, Christophe 126
McDonagh, Luke 109, 110
McGrath, Lisa 157
Mejer, Malwina 126
Melander, Björn 160
Melby, Alan 19
MemoQ 45
MemSource Cloud 44
metadiscourse 97, 137, 155–7, 160,
    167–8, 202
metaphor 157–8, 167, 192
Microsoft terminology 43
modal verb 154, 156, 165, 184
Mongolian 193
Montemagni, Simonetta 54
Montesi, Michela 160
Montgomery, Scott L. 138, 168
Moorkens, Joss 49

Morozov, Evgeny 7
Moses engine 126
motivational information 64–6,
    69–70, 75, 77
Mousten, Birthe 14
move: rhetorical/discoursal 149–55,
    160–5, 187–8
multimodality 55, 201
Mur Dueñas, Pilar 141, 157
Myers, Greg 156, 174–5, 199

National Geographic 173, 192–4, 199
National Geographic Society 193
n-gram 33, 36, 38
Nolet, Diane 12
nominalization 132, 167; see also
    grammatical metaphor
Nord, Christiane 19, 128
Norwegian 144, 157, 160, 193, 195
Nutt, David J. 175–6

Olohan, Maeve 24, 48, 76, 168, 201
Omega-T 45
operative function 52, 80
OPUS corpus collection 38, 41
Organisation africaine de la
    proprieté intellectuelle 121
organization name 195

PACTE 14
ParaConc 48
Partington, Alan 98
patent: abstract 118–19; agent 109;
    application 16, 106–10, 118–19,
    121–2, 127–8, 130–1, 133–5;
    attorney 106, 109, 112, 127–8,
    130, 134; claim 108, 115–18,
    134; claim preamble 116;
    dependent claim 116–17; design
    107; examination 108–9, 130;
    infringement 109–10, 128;
    innovation 107; litigation 109–10,
    128, 135; plant 107; search 108,
    130; specification 106, 108, 110,
    117, 135, 158; utility 107

Patent Cooperation Treaty (PCT) 121–3
patentability 107, 109, 116, 121, 127, 135
Patentscope 118, 121–2, 124, 126, 133
PatentTranslate 46, 120–1, 134
Pavel, Silvia 12, 46
Pearl termbase *see* WIPO
Perales-Escudero, Moisés 163–4
phraseology 27, 28, 44, 66, 104, 118, 130, 133, 148
Pisanski Peterlin, Agnes 140, 157
place name 194
plant patent *see* patent
Polish 144, 193, 194, 201
popularization: degrees of 174
Portuguese 47, 94, 100, 102, 120, 122, 124–5, 139, 142–3, 155, 160, 193–6, 199, 201
post-editing 13, 46
Pouliquen, Bruno 126
precautionary notice 92–3, 101
preformulating device 179–81
prior art 108–9, 112, 118, 121, 126–8; *see also* patent
procedure 56–62; complex action 60; conditional 61; feedback statement 60, 64; paragraph-format 64; rich-step 64; streamlined-step 59–60, 68–9; *see also* action statement
product name 82–3, 90, 95
promotional function 58–9, 71, 77, 80–1, 85, 93–5, 98–9, 102–3, 159–61
proofreading 12–13
proprietary technology 83, 95
proximity 97, 201: of commitment 187–8; of membership 187–8
pseudo-quotation 179–81, 184–6

Quesenbery, Whitney 53
quotation 156, 179–81, 184–6, 190–2

REACH *see* Registration, Evaluation, Authorization and Restriction of Chemicals
readability 53–4, 76
readership 18, 57, 67–8, 83, 104, 141–2, 162, 174, 190–1, 197–8
reader-writer interaction 97, 192, 202; *see also* metadiscourse
Registration, Evaluation, Authorization and Restriction of Chemicals 92
repetition: lexical 35–6, 74, 113–14, 116; 132, 166, 188, 191; phrasal 130
research centre 10, 141, 200
reviewing 12–13
revising 12–13
revoicing 200
Risku, Hanna 14
Robinson, Marin S. 154
Rodríguez-Castro, Mónica 12
Root-Bernstein, Meredith 141–2
Royal Society 173
Russian 83, 94, 102, 120, 122, 124–5, 142, 160, 193, 201

safety data sheet 91–3, 101, 104
safety notice 62–4, 72; *see also* precautionary notice
Salager-Meyer, Françoise 159
Salama-Carr, Myriam 168
Salisbury, Gerald A 10
Samraj, Betty 160
Sauermann, Henry 201
Scarpa, Federica 14
Schjoldager, Anne Gram 49
SCIELO 143
science: defining 6–7
science and technology studies (STS) 7
Science Daily 175
science museum/exhibition 175, 199
Science News 175
Scientific American 174, 192
scientific publishing 136–44, 150

Scott, Mike 28
Scotto di Carlo, Giuseppina 201
screenshot 73–4
SDL: Multiterm 44; Studio 44, 45
SDS *see* safety data sheet
search engine optimization 13
self-mention 156, 167
semantic prosody 98–9
Sense About Science 176
Serbian 193
Shuttleworth, Mark 192
SI unit *see* unit of measurement
simile 188, 196–7
Sinclair, John 29, 37
Sismondo, Sergio 7
Sketch Engine 28–40, 48, 166
Sleurs, Kim 180
slogan 82–3, 95, 100–1
Slovak 144
Slovene 157, 193
SMOG Index 53
Snow, Charles P. 2
source text deficiency 99–10, 129–30
Spanish 47, 88, 90, 94, 97, 100, 102,
    120, 122, 124–5, 141–4, 157,
    160, 162–4, 167, 189, 191–3,
    201; Latin American 94, 143, 193
speech act 108, 110
standards: in technical data,
    87–8, 95
Steehouder, Michaël 52, 62, 65
step *see* CARS
Stoller, Fredricka L. 154
strapline *see* slogan
Strobbe, Ilse 180
Suojanen, Tytti 14
superlative form 98, 154
Swales, John M. 16–17, 139,
    149–50, 156, 159–64
Swedish 9, 120, 125, 144, 160, 193
symbol 54–5; *see also* graphics

TAPTA 126
TAUS 45
Taviano, Stefania 140

tcworld 10, 23
Tech Writing Handbook 74, 77
Technical Communication 76
*Technical Communication
    Quarterly* 76
technical drawing 95, 115, 129
technical knowledge 67, 89–90
technical specification 14, 80, 84,
    86, 95
technical writing 10, 13–14, 23, 55,
    76–7
technology: defining 6–7
TED 201–2; TED Talk 201
tekom *see* European Association for
    Technical Communication
term 27, 31–8, 41–4, 72, 88–9, 92,
    99, 102, 114, 117, 124–5, 129–
    31, 164, 189; candidate 31, 33,
    36–7; complex 27, 130;
    designating construction
    materials 90–1; simple 27, 130;
    see also concept
termbase 12, 42–9, 104
TermBase eXchange (TBX) 43
terminology 2, 10–12, 26–7, 66, 72,
    89, 99, 102, 104, 123, 148, 150,
    168, 177, 188; legal 66, 84, 95,
    101, 118, 130, 133, 198; corpus
    based research 27–41; managing
    and storing 41–9; working in 12
TermWiki 44
text type 17–18
Thai 193
Torrance, Caroline 200
Torresi, Ira 99
trade name 90
trademark 56, 82, 193
Transit 45
transition marker 156, 167
translation: as intellectual challenge
    1–3; competence 6–7, 12, 14–15,
    36, 66; EU 10–11, 14–15;
    freelance 8–10, 13, 23, 24, 47,
    120, 123, 127; in-house 9–13, 24,
    120, 123, 127; workplace 4–12

translation brief 6, 18–20, 22, 24, 104, 167, 203
Translation Bureau (Canada) 11–12, 47
Translation Centre for the Bodies of the European Union 11
translation memory 26, 42–5, 49, 74, 82, 87, 168
Translation Memory eXchange (TMX) 45
translation project specification 6, 19–21
translator training 2–5, 13
translator's note 130
translatorial action 19
transliteration 83–4
tri-gram see n-gram
Trosborg, Anna 18
Tse, Polly 146–8, 155–8, 161, 166
Turkish 90, 143, 193–5

Ukrainian 160, 193, 201
Ummelen, Nicole 52
Unified Patent Court 127
unit of measurement 29, 86–88, 90, 95, 196
unitary European patent see European patent with unitary effect
United States Patent and Trademark Office 107–8, 118
Urdiciain, Blanco Gil 160
usability 51–5, 71, 75–6
utility model 107
utility patent see patent

Van Bonn, Sarah 149, 159, 161–2
Van de Velde, Freek 160
van der Meij, Hans 56
van Leeuven, Theo 55

van Pottelsberghe de la Potterie, Bruno 126
Vandepitte, Sonia 14
Venturi, Giulia 54
Vermeer, Hans J. 19
video instruction 55
visual elements see graphics
Vitek, Steve 134
vocabulary list 54
voiceover 55, 200
Vold, Eva Thue 157
volunteer translation 201, 203

Wang, Fade 83
WebBootCaT 37
WebCorp 48
Werlich, Egon 18
Wiener Sachtextformel 53
Wiens, Kyle 74
Wikipedia 202
Wikipedia Corpus 38, 48
word cluster 146; see also lexical bundle; n-gram
word list 29–41, 48, 145–7; see also keyword list
Wordfast 45
Wordsmith Tools 28, 48, 166
World Intellectual Property Organization (WIPO) 12, 106, 109, 111–12, 121–7, 133; Pearl termbase 123, 133; Translation/ Terminology Fellowship Programme 123
Wynne, Martin 48

Xiao, Richard 160

Yakhontova, Tatyana 160

Zanettin, Federico 48
Zooniverse 201

Printed in Great Britain
by Amazon

67637900R00149